Experts in the Age of Systems

Experts in the Age of Systems

William Ray Arney

FOREWORD BY IVAN ILLICH

University of New Mexico Press : ALBUQUERQUE

Excerpts from *Assessing the Nuclear Age*, Robert R. Wilson and Steve McGuire, eds., © 1986 by the Educational Foundation for Nuclear Science, reprinted by permission of the *Bulletin of the Atomic Scientists*.

Excerpts from *The Nuclear Age* by Tim O'Brien, © 1985, reprinted by permission of Alfred A. Knopf, Inc.

Excerpts from *London Match* by Len Deighton, © 1986, reprinted by permission of Alfred A. Knopf, Inc.

Excerpts from "The Day After Trinity: J. Robert Oppenheimer and the Atomic Bomb" used by permission of Jon Else.

Excerpts from *Life and Times of Michael K* by J. M. Coetzee, © 1983 by J. M. Coetzee, reprinted by permission of Viking Penguin, a division of Penguin Books USA, Inc.

Excerpts from *The Name of the Rose* by Umberto Eco, © 1980 by Gruppo Editoriale Fabbri-Bompianí, Sonzogno, Etas S.p.A.; English translation © 1983 by Harcourt Brace Jovanovich, Inc. and Martin Secker & Warburg Limited, reprinted by permission of Harcourt Brace Jovanovich, Inc.

Excerpts from James Agee's "Dedication Day" used by permission of The James Agee Trust.

Excerpts from B. F. Skinner's *Walden Two* © 1948, renewed 1976 by B. F. Skinner reprinted with permission of Macmillan Publishing Company.

Library of Congress Cataloging-in-Publication Data

Arney, William Ray.
    Experts in the age of systems / William Ray Arney.—1st ed.
      p.   cm.
    Includes index.
    ISBN 0–8263–1268–3
    1. Intellectuals. 2. Expertise. 3. Objectivity. 4. Knowledge, Sociology of.
  I. Title.
HM213.A68   1991
306.4'2—dc20   90–23501
                                                 CIP

Design by Susan Gutnik.

For John Arthur Arney

But in your perishing you will shine brightly, fired by the strength of
the God who brought you to this land and for some special purpose gave
you dominion. . . . The end of living and the beginning of survival.

CHIEF SEATTLE, 1854

[W]e can console ourselves with the thought that we have been obliged
to build our way out into the dark. . . . Other lines of approach are
bound to lead us into much the same region and the time may come
when we find ourselves more at home in it.

SIGMUND FREUD
The Interpretation of Dreams

Contents

Foreword

IVAN ILLICH

In book after book Bill Arney has helped me to get hold of a new experience: living an unprecedented human condition, the system. I know no better word. Because a system knows no ground we cannot compare our age to any other. We cannot say, "We stand on the other side of a break, a gulf or chasm," for that would imply that we are still grounded. A system—as Arney has helped me to see—lies outside the kind of time that I can inhabit only as a historian. No one has moved into this new age: it came suddenly upon us, like darkness or smog.

In this new state of the world, something has gone. Man is no longer the measure. Systems void the common man, on whom common law and common sense were built. The Earth, as Gaya, becomes a global system. The person, as an object of care, becomes an immune system—an enclouded self. And for an enclouded self, there are no points of orientation.

Arney retraces this story, which paralyzes and silences me. His delicacy and wry humor evoke the experience of living in a world in which the long history of Being has resolved into systems. He is intrepid in his refusal to be taken in by an "after all . . . " or "so what?" He knows that now we are finally in u-topia, no-where; we have to live in the sad awareness of our impotence to assume responsibility because responsibility becomes impossible, meaningless, in systems terms. His gentle courage permits two complementary activities: his relentless refusal to let a systems perspective seep into his world-view and our search for a new and demanding probity based on friendship rather than culture.

Acknowledgments

There is no need for me to name names and implicate those who have helped me with this book, both through their caring and through their expertise. They know who they are and I hope they will understand my decision to remain silent.

Various institutions have contributed materially to the project. I am pleased to name them: The Washington State Library, the Library of Congress, the Oppenheimer Memorial Committee, and the library at the Los Alamos National Laboratory provided research assistance. Thanks to the State of Washington for providing sabbatical and travel funds through its agency, The Evergreen State College; to the National Endowment for the Humanities for a fellowship; and to the Rockefeller Foundation for a residency at its Study and Conference Center (justly famous in fiction and in fact) at the Villa Serbelloni, Bellagio, Italy.

Roberto and Gianna Celli at the Villa Serbelloni must be among the finest, most gracious hosts in the world. They provided good food, good company, and good memories.*

WILLIAM RAY ARNEY
Olympia, Washington

---

*I learned of the death, on September 8, 1990, of Roberto Celli. My sadness is somewhat tempered by having this opportunity to acknowledge a brief but fine friendship.

Experts in the Age of Systems

Opening

We hardly know if man is a simple or a compound being. Impenetrable
mysteries surround us on all sides. . . . Nevertheless, we want to
penetrate everything, to know everything. The only thing we do not
know is how to be ignorant of what we cannot know.

JEAN-JACQUES ROUSSEAU
Emile

We live, we hear, in a new age. I characterize this new age as the age
of systems. A "systems theoretic logic" and a "systems approach to
knowledge" undergird modern life, a life that we live, we are told,
supported by layer upon layer of large, complex systems that extend
from the previously unimaginable minutiae of subcellular systems
through the previously unimaginable macroscopic systems of the
biosphere.

There is no question in my mind that the age of the system is new
in this century. What remains a question in my mind is how to live
in this new age. Chief Seattle understood the end of his age and the
beginning of a new one as "the end of living and the beginning of
survival." In order to consider seriously the question of how to live
in this new age of complex systems, we must at least be open to the
possibility that, like Chief Seattle in his day, we cannot.

But we should not be quick to draw a conclusion. We are only
beginning. When this book ends, there may be an opening—but that
will be for the person who closes the book to decide. Authors can
only begin and end. Readers close and open.

How can we pursue the question of how to live in this new age? Surely there are many routes. I have chosen to focus on the place of experts in complex systems. Experts, as a class, seem to be people with a certain vitality about them. They have knowledge; not infrequently they seem to have power; they make decisions and make things happen; they assume responsibility and through all this they seem to find a way to live. If an answer to my question is to be found, it might be found by examining the place and function of modern experts and by examining the operations of expertise in complex systems.

An appropriate subtitle for this book would be "tickling the tail of the dragon," the name given an experiment that is crucial to the assembly of nuclear bombs. This book focuses (though not exclusively) on the atomic scientist as an exemplar of the modern expert, operating in and through complex systems, in particular those scientists who worked on the development* of the first atomic weapons. These scientists and engineers for the most part tried to be vital, responsible, morally conscientious agents of expertise, even as they participated in the construction of uniquely terrible weapons. They tried to live the lives of good, responsible and respectable experts. Arguably, they were among our best and our brightest; if anyone stood a chance of succeeding in finding a way to live, it would have been a member of this rather remarkable group from our recent history. But, as the atomic scientists were among the first to suspect and among the first to say, they were living in a new age. They experienced themselves, not through any fault or error or lapse, as not entirely alive to what they had done or would later do with their lives. They became, in my characterization of them, *dead but real executives of the inevitable*.

It is the argument of this book that complex systems create experts who must be dead but real to the lives that modern systems of expertise provide for experts to live. The argument is a bleak, even a relentless one. As such, I think, it reflects the relentlessness of our new age. Complex systems are relentlessly resilient to change, rapidly

---

*Such tortured constructions, which avoid words like "invented" or "developed" that imply agency, are purposeful. Why they are necessary will become clear as the book proceeds.

responsive to criticism and remarkably stable for it. Indeed, one of the axioms of systems thinking is that, like the self-righting, equilibrium-maintaining behavior of a bicycle, complex systems sustain themselves in response to most assaults from their environments or injuries to their internal workings. (And also like the bicycle, encountering the unexpected, well-placed pebble in the road, when complex systems do change they tend to collapse catastrophically.) One argument has it that if the best and brightest (not to mention the earliest) critics of such systems could not fundamentally alter them, then rehearsals of their arguments so late in the day—well after the systems have developed systematic, virtually automatic responses to every possible critique—are unlikely to be successful. So I will not undermine my own argument by ending with a call for reform or with an urging toward one or another set of ethics. This book will simply end on what I can only hope will be an opening.

Let me try to be clear about my approach. This is another book about the relationship between reason and violence. In previous works,[1] I described the operations of medical reason, changes in the implementation of medical truths, and the effects of the operations of medical knowledge on the people—both doctors and patients—subject to that knowledge. In the present exercise I am interested in the way modern systems of expertise made the atomic scientist their agent and, in that violent process, made it difficult for anyone to speak any more about notions of responsibility, ethics, guilt, commitment, and the like. I will not argue that we are in a "crisis of expertise," for that phrase suggests that if we could but manage the crisis well, we could bring back a time when terms like "individual responsibility" had meaning.* I simply want to describe how modern systems of expertise operate. Complex systems, the systems theorists tell us, are "huge," "gigantic," "comprehensive" and they tend to aggregate themselves so that there is simply no room left in which one can exercise the freedom that is necessary for a person to develop a sense of responsibility and commitment. Complex systems enable us to be what we are; they do not leave free space for us to test ourselves against our limitations and to the extents of our imaginations. Indeed, complex

---

*See the remarks on James Agee's *Dedication Day*, and note 67, in Chapter 4.

systems such as the atomic system make the previously "unimaginable" into commonplace, simple, but seemingly limitless facts of modern life that disable the human imagination. I will describe the amoeboid operation of the reason enabled by complex systems. Relying on data from and about the people who made the first atomic weapons, I will clarify the connection between the contemporary operations of reason and violence.

But this is also a work of ambiguity. It must be. Simply to write about the relationship between reason and violence would run the risk of either justifying (or, at least, coming to understand) violence or it would set the stage—as I argue in Chapter Four—for the development of a strange but powerful identification with violence. I would prefer not to fall into either trap.

The ambiguity toward which I aim has at its center a question about experts and expertise: Is it possible—or, more important, is it even useful—to ask whether experts direct or are directed by the systems of expertise in which they do their work? One focus of this work is a specific expert, J. Robert Oppenheimer, and a specific system of expertise, the elaborate mechanism that built and exploded the first atomic bombs. Is it even important to ask whether Oppenheimer directed (from his position of "Director" at Los Alamos) or was directed by the "atomic system"?

To the extent that I answer this question, I answer it ambiguously. To do otherwise would be either to make a case for the absolution of those involved in some of the acknowledged horrors of our time, or to make a case that pins responsibility on those who were (and are) in positions that, in another age, would have been called "positions of responsibility." In my view, a systems theoretic logic makes these old kinds of arguments rather useless. To try to resurrect them is to engage in self deception of a very high order. Holding the old arguments in abeyance by developing a studied ambiguity may help us appreciate the extremity of our situation a little better.

This is not a book *about* ambiguity or, what would be worse, about *an* ambiguity. It is a work that tries to sustain ambiguity. Allan Bloom recently wrote in his book, *The Closing of the American Mind*, "Natural scientists now project an ambiguous image. Although they may be truly theoretical, they do not appear that way to untheoretical men. Their involvement in human things gives them a public role as curers of disease and inventors of nuclear weapons, as bastions of democracy and bastions of totalitarianism."[2] Bloom's "ambiguous image" is a problem that calls for a solution. He, like most modern experts and critics, wants to teach us how to think correctly. We must, he implies, make a choice between democracy and totalitarianism and install our experts unambiguously as bastions of one or the other. Bloom wants to teach us how to think of the natural scientists, our most obvious experts, and how to organize our lives so that we might come to think of them, without deception, in the proper way, as if we had a choice in the matter. Bloom is one among many—and the many include most of the atomic scientists themselves—who have written *about* the ambiguous position of the natural scientist/expert with an eye toward resolving the ambiguity in one way or another. There have been personal memoirs and confessions; there have been ever more thorough historical investigations into the true facts concerning the development of the bomb; there have been sociological constructions of the actual and optimal functions of experts in modern society. Instead of following this well-worn path of formulating an understanding of experts or of these particular experts, I wish to try to sustain, even nurture, the ambiguity that surrounds and, I think, grips modern experts. This ambiguity is not, for me, captured by Bloom's opposition between the "theoretical" and the "practical." Indeed, this ambiguity is not captured by any simple opposition. In this time when the most atrocious horror can be committed in the name of "democracy" and in which totalitarianism so easily embraces "democratic reforms," we seem unlikely to mount a successful critical campaign if we insist that the way to proceed is to appeal to the proper, crystal clear, true meanings of terms that have become so slippery. A better strategy might be to force ourselves to wallow in the ambiguities that are everywhere around us and get a good feel of them.

In a culture such as ours, with an abundance of tools for acquiring knowledge and with such a terrible thirst for truth, a project that tries to sustain ambiguity risks stillbirth. But the risk of stillbirth is preferable to the certain deadliness of totalizing understandings or explanations of events and behaviors. The men who worked on the bomb were among the morally concerned. They were philosophers, in the best sense, as well as scientists. And yet they became dead but real executives of the inevitable. After their blazing success, their *ex post facto* explanations and their "if only" understandings ring hollow and only serve to reinforce the image of our modern expert as "dead but real." These were men who lived their lives in what Primo Levi has called the "grey zone,"[3] that band of existence somewhere between victim and executioner. This study, if it is not stillborn, reinforces Levi's view that we ought to withhold judgment on those who find themselves in this "grey zone" while we try to appreciate the nature of the situation in which they found themselves forced to live. But it goes a little beyond Levi and raises a question of whether complex systems permit any life outside the grey zone. Is there any black zone anymore? In systems of expertise that make modern experts both their agents and their objects, the frightening prospect is the potential dissolution of the boundary between victim and executioner. The loss of that boundary would take away once and for all the basis for the few judgments of which Levi, for one, could be so certain.

The dissolution of boundaries, one effect of the boundary-breaching logic of systems theory and a theme of this work, has implications for would-be critics as well as for the experts of whom we might be critical. Part of my view, explained in the text, is that the systems that support us leave no place from which to mount effective criticism. Indeed, good, well-functioning systems depend on good criticism and use it well. Systems of expertise incorporate criticism in themselves. To try to be a critic is to double the expert and to become an agent of the system, but with a little disguise, effective principally for hiding oneself only from oneself. In this work I have not concerned myself with being critical in any of the usual senses. I have not tried, for example, to add more subtlety to the latest (or the oldest) sociological arguments about experts and expertise. I have not worried about gaining a "more correct" historical understanding. (If the history of historical understanding of the bomb has taught us anything, it has taught us that the more history we know, the more awful the situation becomes.*) I have no interest in playing an obliging Bohr to

---

*For example, there is evidence in Oppenheimer's files at the Library of Congress that Enrico Fermi proposed, and Oppenheimer considered, a plan to use radioactive material to poison the water supplies and food chains of Axis countries. (See Bernstein, Barton J., "Oppenheimer and the radioactive poison plan," *Technology Review* 88, May/June, 1985: 14–17, and Bernstein, Barton J., "Radiological warfare: The path not taken,"

anyone's Robert Wilson who, with his ear on the great man's lips (Bohr spoke softly) trying to hear Bohr's plan for peace in our time that Wilson was to carry out, demandingly pleaded, "For God's sake, man, speak up." (This story is recalled on pages 211 to 212.) If anything, too much has already been said in response to this all-too-reasonable demand that we all-too-reasonably make of experts of all stripes. If we can develop a little better appreciation of our common, complex, very ambiguous situation, that will be enough and there would be nothing more to say.

But is there anything to be done? I think there is.

In a situation where there is no way out, where violence wears the face of humanism, and where things get the most dangerous precisely as they become the most reasonable, I think there is little left to do but laugh. As Dostoevsky said of human life in societies such as ours, "there seems to be a kind of jest in it all." I will argue that we ought to see the jest for what it is. We should listen to Lenny Bruce who thought people should be taught what is, not what should be. His response to the question of whether there is anything to be done about the horrors of our time is summarized this way:

> *Sometimes I look at life in the fun mirror at a carnival. I see myself as a profound, incisive wit, concerned with man's inhumanity to man. Then I stroll to the next mirror and see a pompous, subjective ass whose humor is hardly spiritual. I see traces of Mephistopheles. All my humor is based upon destruction and despair. If the whole world were tranquil, without disease and violence, I'd be standing on the breadline right in back of J. Edgar Hoover and—who's another real heavyweight?—Dr. Jonas Salk.*[4]

Humor sometimes helps us appreciate our situation a little better, even when it fails to make us laugh. It can point out the absurdity of the situations we are in even if it does not point to a way out.

Candace Lang, in her *Irony/Humor*,[5] has offered a justification for

---

Bulletin of the Atomic Scientists 41, August, 1985: 45–49.) Oppenheimer suggested to Fermi that they not go forward with the plan until they could guarantee killing 500,000 people.

Frankly, I don't know which is more disturbing, the plan itself or the fact that no one was terribly disturbed by the plan until Bernstein "discovered" this evidence in the *open files* of the Library of Congress in 1985.

humor as a "critical paradigm." Lang reads many of the post-struc-
turalist theorists and much of postmodern literature as "humorous,"
not ironic as many critics of postmodern works would have it. Humor,
for Lang, does not have to evoke a laugh, not even a chuckle, to be
"humorous." Humor is a term she uses as a counterpoint to irony.
Irony, Lang says, hides authorial intention. The intention and meaning are there; it remains for the reader to penetrate the instability of
irony to find them. There is always positive direction in the ironic
critic's work; it is just sometimes hard to decode. (And so, the critics
say that postmodern criticism, which is but another participant in the
era of irony, merely seeks to hide its intention, and—some would
say—is not very effective at it.) In contrast, a humorous work, for
Lang, contains "no positive content," it is "an incessant questioning,"
"a nondialectical negation of existing modes of thought."[6] And—and
this is crucial—a humorous work is always political because it contains
the possibility of undermining structures of power "that support and
are supported by the discourse in question."[7] Humorous works are
pregnant. They puncture pretensions and open up fields of meaning.
Humor always takes on the heavyweights but it also respects the
common folk, those who might make meaning if the heavyweights
of meaning making were gone and the fields were open.

Humor works in the service of freedom in that it can be destructive
of the reasonableness of everyday life and the edifices of reason that
fill up the spaces that free human beings must have if they are to act
freely on imagined alternatives. But humor is, as Lenny Bruce knew
all too well, always ambiguous. Even if someone gets the joke, humor
does not guarantee he or she will get the point, since most humor is
pointless. Humor never guarantees that people will act into the spaces
it opens. Maxine Greene writes of our modern situation,

> it may be that we no longer know how to create the kinds of situations
> in which persons are likely to choose themselves as committed and as
> free. As we have said, they may have the liberty to speak, to buy books,
> to change jobs, to leave home; but they do not know what it is to reach
> out for freedom as a palpable good, to engage with and resist the
> compelling and conditioning forces, to open fields where the options can
> multiply, where unanticipated possibilities open each day.[8]

All a humorist can do is keep trying to make the most, politically, of
"destruction and despair." There is no "positive content," no direction

or program in a good joke. The humor that opens fields of meaning to the activity of freedom at the expense of edifices of reason and at the expense of "compelling and conditioning forces" must be freely accepted.

In this work, as in the others, I tend to take my cue from one of Lang's humorists: Michel Foucault. In his writings on specific and universal intellectuals and in his work on structures of power, he has framed the issues about experts and expertise I explore here.

But Foucault a humorist? His work hardly evokes laughter. But still, I find him *humorous* in the sense that Lang wants us to use that term. How else are we to understand a person who would write a book, *The Archeology of Knowledge*, responding to his critics' demands for definitions of terms and an outline of his method, and then never use those terms or that method again? How else are we to understand a person who explosively juxtaposes the gruesome scene on the scaffold to the humane severity of a prison timetable, only to have this juxtaposition work to the detriment of the "humane"? Foucault's work is conclusive, directive, and has positive content only posthumously in the hands of his disciples and, especially, his interpreters. In his own hands, his work was ultimately inconclusive, shall we say ambiguous, and ended with the pregnancy, open-endedness, directionlessness, and threat of a good joke. He sometimes tempted us to think he was making a point by holding up as a sort of goal such high-sounding phrases as "a different economy of bodies and pleasures." But such terms can be taken seriously only by very serious people. I imagine Foucault laughing. (And the authorities [the disciplinarians of all sorts]* understand that laugh better than anyone else.) Foucault was Mephistophelean in the laughter he directed toward structures of power and edifices of reason, but at the same time, he had the greatest of respect for those who were agents of "censored and subjugated knowledges." I imagine him imagining himself opening a way through the violence of reason for them.

The humor of Foucault finds an analogue in the work of Ivan Illich

---

*Recall Foucault's response to the interlocutor who worries that Foucault might change again and laugh at all of us who are trying to understand him: "Do not ask who I am and do not ask me to remain the same: leave it to our bureaucrats and our police to see that our papers are in order,"[9] or recall Bruce's troubles with the law.

and some of his friends.[10] In their recent studies they have moved away from Illich's early call for "deinstitutionalization" toward a stance of saying "no" to the new idols, the new "sources of axioms," the new "modern certainties" that ground our existence.*

What could it mean to say, simply, "no," with the laughter that act engenders, to those modern certainties and the sources of axioms, first among them systems theory, that make our new idols so compelling? Some will get the joke if I say only what this activity can *not* mean. It cannot mean the mounting of a programmatic or principled No. It cannot mean the formation of a loyal opposition. Saying a simple "no" to the reasonable and rational will make one look ridiculous.[14] Ridiculousness can drive one to want to begin to behave normally, something that inevitably leads one not to say "no" but "maybe" to our new idols and our new sources of axiomatic truths. It is very difficult not to respond positively to the warmly posed, understanding, always reasonable request that goes, "I understand that by your 'no' you are expressing an opposition; so what exactly do you propose?" If it is to retain its vigor, the stupidly simple "no" that makes one ridiculous must be accompanied by laughter, the laughter that Rousseau's implication that we come to "know how to be ignorant" must engender in our modern situation.

There is vitality in the laughter that humor makes available if not inevitable. And laughter is one response to ambiguity. But we have access to the laughter only if ambiguity can be sustained. We have known since Nietzsche of the difficulty of maintaining vitalizing laughter, of creating the ambiguity that sustains our aliveness, something difficult but important to distinguish from that icon of Life which demands obeisance and sacrifice. This book is an attempt to create some ambiguity around our modern effort "to penetrate everything,

---

*They have called, for example, for people to say "no" to New Life emblematized on the one hand by the publicly visible fetus and on the other hand the view of globe from space. This New Life has been created as an undefined entity[11] that can claim anything under its rubric and that can equally reject anything. Regardless of what it claims or rejects, however, it demands reverence and commands protection. As Illich put it, "Life is an eminent example of an assumption that is convenient for the expansion of institutional control over resources, which, by going unexamined, has taken on the features of a certainty."[12] Not incidentally, Life is one of those certainties that has been made possible by systems theoretic thinking.[13]

to know everything." This book tries to create in the midst of our concerns for certainties an ambiguity that favors living through our difficult times over the temptation to just survive them. It strives not to be a contribution to knowledge but a rehearsal of a plea for ignorance in its place. This book will have been successful in that effort if, some 205 pages from now it closes and does not simply end.

CHAPTER ONE:

Introduction to Extremity

*On that first road, which now can be completely surveyed, arise
adaptation, leveling, Higher Chinadom, modesty in the instincts,
satisfaction in the dwarfing of mankind—a kind of stationary level of
mankind. Once we possess that common economic management of the
earth that will soon be inevitable, mankind will be able to find its best
meaning as a machine in the service of the economy—as a tremendous
clockwork, composed of ever smaller, ever more subtly "adapted"
gears. . . . It is clear, what I combat is economic optimism: as if
increasing the expenditure of everybody must necessarily involve the
increased welfare of everybody.*

FRIEDRICH NIETZSCHE
The Will to Power

"Ours is a society of experts." It is an old cliché, but today its truth
seems a little tame. Ours is better called a society of *expertise*. It is not
just that we defer to the expertise manifest in the person of an expert,
but rather, expertise is something that teaches us all how to talk.
Expertise infuses thought and language and marks a person as rational or not, thoughtful or not.

Consider an exchange on a radio program. A couple was being
interviewed. The husband was a scientist, a specialist in ecology, one
of the sciences of our new age. In response to a question about the
bomb, he said something like, "After the next thermonuclear device
is used against a civilian population, there will be a window of opportunity—a small window of opportunity—during which we will be
able to mount the political and moral discussions necessary to ensure

that these weapons are never used again." The wife followed and said something like, "I don't want any bombs to be used. I don't want my children killed. I don't want anyone's children killed. I think we should just stop now." In comparison to the husband's unstudied utterance, the wife comes up a little short in the exchange. We might think that she has said the only responsible thing that might be said. We want her view, an essentially moral view, to carry the day on a question we want to be an essentially moral question. She has appealed to our hearts. We should, of course, "just stop now." But then there is the husband, an expert, speaking expertise. We know, even in our hearts, that *he* is right. There is an appeal in his techno-talk that tells us he knows what he is talking about—"thermonuclear device," "civilian population," "window of opportunity"—and there is the evidence of his scholarly study of future "scenarios": the opening of that window will be, he tells us, "small." "Stop now" in an ideal world, but in this world, realistically and rationally, we should ready ourselves for the opening of that window, look past the violence it will involve, and prepare to speak technically, quickly and well before the window slams shut. Speak back to violence with expertise. That is the only rational thing to do.

This study is an exploration of what Michel Foucault called "the rationality of the abominable." The attendants of our rationality are our experts. (Whether the experts are the "keepers" of rationality or not is a question that should remain open for now.) One route of inquiry into the rationality of the abominable is to examine the place of experts in modern society. There are, not surprisingly, several rational, contained and thoughtful, if competing assessments of the current status of experts, and then there is a more extreme position which I find necessary to address the extremity of our situation.

Experts on Expertise

As we begin to consider contemporary expertise, we can look first to the experts on expertise. Sociology has been the disciplinary locus for many of the commentaries on and the debates about expertise. The power, the authority, the legitimacy, the function, the production of experts and of expertise are questions that harken back to the foundational questions of the discipline, so it is not surprising that all corners of the field have had something to say about expertise.

One school of sociology seeks to elaborate the functional characteristics of experts and to outline the social contributions of expertise in various forms of society. Expertise in capitalist society is different from expertise in prior times and this difference is best expressed in the amount of authority attributed to experts, according to this school of thought. Experts in the modern era—since perhaps the end of the eighteenth century—have acquired a certain amount of power and authority that was once reserved to the lords or more generally to the state because they have specialized, esoteric, socially useful knowledge. The aphorism that "knowledge begets power" is true and analytically informative as society is viewed from this perspective. The state, this theory says, grants a franchise over specialized, expert knowledge and its attendant practices because it is in the interest of the state and its citizens to do so. In return for the franchise, experts in their professions implicitly or explicitly agree to certify valid practitioners and to police their ranks to protect the public that cannot on its own judge the competence of each specialist. The professions are necessary in modern societies built on complex divisions of labor to allow people to enjoy the fullness of life such societies have to offer. As Eliot Freidson, one contemporary exponent of this view, put it, "without reducing population to seventeenth century levels, or without assuming a complex technology and economy which covertly relies on experts to form a supportive technological structure around such communities, the abolition of full-time, specialized experts is really inconceivable."[1]

This school of sociology is sometimes accused of simply rationalizing the existence of the professions, professions that contribute directly and indirectly to inequalities and injustices in modern society. The radical argument against the liberal politics of the functionalist school has it that professions and the professionals themselves are artificially advanced up the social ladder due to the fact that they work outside the competitive market and due to their successes in commanding state support for their monopolies over practices and, thereby, over markets. Professional experts tend to serve those who can afford them and give short shrift to those who cannot, a practice that enhances extant structures of inequality. This is the first volley from the more radical critics of experts.

The politically liberal sociologists are not completely uncritical of the professions, however. They are quick to recognize the abuses of power which common sense suggests will always exist whenever power is allowed to become concentrated as it is in the professions. Their response is usually some variant of a proposal to "fine tune" the professions. A little less emphasis on credentialling here, a little more accountability to the public there, a little more regulation, a little less regulation. The professions pose a technical problem in want of a technical solution (which these professional sociologists are usually ready to offer), this understanding of expertise tells us. Regardless of the problems caused by professionalism, the argument goes, the professions are a social good, they serve the public well, and they must be preserved, even as their problems are addressed. In fact, if society does not wish to retain the specialized professions in their current form, society will have to invent some other social form to do the job just as well. Indeed, in those modern instances during this century and the last where a society has tried to do away with the professions, they have been regenerated. Freidson says,

> *my suspicion is that this re-emergence [of the professions in a post-revolutionary period] occurs not because of counter-revolutionary political winds, or because of class politics, but rather because of a generic problem that has little or nothing to do with political issues of equality and unjust privilege. At the foundation of professionalism . . . is specialized knowledge and skill thought to be of value to human life.*[2]

The professions are just another of Nietzsche's "ever more subtly 'adapted' gears" needed to keep the clockwork of society running. If these particular gears ever begin to grind against the mechanisms that produce and support Freidson's "human life," sociologists like Freidson will be there to help adapt the gears ever more subtly. The optimism of this school of thought derives from its confidence in its own technical skills even if it sometimes calls into question the technical capabilities of other professions.

Those sociologists who have criticized the liberal wing of the discipline by accusing them of unnecessarily rationalizing privilege, prestige, and inequality have not been, in their turn, simple naysayers. Their critical histories lead to some (re)constructive proposals. Their studies have shown that the professions came into existence not through the rational process of developing a body of socially useful knowledge, purveying it to the general public in a beneficial manner, and gradually acquiring the social recognition and protection such a service might arguably deserve. The historical record (as interpreted by these politically more radical theorists) says it is not the case that knowledge naturally and legitimately leads to power and authority. Instead, the power which socially well-placed, specialized practitioners were able to acquire by aligning themselves with the proper social classes and, in some cases, with power brokers and influence makers permitted some groups of practitioners to do away with their competition. With the competitive field narrowed, the professions could develop, transmit, elaborate, and sell their own forms of specialized knowledge and practice on their own terms. Shrewd political maneuvering was abetted by the breakdown of political society in the nineteenth century, according to this view. The professions situated themselves in schools and universities to which more and more people were being admitted and there the specialists could demonstrate to the masses their obvious superiority in technical fields characterized by and insulated by impenetrable jargon and mysterious, shared, state-protected practices. Ideologies of objectivity, personal disinterestedness, progress being dependent upon technical advances, and so on, developed around the professions and sustain them and their experts today. But such ideologies are simply collective rationalizations, facades that accord a group political protection for continuing privilege, this line of reasoning reminds us. The politically more radical sociologists would have us re-think the position of experts and our reliance on expertise in light of (their reading of) history. Perhaps we do ourselves a disservice by unquestioningly continuing the monopolies of experts, but perhaps we would do ourselves an equal disservice by doing away with specialized knowledge entirely.

The most radical social theorists have called for the abolition of the institutions that sustain our experts. Illich, in his early work, argued that thinking that experts merely fulfill social and individual needs obscures the fact that experts first define our needs so that they might then fulfill them. This leads to alienation. Illich argued that we ought to consider the damage done by all institutions that move us away from a level of subsistence at which each person understands well and is intimately in touch with the factors and forces that sustain him or her.[3]

Most sociologists, even those of the left, stop short of Illich's position, however. Radical theorists tend to argue instead that experts might align themselves with average citizens, might open the doors behind which they closet their socially useful knowledge, and might, thereby, contribute to the democratization of society. They can become part of the solution instead of continuing to be part of the problem. By reversing the mechanisms that led to the concentration of power (and privilege and wealth), experts can help make society more open and just, so these left-leaning experts on expertise say. Radical theorists are also optimistic about the operation of expertise. They call for a bit more radical reorganization of the gears, but they do not tend to align themselves, like Nietzsche, in opposition to "economic optimism."

At the risk of oversimplification, it might be said that sociology has involved itself in a chicken-or-the-egg problem. Most of the sociology of experts and expertise can be divided into two camps based on which variable, knowledge or power, a theory posits as prior to the other. Liberal theorists believe knowledge comes first, power follows, eventually power evolves into authority, and the continuing, publicly beneficial activities of the experts reinforce the legitimacy of the experts. Radicals show that, in historical fact, power comes first, knowledge—and the *apparent* legitimacy of a particular body of specialized knowledge—follows.

Whether knowledge or power comes first may be worth debating, but the debate impresses me as an endless one. And it is not entirely clear that the two dominant theoretical postures lead to wildly different conclusions, as one might expect. With a few exceptions like Illich, radical theorists have not been quick to call for the fundamental undoing of the professions and their expertise. They have attacked the closed, guild-like structure of the professions. They have urged more open debate among experts themselves. They have called for easier access to expert knowledge and data so that the public might judge for itself some of the knowledge claims experts make. They have called for the political realignment of expertise with the citizenry. But these kinds of criticism sound a lot like the "fine-tuning" that liberal theorists advocate. Radicals want to adjust different factors, to be sure, but few have suggested undoing the system.

There is a threat that lurks behind all the sociologies of expertise. The critical work of the radicals begins to approach the threshold of this threat, but only just looks over the edge. If the knowledge claims of experts are dependent largely on acquired power, if the knowledge experts possess and profess is, as some sociologists have argued, absolutely constitutive of reality and not at some level or in some sense reflective of it, then relativism rears its head and one knows that the tail of anarchy cannot be far behind. One is forced to admit that any knowledge claim has the same force and legitimacy as any other and one is led to doubt the sanctity of all large, stabilizing institutions like the state, like the market, like the knowledge industry itself. If we follow some historically based critiques too far, we enter a space where there are no standards of judgment, not even standards by which to judge the claims of expert sociologists that carry us onto this perilous ground.

Some recent sociology has tried to bridge the gap between the radicals, whose arguments rely primarily on historical investigations, and the liberals, whose arguments tend to be of a static sort. Arthur Stinchcombe, for example, has tried to add a historical dimension to the liberals' analyses of social formations of expertise by arguing that social institutions are repositories of "precedents" developed

> by a long line of people professionally concerned with trying to embody
> rational decision-making in a set of institutional practices. . . . What
> this means . . . is that there may be an "institutional wisdom," a
> rationality at a deeper level than is routinely understood consciously by
> its practitioners, so that by following the tradition of the institution
> people do better, behave more rationally, than they would do with their
> unaided rational faculties.[4]

This view, which Stinchcombe calls "a reserved and somewhat cynical Pollyanna view of the institutions of reason,"[5] leads to a call for the predictability of markets and the maintenance of order in the state on which the institutions of reason depend. He has sensed the threat implicit in the general sociological critique of expertise and he has come to the defense of the realm.

On the other side, the side of those who are inclined to the radical view, there is an unwillingness to follow their own argument too far. There is a tendency to stare into the void of relativism, into the face of potential anarchy, and to withdraw at the last moment. Thomas Haskell, editor of a volume on *The Authority of Experts*, seems attracted to an essay that concludes "our deference to . . . experts may not be warranted, at least not for the reasons customarily given." But even Haskell falls back on the weak notion that social conventions, emanating from and sustained by the institutions of reason, "certainly possess more holding power than conventions that simply descend from past usage and tradition, or from arbitrary deference to a Hobbesian ruler. We know they won't hold under the severest strain, but in high wind and shoal water, even a light anchor is vastly superior to none at all."[6] Out of a sociology that points directly at a possible "philosophy of pessimism,"[7] Haskell is among the many who seek out the glimmers of optimism favoring a stable future, no matter how faint those glimmers might have been made by the assault of a thoughtful sociology. On all sides, then, there is hesitation in the face of the standardlessness toward which competing theoretical positions point.

An Extreme Position

One thinker who has not pulled back from the brink, who based his work on the premise of "a derelict present," who wished "to leave the extant world in ruins,"[8] is Michel Foucault. Foucault refused to be trapped by the academic (and the word is apt) question of which comes first, power or knowledge? He dissolved the distinction and employed the hybrid concept of *pouvoir/savoir*, "power/knowledge." Knowledge *is* power, period, for Foucault. No intellectual turns of a phrase, no historical explorations, reconstructions, or representations to get from one to the other. They are one in the same.

This simple act of joining familiar terms is, first, an act of destruction. Power/knowledge admits none of the old analytics of either power or of knowledge. Knowledge is no longer that which penetrates reality and permits one to apprehend the so-called objects of knowledge that are "out there" in our more-or-less common world. Knowledge only plays back over the "knowing subject," and disciplines him or her to begin to speak well and truthfully about a world that knowledge, through its power, made more-or-less common. Power is not a constraining force in Foucault's scheme. Power is that which enables us to be what we are. Power is that which, via knowledge, produces the "knowing subject," the celebrated center of modernity.

Even though Foucault once said all of his work was fundamentally about power, he was never to be pinned down on a precise definition of the term. For him power was not a thing that one could grasp, say, by acquiring knowledge or by aligning oneself with powerful people or by orbiting known centers of power. "The idea that there is either located at—or emanating from—a given point something which is a 'power' seems to me to be based on a misguided analysis," Foucault said. "In reality power means relations, a more-or-less organized, hierarchical, coordinating cluster of relations."[9]

By refusing to accept and employ conventional notions of power, Foucault became a destroyer of a cultural myth that permits a sense of individuality and individual centering. Indeed, Foucault can be added to a series of cultural iconoclasts that Freud first articulated and put himself at the end of. First, Freud recounts, Copernicus said we are not at the center of the universe but at its periphery. With that demotion, we could still rest assured that we were the first among species with dominion over a planet, albeit a marginal one. Not so, said Darwin. We are the last among species and but the mere result of a long series of ecological accidents. After Darwin, there remained the self, a sanctified center. But Freud showed that we are not even masters of our own psychological houses. Freud, in his turn, left us power to be acquired and used by people in violent but usually unconscious ways in order to gain a sense of self. But after Freud, Foucault enters and turns this new, most modern reality into myth. Power is no thing, no where, and it operates according to its own rules to produce that which we are. To imagine controlling power is modernity's last delirium, according to Foucault.

If power, manifest in and through the use of true words about the true nature of things, plays over us and makes us its agents as well as its objects, what then is Foucault, this man of so many words? It is tempting to think him a critic. If that label is to apply, we must be quick to add that he came from other than the usual critical molds. He was always cautious about being drawn to a critical posture, especially if such posturing seemed to align him with some system of critical thought. Critics are experts too. Indeed, experts need critics to help them refine their systems of thought and critics, of course, need the experts for their fodder. Each is indispensable to the other. Critic and expert both use to their own benefits the myth of knowledge, while both obscure the question of power by encouraging us to understand the present in terms of "its" (true) history (from the experts' points of view) or in terms of one sort or another of "critical" history (from the expert critics' points of view).

The system is telling you, in effect: "If you want to understand and

perceive events in the present, you can only do so through the past,
through an understanding—carefully derived from the past—which was
specifically developed to clarify the present." We have employed a wide
range of categories—truth, man, culture, writing, etc.—to dispel the
shock of daily occurrences, to dissolve the event. The obvious intention
of those famous historical continuities is to explain: the eternal "return"
to Freud, Marx, and others is obviously to lay a foundation. But both
function to exclude the radical break introduced by events.[10]

To become a critic, for Foucault, would have been simply to double
the expert. To uncover the power that lies behind the powerful, how
powerful that would be! And, Foucault might reply, how hypocritical,
how presumptuous, how ironic.

How Foucault was reproached with neglecting, in his analysis of power,
the importance of a fundamental power! And from this was deduced his
so-called apoliticism, his refusal of a battle (a final struggle) that might
one day be decisive, his neglect of a project of universal reform. But
there is silence on the subject not only of his immediate and local
struggles but also his refusal to enter the fray with "grand designs"
which would be but an alibi in the service of daily servitude.[11]

Foucault, like Lenny Bruce, wanted merely (if we may use such an
understated qualifier) to help people understand things as they are.
I imagine him thinking, with Paulo Freire, Maxine Greene, and others,
that once an understanding is developed the people will call for changes
where they think them necessary.

Foucault was not a disciplinarian whose job it was to use disciplinary knowledge to penetrate and bring to order some "vast, silent
narrative, a continuous, immense, and unlimited murmur of something enigmatically unspoken or unthought that would not only await
its revenge but would obscurely gnaw at thought, rendering it forever
dubious." He was not interested in engaging in the endless debates
of academe. His project was superficial. Instead of "demystifying,"
"unmasking," or "de-concealing" the "obscurantist" speech of the
"ideologues," he took seriously what serious people said seriously
from their very serious positions in society and then asked, what
makes it possible for them to say *that?* He explored "conditions of
possibility" instead of plumbing the depths of "meaning, that buried
treasure of concealed meanings"[12] where disciplinarians mine forever

in all directions, never knowing when they are passing one another, never having the possibility of meeting on common ground for a friendly but serious chat.

Foucault's writings had no aim. He had targets. His principal target was "what threatens us, as well as what serves us, . . . less reason than the various forms of rationality."[13] His studies were always particular, his struggles local. He understood the irony involved in intellectuals trying, in our societies, to assume their traditional positions "outside" of power. He tried harder than anyone else, I think, to heed his own advice that a would-be "intellectual" should "struggle against the forms of power that would transform him into its object and instrument in the sphere of 'knowledge,' 'truth,' 'consciousness,' and 'discourse.'"[14] His writings were to be impermanent. He "regard[ed] his writings as bombs directed against extant reality, [he wanted] them to 'self-destruct' after use, like fireworks."[15] He wanted the impossible: to stand nowhere. Failing that, he moved, always, quickly. Rather than adopt and elaborate a particular critical posture, he darted among subjects in order not to be pinned (or penned, which is the risk in our profession) down.

One of Foucault's critics, Michael Walzer, has said he has no quarrel with Foucault's attacks on the disciplines as long as he can still be held to traditional standards of truth-telling. "I take him to be making an argument," Walzer writes, "that is right or wrong or partly right or partly wrong."[16] But this strikes me as misunderstanding Foucault's work entirely. In what sense can a firework or a self-destructing bomb be said to be "right or wrong or partly right or partly wrong"? Fireworks and bombs either work or they do not. They impress those who happen to see them or they do not. There is destruction or not, ostentatious violence or a fizzle. Only later is there time for the ethicists and the other expert critics to debate right and wrong according to extant conventions. "Should it have been made?," "Should it be used again?," "Was the target the correct one?"—these are *post hoc* questions, as we shall see once we turn to the principal subject of this study.

Foucault did not engage structures of rationality on their own terms like a good critic does when she writes sober, thoughtful, truthful, but contrary accounts of things as they are. He realized, as Philip Roth put it a full three decades ago, that "what is particularly tough about the times is writing about them." "The [American] writer in the middle of the twentieth century," Roth said, "has his hands full in trying to understand, and then describe, and then make *credible* much of [American] reality. It stupefies, it sickens, it infuriates, and finally it is even a kind of embarrassment to one's own meager imagination. The actuality is continually outdoing our talents."[17] Foucault realized it was futile to take on this reality in a critical way, so he did the next best thing: he made light of it, but in the most serious and high-minded of ways. His writings are like mirrors in the funhouse, distorting, de-centering, disruptive, at times humorous, at times sickening, but always reflective of what is, simply, present in our life together. Foucault was, as Maurice Blanchot put it so well, "on a perpetual slalom course between traditional philosophy and the abandonment of any pretension to seriousness."[18] He relied on rhetoric. His language was extravagant, given to excess. It had to be or he could have been construed as trying to make a point. His precursor, according to Richard Poirier, was Emerson who

> *was ready to teach us, long before Foucault, that if we intend to resist our social and cultural fate, then we must first see it for what it is, and that its form, ultimately, is the language we use in learning to know ourselves. Language is also, however, the place wherein we can most effectively register our dissent from our fate by means of troping, punning, parodistic echoings, and by letting vernacular idioms play against revered terminologies.*[19]

For even though Foucault's target was rationality, he did not feel compelled to abandon reason and flee to a critical position, for example, staked out by some neo-Freudians over which they fly the flag of Eros. As he put it, "The rationality of the abominable is a fact of contemporary history. The irrational, however, does not, because of that, acquire any indefeasible rights."

Foucault's vision of power left no escape routes, not even for Foucault. His use of the image of Betham's Panopticon[20] at once illuminates the operations of a power that expresses itself only in relations and simultaneously obliterates the promises of traditional philosophy that there is a position, a critical position, that permits one to stand on neutral ground sufficiently distant from the scene to write critical commentaries. No one can hope, according to Foucault's relentless vision, to be the guard of reason because the Panopticon imposes certain kinds of equivalencies on the guard and the guarded.

Both acquire "records," both have their capabilities and their limitations inscribed in their histories, both are subjected to surveillance, experimentation, and the discipline that comes from correct action. General notions like correct order, right living, or social harmony give way to the contingent criteria of judgment which the next social experiment may bring to the fore.

The world of the Panopticon is no place for what Foucault elsewhere called the "universal intellectual," the figure who "derives from the jurist/notable and finds his fullest expression in the writer, the bearer of values and significations in which all can recognize themselves."[21] In the panoptic structures of our world, there is no true, deeply embedded self to be recognized in the "values and significations" of the writer, not even among those who are regular commentators on "MacNeil-Lehrer." Panopticism demands an always vigilant commitment to improvement, embellishment, judgment that is only temporary, fluid, and directed toward the constitution of a better life. Critics and experts alike are committed by the structures of rationality under which they serve to exactly the same ends.

Even Foucault was subject to the normal and normalizing demands of the modern era. Foucault's critics "believe that he fails insofar as he has no social alternatives to offer, and no moral or political standards on which to base his angry charge that modern society is becoming like a prison, however progressive and benevolent it appears to those who have let themselves be successfully normalized."[22] Even though he could not escape the usual, common, inviting insistences of his critics, he was among the few modern thinkers who refused to meet his critics on their own ground. He remained "a silent being, . . . compulsive in keeping his silence when benevolent or malevolent questioners asked him to explain himself."[23] He would not explain; he refused the all-too-reasonable requests for elaboration. A guerilla fighter in the intellectual world, he simply moved on to the next device that might cause the gears of the clockwork to grind a little more slowly, if only for a little while.

The only alternative to Foucault's silence in response to the ever-so reasonable demands of his critics would have been for him to become yet another "specific intellectual," one who "derives from quite another figure [than the 'universal intellectual'], not the jurist/notable, but the savant/expert."[24] The alternative would have been to become one of the impersonal "anyones" who could always, at any time, enter the Panopticon and run it—expertly (eventually)—so simple was it to see when something was going wrong. It would have been to respond, as so many social critics do, with a line so well thought out and so well rehearsed and so well shaped in response to the critical commentary it has drawn over the years that the shock of everyday abominations cannot cause it even to pause. To engage his critics and the modern situation on their terms would have meant developing a specialty and struggling for support; it would have meant saying "yes" to the demanding operations of great structures in need of expertise. Foucault did not choose the path of the specific intellectual. But neither could he presume to be a universal intellectual on the models of old for along with Russell Jacoby, who argues that "the last intellectuals"[25] disappeared in the 1950s, Foucault believed that the universal intellectual gave way to the specific intellectual around the middle of this century. "It seems to me," Foucault said, "that this figure of the 'specific' intellectual has emerged since the Second World War. Perhaps it was the atomic physicist—let's say in a word, or rather a name: Oppenheimer—who acted as the point of transition from universal intellectual to specific intellectual."[26]

The Extremity of the New Age

"In the hour before dawn one day last summer," J. Robert Oppenheimer told a radio audience two days before Christmas 1945, "the hills of the Jornado del Muerto, a desert stretch in New Mexico, were briefly lighted with a light no man had ever seen before. We who were there knew that a new world lay before us." Oppenheimer was quick to note that this first test of an atomic bomb did not represent a technological rupture in history. The bomb was based on a few physical principles that had been brewing in the scientific laboratories of the world for about a hundred years. The success of the Manhattan Engineering District, as the U.S. Army named the venture that brought us the first bombs, was that it brought together pretty good engineers who were able, in a relatively short amount of time, to create the conditions under which some of the power of natural forces might make itself manifest. "If there was any surprise in this first explosion," Oppenheimer said, "it lay not in any great new discovery. It lay rather in the fact that what happened was so like what we thought would happen—that the physical science which had been built into this new weapon was such a sure and reliable guide."[27] The extremity implied by a few equations on the blackboard was realized on that "way of the dead" in a corner of the New Mexican desert.

But without a doubt the bomb heralded a new age, an age of new relationships, of new structures of power emblematized by "systems thinking." Just after hearing the public announcement of the use of the atomic bomb against the city of Hiroshima, Norman Cousins wrote his famous editorial for *The Saturday Review of Literature* in which he declared, "Modern Man is Obsolete." "It should not be necessary to prove that on August 6, 1945, a new age was born," he wrote. The bombing of Hiroshima

> *marked the violent death of one stage in man's history and the beginning of another. Nor should it be necessary to prove the saturating effect of the new age, permeating every aspect of man's activities, from machines to morals, from physics to philosophy, from politics to poetry; in sum, it is an effect creating a blanket of obsolescence not only over the methods and products of man but over man himself.*[28]

We may try to comfort ourselves by rehearsing in our minds and on appropriately ceremonial occasions how little the "basic nature of human beings" has changed, how it is possible still to be "human" despite all the changes that have occurred in the last half century. But it seems to me valuable to take Cousins seriously and reflect for a few moments on the possibility that modern man is, actually, obsolete.

The many people who tried to express the nature of our new age hold in common the view that the notion of a boundary, the notion on which we have always relied for our definition, was suddenly no longer meaningful. The boundaries of the classes, across which extended the relationships of power that defined our modernity, were obliterated by the great equalizer qua leveler whose first names were Trinity, Fat Man, and Little Boy. The boundaries of the nation-states, in terms of whose shifting relationships we have always, in the past, written history, were no longer defensible, literally, rhetorically or figuratively. Even the self lost definition because the final boundary of the self, which it has always been the social obligation of others to mark well, was transformed from the ritually loaded notion of "the hour of our death" into something common, not to say vulgar. We comfort ourselves by being concerned about injustices across the still all-too-palpable boundaries of race, class, gender, and global inequalities, and there is still some growth potential in the sectors of the knowledge industry that mount these critiques. But the fact that problems still persist around and violence is still practiced across these boundaries on which social science has based much of its critical case should not stop us from reflecting on the violences exacted in the name of a rationality that begins with the obliteration of all definition-giving boundaries.

The elimination of boundaries by new forms of thought and by the practices that thought enabled caused Cousins, for one, to suggest that there are only two alternatives open to those who live in the new age: boundary breaching world government equal in power to the potency of the new weapons or the boundary breaching abolition of all nations, all civilization, all progress, all literacy, so that once again the tribe would be sovereign. The new age is not tolerant of the boundaries that have been built by history and defined and defended by philosophy. As Robert Jay Lifton put it in his book, *Boundaries*, "There is a very real sense in which the world has become a 'total environment,' a closed psychic chamber with continuous reverberations bouncing about chaotically and dangerously."[29] Without walls that help us come to know who we are through the limits they impose on our freedom, the self which can be a limitless anything threatens to dissolve into nothing.

If there is a modern—that is to say, pre-mid-twentieth century—figure whose existence is tied to the notion of boundaries, it is the traditional expert. The expert might push back the frontiers of knowledge, as we say, but always by digging deeper into the subject matter bounded by his or her expertise. Expertise was always a personal matter locatable in a person who could be held accountable for her or his expertise. Expertise was personal "because it remain[ed] partly tacit and mysterious, [and became] inseparable from the person of the knower."[30] The expert gained a large, often determinative part of his or her identity through the boundaries of the knowledge for which she or he was personally responsible. Whether the world divided knowledge or knowledge divided the world, there were in the persons of the experts identifiable people responsible for the boundaries that held everything together. The world was an ethical place in the old sense of that term. That is, beyond the boundaries of expert knowledge there remained a space into which human meaning could be projected.

In the new age the very notion of "expert" is called into question. Some say there are more experts now than ever before. Some say we are more dependent on experts now than ever before. There is little reason to dispute such claims. However, the expert who is responsible for a disciplined definition of subject matter and for an ethically grounded, asymptotic approach to truth within a subject is an anachronism. This is the new age of boundary breaching logic and practices. Even Peter F. Drucker, whose work on management gave some impetus to contemporary reliance on experts, suggests that we live with a set of "new realities" that "are different from the issues on which politicians, economists, scholars, businessmen, union leaders [experts of all sorts] still fix their attention, still write books, still make speeches."[31] A review of Drucker begins,

> Times have changed, but we still talk about nation-states and nation-based corporations in a world increasingly defined by economic regionalism and transnational enterprises. We celebrate capitalism or socialism in a global economy that has moved beyond class and ideology. We worry about securing justice in America through government and about securing justice in the Soviet Union through liberation from government, when the very idea of government has become obsolete. . . . Faced with recurrent crises today, we put the big adjustments off till tomorrow. But tomorrow has arrived.[32]

This "tomorrow" was characterized by Norbert Wiener at mid-century who wrote, "The thought of every age is reflected in its technique. . . . If the seventeenth and early eighteenth centuries are the age of clocks, and the later eighteenth and the nineteenth centuries constitute the age of steam engines, the present time is the age of communication and control."[33] It is the age of information exchange (or information markets), strategic planning, tactical response, flexibility, social athleticism, all terms that gain meaning only as one thinks across traditional boundaries. Of course, there have appeared those people who claim to be experts in the new fields, communications, ecology, interdisciplinary studies, and other fabrications of the academy that try to force our "tomorrow" into the molds of yesterday. But those molds will not hold. One might zone off a small portion of these new fields—which have no boundary and encompass everything—and develop one's expert authority by placing boundaries around that portion. But honest experts recognize that such boundaries are artificial, that at best individual "experts" can only make small contributions to the whole that is everything.

Walzer, again, can follow Foucault "so long as [he] takes on the disciplines one by one, medicine, psychiatry, criminology, political science, and so on." But for Walzer the game must stop at the boundary of each discipline because "each of these [Foucault's] campaigns must still take place within the overall discipline of language and the rules of plausibility (if not Truth)."[34] In this Walzer is taking only the modern stand of the expert interdisciplinarian. The trouble that Walzer (correctly) senses is that Foucault, the self-styled anti-disciplinarian, may, if his argument is taken seriously and pushed beyond its limit (where, after all, it points), turn out to be anti- the new "disciplines" of interdisciplinarity which are the last stands for modern expert critics including Walzer himself, Habermas, and others.

To an extent that he did not intend, Oppenheimer may have gotten our time right when he said, in response to General Groves's request for names of the best people in the new field of atomic physics, "There are no experts."[35] That phrase would acquire a new force during and after the creation of the atomic bomb, a period that involved not so much the actions of responsible experts as the successful mobilization of new structures of expertise. Contra Walzer and the many others who think they can find a ground for criticizing our new age by expertly articulating ever more broadly conceived theories, it may be the case, as Foucault put it, that there is no outside anymore.[36] Expert critics may be simply mirror images of the experts and may be part and parcel of the new structures of power that make it impossible for anyone to be a responsible expert in the traditional sense anymore.

In this work I am not interested in making an expert contribution to the debates about expertise. I am not inclined to take up the old questions about experts and expertise. Are experts necessary? I suppose they are until we opt for Cousins's second course: punish literacy with death, as he put it, and return to the tribe with all *that* has to offer. But, finally for me, the question is most uninviting. Did experts appear on the modern scene because of their ability to create protected markets or did they emerge as the victors in a free competition among esoteric knowledges? I am persuaded by the arguments of the sociologists and historians that, probably, something like the former happened. But unless I had some technically oriented, monstrously presumptuous plan of social action that might flow from such knowledge about experts, I am not sure I should take a side.

I prefer simply to describe the position of experts in the new age captured as they are by the operations of modern expertise. Philip Rieff said that for scholars and teachers, "the last thing we have to do, if then, is to deliver a message, even to our little world." Unless we remain "re-cognizers," then "we professors of the present may become minor actors in more or less provincial roadshows."[37] The chapters that follow are descriptions through illustrations. Each moves from the general to the specific. This is partly to avoid the implication (or the imputation) that I am offering anything resembling a theory of expertise. Robert Oppenheimer and the other components of the bomb system are, for me, only the most extreme illustration of the position of experts and expertise in our time. But we must rely on extreme examples to help us grasp an extreme situation. Those looking here for a message about experts and their expertise will be disappointed. What follows is nothing but description—excessive at times, extravagant of course—of some of the activity at the leading edge of the rationality of the abominable.

The decision to "describe" what I see on the horizon of modern expertise is not an attempt to resurrect the old fact-value dichotomy and stand safely on one side of the divide. In fact, I make the decision to describe as part of an effort to reveal the values and (an ugly notion) "valuing processes" required by our commonplace "facts." As the next chapter makes clear, systems thinking presents itself as a "perspective," but it is not a perspective in the traditional sense of that term.[38] It provides no position from which to see anything; instead it offers a set of axioms by which to apprehend everything, including all that is invisible from any true perspective. To describe something is to try to recover from our "new epistemological mode" (as one writer calls systems thinking) the very notion of perspective. This book is an exercise in trying to say what can be seen from a particular view point.

There are other "lines of approach," as Freud put it, to this problem. Foucault and Illich reclaim perspective by gaining historical distance on our present by tracing back over the "histories of the present" or over the "histories of modern certainties." I try to reclaim perspective by using the words that have become commonplace in ways that are ever so slightly out of place, by extracting them from their usual contexts and embellishing them with a few provocative descriptors. Jokes often function by forcing us to see ourselves—our everyday, well accepted, historically and culturally grounded selves—just slightly differently. And to the extent a joke works, it might help us rethink our selves, if only for a moment.

Rousseau lamented that the authors of his time said little and made "many pronouncements." He urged his Emile toward authors "rich in facts and sparing in judgments."[39] With that notion as our guide we can begin to examine the bases of our modern rationality of the abominable.

CHAPTER TWO:

The Complex and the Simple

Our job is to trace the connections and reveal them.

"JACK LINT"
Ministry of Information Retrieval
Brazil

I want to invoke Drucker without endorsing him.* He employs a topographic image to discuss some types of historical changes. Most passes across rises or peaks in the landscape, he says, mark only the smallest geographical change from one valley to the next, from one undulation to the next. "But some passes are different," he writes. "They are true divides. They are often neither high nor spectacular." Sometimes, looking back on what one has experienced as a most gradual shift in one's position, one knows that there is no return. Things are different. One's old world may still be in view; it may still be recalled with the mixture of bitter and sweet that accompanies most memories of the recent past; but once one is on the down slope of the other side of such a pass, regardless of how gentle the slope, one cannot go back. *"There are new realities,"*[1] as Drucker puts it.

---

*Frankly, Drucker's analysis impresses me as one of the most thoughtful considerations of our time in terms of the disappearance of boundaries and the reconstruction of the world along system theoretic lines. He and I obviously differ on our understanding of what is "political." I am concerned with new structures of power enabled by systems thinking. He is interested in new approaches to managing this new reality.

Sometime in this century our society crossed a pass in its dominant mode of thought that enables peculiar new forms of practice. We moved from an analytical approach to knowledge to a systems approach to knowledge. Crossing this pass changed thought and practice, irrevocably in my view. An analytical approach to knowledge directed inquiry into the so-called complexity of one's world through the simplifying Method of Descartes and Bacon. One knew the complex, analytically, in terms of its simple components. A systems approach to knowledge stands this old approach on its head. Now the task of inquiry is to determine the location of the simple in terms of the complex. The task begins by taking for granted the grand and newly obvious simplicities of our world—the simple beauty of the explosion of the first atomic bomb (for which, see page 61 below), the simple fact of flight in hopelessly sophisticated modern jet aircraft, the simple fact of Life itself—and proceeds to understand these simplicities in relation to the enormous, complex systems—both those that are components of the object of inquiry and those that surround the object and of which the object is but a sub-system—that enable the simplicity to make itself manifest. Just as systems thinking turns inquiry on its head, so does it change fundamentally the role of the expert. Experts based in the analytic tradition sought mastery and domination of nature and the social world. Problems admitted solutions and one only had to find the right solution whenever a problem revealed itself. Now, what Drucker says of social problems is true for all problems: they "are much too complex to admit a simple 'right answer.' If they can be solved at all, they always have several solutions—and none is quite right."[2] Dreams of mastery and domination have given way to management, optimization, and the task of enabling a system to realize its potential.

There will be much more to say about the changes involved in crossing the pass from analytical thinking to systems thinking. For now, consider our position on the pass. In writing of this shift in the context of medical thought and practice, Bernard Bergen and I suggested that systems theory and analytical thought stand in the same relation to one another as the two images in a pentimento. In a pentimento one image overlays and obscures the other, but hints and suggestions of the underlying image can still be discerned. There are analytically oriented thinkers and experts around today. Some are quite prominent. Isn't it, then, just so much rhetoric to say that systems theory has eclipsed analysis? No. Systems theory needs analysis and analytically inclined experts. Indeed, systems theory creates the prominence of some analysts and their analyses.* In fact, one of the rude truths of systems (explored more thoroughly in the next chapter) is that systems both *create* and *dispose* of experts according to the whims of the system. We can comfort ourselves by interpreting images from our present surroundings in terms retained from our past, but I think this is equivalent to looking backward as we progress (progress backwards, shall we say?) down the far side of that gentle pass that divides our thinking and our time from nearly four centuries of one mode of thought and one approach to practice.

But systems was a fad of the seventies, wasn't it? No one even teaches systems theory anymore. And in those disciplines like biology that introduced us to systems thinking, there has been an admission of failure and a retreat from this clearly ineffective approach to their work. To the contrary, my contention is that, today, no one has to teach systems thinking anymore because it is the only way to think. Rational speech is, of necessity, cast in the systems idiom of information, communication, coding, regulatory mechanisms, mobilizations of resources, windows of opportunity, threshold conditions, feedbacks, feed forwards, and the like. And the complaint that some disciplines have abandoned systems thinking in order to advance their disciplinary knowledge begs the question. Systems thinking does away not with the disciplines themselves, but with the prominence of the disciplines. This kind of argument is equivalent to pointing at a painting of a dog, seeing the ghostly suggestion of a landscape that was the first painting on the canvas, and insisting that, in fact, the painting is actually of a landscape and that anyone who could see well would see this (and not, erroneously, the dog). Such an argument will go a long way in the circles of investors who hope against hope for a rebound in the landscape painting market. It is fine to look backward and remember the territory left behind; it is fine to hope

---

*Recall, for example, Richard Feynman at the Challenger inquiry dunking the piece of O-ring material into a glass of ice water and demonstrating how that proverbial "pebble" caused the catastrophic collapse of that most prominent part of that most complex system. Analysis at its best, some would say. But then recall Feynman's admission that some anonymous someone deep inside the space exploration system prompted him to this stunt.

against hope that this pass will be one of those many passes that mark only minor transitions in our traverse of the territory. But it may be of some value to spend a little time considering the question of how we are going to live—or, prior to that, whether it will be possible to live—in what may be, in fact, a new land.

Now review with me the historically vast territory of the analytical tradition. Then consider the land of systems. You will decide if we have crossed a pass into "new realities."

The Complex from the Simple: The Regime of Analysis

Descartes' dream, literally and metaphorically,[3] was that all science should be unified. Descartes wrote he did not wish to "embroil" himself in the "many questions which are in dispute among the learned." He took instead a tack that permitted him, he said, to work his way from a few, basic, simple truths to a complex "chain of other truths" including "all the principal difficulties usually treated in philosophy," "certain laws which God has so established in nature . . . that after sufficient reflection we cannot doubt that they are exactly observed in all which exists or which happens in the world," and sundry other "truths."[4] Descartes's path to understanding the complexities of this life was his Method, which he outlined in four steps:

> *The first rule was never to accept anything as true unless I recognize it to be certainly and evidently such: that is, carefully to avoid all precipitation and prejudgment.*
>
> *The second was to divide each of the difficulties which I encountered into as many parts as possible and as might be required for an easier solution.*
>
> *The third was to think in an orderly fashion when concerned with the search for the truth, beginning with the things which were simplest and easiest to understand, and gradually and by degrees reaching toward more complex knowledge.*
>
> *The last was . . . always to make enumerations so complete and reviews so general, that I would be certain that nothing was omitted.*[5]

To know a thing under this regime of knowledge that grounded our culture for such a long time, one merely had to analyze it—take it apart. One knew the complex in terms of its more simple components. And if those simple components were themselves too complex to understand easily, they could be subjected to analysis as well.

Events could always be analyzed into their component parts and articulating forces. Behind blinding complexity lay, always, clear simplicity. This was the faith of the analyst. Analysis of a very complex event might take time, but time was irrelevant to the analyst because his objects of interest were timeless laws of cause and effect, relations of things and forces that are valid everywhere and always and that stand at the service of understanding. The physicist Ilya Prigogene answers the question, "What are the assumptions of classical science?" this way: "Generally those centering around the basic conviction that at some level *the world is simple* and is governed by time-reversible fundamental laws. . . . Here time is apparently reduced to a parameter, and future and past become equivalent."[6] Scientists working in the classical, analytic tradition apprehend the true natures of "all events" which "were considered to be subject to a universally valid law in the fullest sense of the word, which means, among other things, valid beyond the reach of human sense experience. . . , valid beyond the reach of human memory, . . . valid even beyond the coming into existence of organic life on earth herself."[7]

The classical tradition of scientific inquiry was exemplified by that great Victorian analyst, Sherlock Holmes. Recall that according to Dr. Watson, Holmes sometimes put pen to paper himself to describe his technique, to report findings of his researches, and, on rare occasions, to recount a case. In his article, "The Book of Life," Holmes wrote, "From a drop of water, a logician could infer the possibility of an Atlantic or a Niagara without having seen or heard of one or the other. So all life is a great chain, the nature of which is known whenever we are shown a single link of it." The complexities of life, including "a man's inmost thoughts," could be known via the route of the simplest of outward signs: "Deceit . . . was an impossibility in the case of one trained to observation and analysis." Admonished Holmes,

> Before turning to those moral and mental aspects of the matter which
> present the greatest difficulties, let the inquirer begin by mastering more
> elementary problems. Let him, on meeting a fellow mortal, learn at a

glance to distinguish the history of the man, and the trade or profession to which he belongs.[8]

Nature, including human nature, is an open book for the observant analyst to read. And entering the book at any page allows one to know it, eventually, cover to cover because the latter, more complex parts of the Book of Life are built rigorously from the earlier, simpler parts.

Dr. Watson may have thought Holmes's approach to the "Book of Life" to be "ineffable twaddle,"[9] but it was Watson's own profession, during his own time, that institutionalized Holmes's "decomposition procedure" as the profession's ideal approach to its subject, disease. Medicine found its truth in the decomposable body. Scientific medicine's ideal disease would always be found to be a disruption in some part of the body reached through an analytically based diagnostic inquiry. Medicine of the nineteenth and early twentieth centuries ostensibly dealt with people, but medical knowledge sought to bypass, quickly, the person suffering from a disease. "It is in the science of biology and the enterprise of medicine," writes Marsden Blois, "where we encounter a particular need for vertical explanation and where we experience an urgency to account for a phenomenon at one level by referring to states of affairs lying at lower or higher ones." Suggesting that a "reductionist (a *decompositionist*) procedure would seem to be more of an historical fact than a deliberate research strategy," Blois nevertheless admits, "the most striking achievements in explanation have been attained by carrying out a 'downward' analysis and in detecting 'upward causation' (i.e., explanation and causality flowing in opposite directions)."[10] Like other objects of analytical inquiry, the decomposable body was divided into levels of inquiry such as organ systems, organs, organ structures, cells, subcellular structures, and so on. The ideal of medicine was to understand illness at the highest level—the person experiencing an illness—in terms of disruptions and their causes observed at lower levels. Medicine always found Morgagni's "tracks" of disease in the body of the dead person lying on the anatomist's table. It was the anatomist's job to retrace those tracks, which were left in the body by that ultimate analyst, medicine's enemy, death.

As the body, medicine's object of knowledge, was divided into its parts, so was medicine divided. The nineteenth century was the century of specialization. Medical knowledge and practice fractured into specialties precisely along the lines of analytical decomposition medicine mapped through the body. The same happened with other forms of knowledge and practice as disciplines took their modern form in the latter part of the nineteenth century. The disciplines and their enabling mechanism, the examination, divided nature through inquiry and investigation. Harsh, universal judgments and crude moral classifications were undermined by the disciplines that "characterize, classify, specialize; [that] distribute along a scale, around a norm, hierarchize individuals in relation to one another."[11] Statistics, the study of variation based on probability, the science of uncertainty, was invented and permitted the study of classifications, cross-classifications, correlations, and the other manifestations of complexity that the disciplines, through their inquiries and examinations, broke down.[12]

Somewhat ironically, disciplinary knowledge ensured ignorance among the disciplinarians. As Watson observed of Holmes,

> His ignorance was as remarkable as his knowledge. Of contemporary literature, philosophy and politics he appeared to know next to nothing. . . . My surprise reached a climax, however, when I found incidentally that he was ignorant of the Copernican Theory and the composition of the Solar System. That any civilized human being in this nineteenth century should not be aware that the earth travelled around the sun appeared to me such an extraordinary fact that I could hardly realize it.

But Holmes was not so much concerned with being a "civilized human being" as he was with being an *expert* Consulting Detective. He did not wish, he said to Watson, to have "useless facts elbowing out the useful ones" in his brain.[13] The disciplinarian is necessarily concerned with the minutiae of the world—and will engage in even the most seemingly bizarre examinations to apprehend life's little details[14]— for it is through the knowledge of little, simple things that big, complex things are understood by the analyst.

The disciplines distribute expertise. They create a matrix of knowledges and ignorances with cells to be filled by specialists. But the dream of Descartes remains viable under this scheme because the matrix as a whole, in theory, includes all knowledge and the truth of all things. Indeed, the matrix of knowledge mirrors Descartes's Method in that it constitutes the analysis of knowledge itself. The matrix of knowledge imposed boundaries within which experts had to speak their known truths and outside of which they would not dare to speak.

At various times, various disciplines—mathematics, sociology, philosophy—have imagined themselves to be the "discipline of disciplines" and the practitioners in these would-be meta-disciplines have aspired to the role of "cultural observer," as Richard Rorty puts it. Such an observer, he says, presumes that "he knows everyone's common ground," "knows what everybody is really doing whether *they* know it or not, because he knows about the ultimate context (the Forms, the Mind, Language) within which they are doing it." Susan Bordo comments, "The dream of establishing such a context, itself transcending all particular contexts, is thus a dream of being able to adjudicate all particular contexts."[15] Disciplinary knowledge is necessarily limited, narrow—and for that, potentially biased or even mistaken—knowledge. But within the dream there is the possibility of corrective action provided by a meta-discipline. Each discipline has little hope of knowing all things, but the epistemological framework that pushes one toward knowledge of the elemental holds out the hope of knowing, ultimately, the essential.

Under this centuries-old approach to knowledge, one apprehends the truth of a thing by reasoning from the particular to the general. Things of the world are little more than instances to analytical science. The particular event holds one's interest only until it is classified. After that, the general truth of the classification flows back—downward, in Blois's terms—over an instance or a particular to explain it. Adolphe Quetelet early in the nineteenth century invented the term *l'homme moyen*, the "average man," that permitted people to speak of Man without direct reference to the women and men one encountered from day to day. Particular people became mere data in the general, multiple classifications of Man. The truth of particular people came to be known by the extent of their deviations from the "average man."[16] The particular held no particular interest. One recalls Holmes's seeming lack of engagement with most of his cases, even those that intrigued him or that offered something "singular." Cases were "of some interest" to the extent that they put his general knowledge—of cigar ashes, of dirts, of plants, of people—to the test or to the extent that they suggested needed reforms in his classificatory framework of general knowledge. Solutions to "inexplicable" crimes or recountings of mysterious chains of events were "elementary" once their general features were understood. In only a few cases, as for example in the case of *the* woman, Irene Adler, was Holmes taken by the particular. And when he was, his general knowledge failed him. (One also recalls that other would-be detective, Oedipus, who could answer the perplexing riddle about that most general category of Man but who, when it came to the task of discovering a particular man in the context of a particular riddle—the murderer of Laius—experienced a few problems.) All things are, in the approach of the classical tradition, knowable because all things are classifiable. Particular instances, conceived as variations on themes, are explained through general knowledge of universal laws.

Knowledge through abstraction was guided by the overarching, underlying metaphorical and practical understanding that the cosmos, the world, and all their parts were machines. Everything was a more or less competent mechanical device. The solar system was a well regulated mechanism. A particular woman's uterus was a more or less competent gestational niche and extrusion device. The body as a whole was a marvelously complex machine that consisted of well articulated machines that served their various functions more or less well. Social organizations and institutions, even society itself, were conceived as great machines whose laws of operation could be apprehended in precisely the way physicists understood the solar system or medicine understood diseases tracking through the bodies of ill people.

The mechanical metaphor enabled people to think in modern terms, in terms of "control," in terms of "improvement," and in terms of "progress." Machines that *were* made, whether by a First Maker or by a lesser deity, could be remade to do their jobs better: more efficiently, more carefully, more accurately, or whatever the reigning notion of "better" might be. Machines invite intervention and the analysis of a mechanism guides intervention to precise points. The productive forces of a machine can be harnessed to serve while their counterproductive forces can be resisted or attenuated by the just application of counterforces. Hannah Arendt said that one of the "outstanding characteristics of the modern age from its beginnings to our own time" is the

typical attitude of homo faber: *his instrumentalization of the world,*

> *his confidence in tools and in the productivity of the maker of artificial
> objects; his trust in the all-comprehensive range of the means-end
> category, his conviction that every issue can be solved and every human
> motivation reduced to the principle of utility; his sovereignty, which
> regards everything given as material and thinks of the whole of nature
> as of "an immense fabric from which we can cut out whatever we want
> and resew it however we like"; his equation of intelligence with
> ingenuity. . . .*[17]

Arendt reminds us that it was not simply that the modern age witnessed an inversion in the value attached to contemplation and the
value attached to fabrication wherein questions of what a thing is
became idealized guides for the making and remaking of things. The
relationship between the idea of a thing and the thing itself, around
which Western philosophy had originally constructed itself was, she
says, "forced wide open [when] the emphasis shifted entirely away
from the question of what a thing is and what kind of thing was to
be produced to the question of how and through which means and
processes it had come into being and could be reproduced. . . . Contemplation was no longer believed to yield the truth."[18] If one was to
read the Book of Nature or the Book of Life, it was not now for
revelation and personal enrichment or out of a sense of responsibility
for life and nature. One read nature and life to tame them. Prince
Albert's Great Exhibition of 1851 at the Crystal Palace assembled not
"The Ideas of Civilization" but "The Industry of All Nations." As one
commentator put it, "The Great Exhibition stands as a striking record
of all that the world has done—it marks the point to which mankind
has arrived—and it indicates what he has yet to subdue."[19]

Descartes's dream was of the mastery of nature. The intellectual
and the practical mastery of nature were to become one. The early
theoretical physicists, whose successors are principals in this essay,
are sometimes imagined to be the purest of intellectuals who dealt
only with problems whose truth could only be spoken in the nearly
opaque language of higher mathematics. However, we learn that for
them, "mathematics was an indispensable tool of their work, but it
was not their goal. Physical understanding was their goal, to which
they brought to bear all kinds of mathematical techniques."[20] That
God made humankind in His image became an irrelevance for the
modern age because the modern age was the first in which human-

kind would set for itself the dream of making nature conform to any image it wished. The Method of reason—in which the complex is understood in terms of the simple, in which the particular is under-stood in terms of the general, and in which timeless, universal laws are there to be apprehended by the careful examiner—would master the complexity of a profusely productive world to produce anything that might satisfy whatever demands the age might have. Arendt, of course, argues that the modern age has stripped the species of the classical demands of the *vita contemplativa* so that what is left is "a 'natural force,' the force of the life process itself to which all men and human activities [are] equally submitted . . . and whose only aim, if it [has] an aim at all, [is] survival of the animal species man."[21] Her words echo those of Chief Seattle no doubt because she was describing our entry into precisely the period that Seattle knew was at hand. The complexity of a productive world can be, imaginably at least, mastered to produce Life itself, the Life to which, Illich argues, every-thing can be sacrificed. The paradox of the age is that life itself is produced through a certain indifference to human lives. The power of this paradox will become clear as we see what form the dream has assumed in this most modern world that we now inhabit.

Pursuing Simplicity Through Complexity: The Regime of Systems

A 1983 newspaper story describing Boeing's then-new airplanes, the 757 and 767, began,

> No one really understands the Boeing 757. No single person knows how to design or build it. No one human, or even a modest group of humans, could fully fathom its complexities.
>
> But anyone could fly a 757—even a nonpilot, under ideal conditions.
>
> Advancing technology, be it in an airplane, a telephone system or a computer program often seeks simplicity through complexity.

These new airplanes achieve their simplicity by layering com-plexity on complexity. Aircraft systems are composed of modules, each of which has its own internal set of systems.

> *On-board electronic systems are in modules, and built-in computers tell*
> *maintenance workers which modules, or boxes, should be replaced to get*
> *a plane flying again almost immediately. Boxes removed from the plane*
> *are taken to repair shops where more new technology is used to diagnose*
> *and repair problems.*
>
> *So the 757 is an amalgamation of hardware that can be repaired*
> *quickly by maintenance personnel who may not really understand what*
> *they are repairing, and flown by pilots who may have little grasp of the*
> *technology they command.*[22]

And, of course, the new planes cannot realize their full potential
without global support systems of aviation administrations, radars
and route controllers, meal preparation systems, and so on. The new
planes are, in a sense, substitutable components in the vast systems
of transportation for Life as we know it.

Traditional science sought to master and dominate complexity
through the simplifying activity of the analytical Method. Modern
science pursues simplicity through complexity. But there is no dream
of mastery anymore. The best one might hope for is the optimal
realization of a system's potential, something that requires a new
kind of expert constitutionally attuned to the demands not of machines but of systems. Some pilots like the new airplanes. Those who
love to dabble with computers enjoy flying the 757 because at the
touch of a button they can get a quick, clean, simple display of information about any aspect of their plane without having to worry
about finding (and interpreting) the right dial or gauge in the myriad
of instruments in the typical jet aircraft. The engineer in charge of
designing the 757's flight deck said, "The crew procedures are simple
and the workload is the lowest of any commercial airplane."[23] Behind
this simplicity, though, lies more than one hundred computers and
an electrical system with nearly forty thousand wires. Some of these
pilots even laugh at the joke that tells us that planes in the future will
be flown by one pilot and one dog. The pilot will be there to feed the
dog and the dog will be there to bite the pilot if he even thinks about
touching the controls.

There are those who don't find that joke funny. There are pilots
who think that flying a plane is an activity in which a person actively
and consciously oversees and uses the technology at hand to *fly* the
machine (much as Neil Armstrong *flew* the first lunar lander, pro-

ducing much embarrassment, exasperation and anxiety among his "mission controllers"). They point out that if the electricity goes out in the new planes, they are left with two instruments: one to tell how high the plane is and one to tell if it is flying upside down. Simplicity comes at the price of relatively opacity. One need not know and often one cannot know what is going on behind the simple data displays that monitor, record, and actually enable the flight. It flies. It is as simple as that.

"The pursuit of simplicity" is the hallmark of a new way of thinking. Prigogene writes, "our vision of nature is undergoing a radical change toward the multiple, the temporal, and the complex." And Alvin Toffler, commenting on Prigogene's work, says,

> the Age of the Machine is screeching to a halt, if ages can screech—and ours certainly seems to. And the decline of the industrial age forces us to confront the painful limitations of the machine model of reality. . . . The notion that the world is a clockwork, the planets timelessly orbiting, all systems operating deterministically in equilibrium, all subject to universal laws that an outside observer could discover—this model has come under withering fire ever since it first arose.[24]

The new way of thinking emphasizes information over structure, temporality over long-term equilibria, change over stability, probabilistic statements over deterministic pronouncements. To capture this new way of thinking in a single term, one would say we have come under the sway of "systems theory," but the term carries much freight and merits consideration.

To invoke without endorsing another modern thinker, consider the work of Jay Forrester. Forrester was one of the first to link systems theory with that modern systems icon, the computer. He tells us that his interest in systems theoretical thinking arose in part out of the "pervasive sense of failure and frustration among men concerned with management."[25] Forrester was intrigued by these people—city managers in one case study—who thought, indeed *knew*, themselves to be "in charge." They had the requisite skills for analyzing the nature of complex urban phenomena and for using that knowledge to improve the workings of their cities. They had command of the intellectual and material resources that were needed to make cities better places to live. Yet, they were constantly frustrated by the effects of their efforts. Forrester explains that their failure was most likely in the *form* of their thinking, not in the substance of what they thought. The city managers of that day were, after all, experts on the substance of the bounded knowledge of cities. They knew what they knew; their mistake was in how they used what they knew. They saw problems, resolved to solve them, diagnosed the problem's causes in the immediate, local circumstances, implemented policies that used knowledge of appropriate cause-and-effect relationships to achieve desired goals, and waited as evaluators brought in results. Often as not the evaluators brought bad news.

Forrester describes the city managers' form of thought as a "first-order negative-feedback loop" thinking: They began with the idea that something is wrong. That is, some variable that indicates the state of a system is not at the level it should be. A manager imagines being able to make things right by manipulating one variable that stands in an expertly known, direct, causal relationship to the variable of concern. The manager manipulates the cause. The effect follows. The system is found to be less wrong but not quite right, yet. This information feeds back to indicate the causal variable should be manipulated more. The effect follows. The cycle continues until the wrong with which the process started is right. The negative-feedback loop, which is "first-order" because it operates through one cause-effect-assessment loop, indicates that no more manipulations are necessary, interventions stop, and the system stands in a new, improved state. First order, negative feedback loop thinking flows directly from analytical methods. We are conditioned by the analytical method to believe that simple relationships among a few variables lie at the root of any problem.

The problem with this approach, Forrester says, is that

> in complex systems cause and effect are often not closely related in either time or space. . . . The complex system has a multiplicity of interacting feedback loops. Its internal rates of flow are controlled by nonlinear relationships. The complex system is of high order, meaning that there are many system states (or levels). It usually contains positive feedback loops describing growth processes as well as negative, goal-seeking loops. In the complex system, the cause of a difficulty may lie far back in time from the symptoms, or in a completely different and remote part of the system.[26]

All the common sense notions that come from an analytical form of reasoning no longer apply. The world according to systems theory is a different place.

Systems theory offers not a set of rules that constitute a Method of inquiry, but a so-called perspective, a way to see.* (We should employ system theory's own terms with the acknowledgement of the caveat on page 32.) Ervin Laslo's introduction to systems theory is titled, instructively, *A Systems View of the World.* Systems thinking is offered as a corrective to vision that apprehends a thing by seeing the thing in terms of the simple parts that compose it and in terms of the simple relations that drive it. To see the world from a systems perspective one must see connections instead of boundaries, irreducible organization instead of well articulated, interacting parts. Niels Bohr apparently liked to tell the story of how his father explained to him, when he was about three years old, the balanced structure of a tree. His father described for his son each of the parts and how the parts linked together to form the whole. Young Bohr, who would later say that he "dreamed of great interrelationships,"[28] looked at a tree and "saw the wholeness of the organism and dissented; if it wasn't like that, he said, it wouldn't be a tree."[29] New eyes see a new world.

Laslo[30] has outlined the precepts of a systems view of the world. He calls his principles "organizational invariances." Laslo says these invariances are the characteristics an object must have to be considered a natural system. His work can be seen just as well as a handbook on how to adopt a systems perspective. His precepts must become percepts and one must train oneself not to take one's own vision seriously. From a "systems view" one can see everything if one will

---

*For a discussion of the way in which systems concepts become percepts and bring about "new realities," see Wolfgang Sachs papers on the "development idea" in the "world system." Speaking specifically of technology, Sachs writes,

> *Any technical device is much more than an aid; it is culturally potent. The overwhelming effects of its power dissolve not only physical resistance but also attitudes to life. Technologies shape feelings and fashion worldviews; the traces they leave in the mind are probably more difficult to erase than traces they leave in the landscape.*[27]

In fact, few people think anymore about the traces left in the landscape by the atomic system. The shallow dish-shaped indentation at the Trinity site is visited by a few people on the one weekend of each year the site is opened. But the traces left in our minds by the atomic system are sharp and very potent.

but look correctly. His "characteristics of natural systems" are instructions for beginning to see the old world with new eyes.

The first precept is that "natural systems are wholes with irreducible properties." The tree is a tree and if, as Bohr said, it wasn't like *that* it would not be a tree. But beyond this homily, this characteristic/instruction forms the ground on which a systems perspective rests. Systems theory encourages one to adopt an encompassing view. "The systems approach is . . . a 'grand' approach, by which I mean 'large,' 'gigantic,' or 'comprehensive,'" says C. West Churchman.[31] Though she did not use the term "systems theory," Arendt anticipates its perspective in her outline of "the human condition." We exist in the grip of a "new science that considers the nature of the earth from the viewpoint of the universe" and in the shadow of "the great boldness of Copernicus' imagination, which lifted him from the earth and enabled him to look down upon her as though he actually were an inhabitant of the sun." Arendt says that as a consequence of this perspective people "now live in an earth-wide continuous whole."[32] Old-time science mistakenly circumscribed its area of attention, systems theory tells us, and the laws of cause-and-effect that operated in those artificially, if expertly, narrowed spaces were, at best, local laws that permitted one to believe, falsely, that human beings could control the world. Widen your view, systems theory says, and do not fail to attend to the larger system in which all local phenomena are embedded, for it is only by appreciating the characteristics of the larger wholes that one can gain an understanding of local events.

Laslo's other precepts speak to the behavior of natural systems and have implicit in them instructions about how one operates in and around complex systems to understand them (but not, definitely, to *control* them). Principles two, three and four are:

2. Natural systems maintain themselves in a changing environment.
3. Natural systems create themselves in response to the challenge of the environment.
4. Natural systems are coordinating interfaces in nature's hierarchy.[33]

In Forrester's summative term, complex systems behave "counterintuitively."

Counterintuitive behavior gains meaning when contrasted with the common-sensical, first-order negative-feedback loop understanding of the world. Our historically documented, materially palpable "mastery of nature" encourages us to believe that when we apply a force to a well-selected variable, other variables change and the world changes with them. Systems theory answers: "But it usually doesn't." Radical changes in the environment of a system can be accommodated. Even changes in the loop structure of the internal environment of a system have little effect on its overall behavior. In Forrester's jargon, "multiple loop realignment along various nonlinear functions makes the complex system highly insensitive to most system parameters. The same nonlinear behavior makes the system resistant to efforts to change its behavior."[34] You can bash a system all you like; you may dent it; you are unlikely to change it. Information, not force, is the new basis for thinking about change. Because "natural systems are coordinating interfaces in nature's hierarchy," whole subsystems can be lost and a system can continue to function. Systems adjust and accommodate, until, of course, the "pebble in the road" brings about a catastrophic collapse.

Thinking that one can master and control complex systems can lead to problems. It is not just that causal forces are usually located in distant parts of the system. Rather, a "complex system is even more deceptive than merely hiding causes" in outback regions of the system. "In the complex system," Forrester writes,

> when we look for a cause near in time and space to a symptom, we usually find what appears to be a plausible cause. But it is usually not the cause. The complex system presents apparent causes that are in fact coincident symptoms. . . . Conditioned by our training in simple systems, we apply the same intuition to complex systems and are led into error. As a result, we treat symptoms, not causes. The outcome lies between ineffective and detrimental.[35]

You might affect a symptom somewhat through your efforts at mastery and domination. You are unlikely to affect the underlying problem. And systems, like the bicycle, are "self righting"; they tend toward previously established equilibria; sooner or later, the symptoms reappear.

In *Normal Accidents*, a book on system catastrophes, Charles Perrow argues that complex systems develop a degree of opacity. Layered and looped nonlinear interactions create a certain incomprehensibility. Starting from a study of the accident at Three Mile Island, Perrow shows how (presumed) common-sense "understanding" can lead to problems that can, in turn, lead to system-wide catastrophic failures. Even though later studies would say that the operators at the Three Mile Island nuclear reactor should have known about a valve that was stuck open, Perrow argues that there was no way for any *person* to know that this very distant *safety* valve was the cause of the disaster in the making. One operator said later, "I think each time we made a decision it was based on something we knew about. . . . There was a logic at that time for most of the actions." When a new shift arrived at the plant two and one-half hours after the start of the accident, checked the valve, found it open, and decided to close another valve to stop the flow of water to the open valve, one operator described that decision as "more of an act of desperation . . . than an act of understanding. After all, he said, you do not casually block off a safety system."[36] Trying to control complex systems as if they were machines with simple, goal-oriented purposes is illusory and occasionally catastrophically dangerous.

Systems theory leads to a particular perversion of the general notion of "understanding." Simple (goal-directed, single-loop, negative-feedback) systems have a certain continuity of action. Effect follows cause until the system monitoring devices force the cause, through their *negative* feedback, to be removed or attenuated. When the cause is removed, the effect ceases. Complex systems sometimes behave discontinuously. Systems simply change states. In models of complex systems, a controlling loop may reach a threshold state and transfer control to another loop altogether. The system appears to have experienced a discontinuous jump from one set of apparent relationships dominating the action to another. But appearances apply only to models and models are designed to mimic—in understandable, essentially linear, essentially simple terms—the behavior of complex systems. Systems *theory* suggests that complex systems experience discontinuities in fact and not just in appearance. This fact—that states of a system may alter fundamentally, that laws may apply only then and not now—contributes to the opacity of a complex system to one who would approach a system with only common-sense understanding. Systems demand new forms of understanding. (The ability to accept the possibility of fundamentally discontinuous change, we shall see, played an important role in the development of atomic theory, and Bohr, that precocious seer of systems, was a principal actor in this.)

In contrast to analytical thinking, which forces one to develop an understanding of the general, systems thinking binds one's interest to the particular. Laws are local and time dependent under the new regime. "Our universe has a pluralistic, complex character," writes Prigogene.

> Structures may disappear, but also they may appear. Some processes are, as far as we know, well described by deterministic equations, but others involve probabilistic processes. . . . The natural contains essential elements of randomness and irreversibility. This leads to a view of matter in which matter is no longer the passive substance described in the mechanistic view of the world but is associated with spontaneous activity.[37]

Investigators studying processes and structures that are active cannot continue to imagine themselves engaged in the business of apprehending general, immutable, timeless, universal laws. They, like their objects of study, are time bound and place bound, and their object of study must be the particular event with its own particular history and its own singular and, to a degree, unpredictable future.

SYSTEMS AND EXPERTS

With these general remarks on systems thinking in place, we are now in a position to ask the fundamental question of this study: What does an expert do under a systems theoretic perspective? Mastery and domination are no longer possible as the mechanical metaphor that supported that form of practice is no longer available. At this stage we can only glimpse the outlines of an answer to this key question. We know analysis creates specialists. A systems perspective requires generalists, but not dilettantes or know-it-alls. The proponents of the "new sciences" that have sprung up around the systems theoretic view of the world give us an indication of the perspective's mandate. William Ophuls, for example, says the "science of ecology . . . is an effort to bridge the gap between specialties and make possible the rational management of the whole human household," not just one part like "the economy," or "waste," or "energy needs." So, first, we are told that experts must be managers, not masters. But to approach this gigantic, comprehensive management task "will require us, in effect, to become specialists in the general." Ophuls believes

> *there will be a decisive movement away from scientific reductionism, the assumption inherited from Francis Bacon that nature is to be understood by dissecting it into its smallest constituent parts, toward holism, the contrary assumption that nature is best understood by focusing on the interrelationships making up the whole system. . . . The "systems paradigm" will become the dominant intellectual and epistemological mode.*

Those who can see great interrelationships and understand phenomena in terms of boundary breaching processes like the encoding and decoding of information will be more valued than those who expertly discern boundaries and are able to understand local events in terms of laws that the local structures always obey. "Embracing holism," Ophuls contends, "will tend to make thinkers generalists first and specialists second, instead of vice versa as at present."[38]

The systems generalist does not have general knowledge that helps one understand and control the particular event. The systems generalist has skills in the mobilization of any potentially relevant knowledge that might assist in the task of estimating or modeling a particular process.

In order to understand the meaning of the terms "estimating or modeling" in the systems context, we must return for the moment to the realm of the less gigantic, less comprehensive science that sought nature's Laws. Models are an essential part of that kind of science. H. R. Post notes that, "Traditionally there have been two kinds of models. There is the model in the strict logical sense, an articulation of a particular theory. . . , the Deductive Model. . . . There is also the model that has its origins in empirical evidence and some conjectural generalization. . . , the Inductive Model."[39] Both models are incomplete guesses about what is occurring in some local part of nature. In idealized science, theory and data are eventually linked, and the circle of scientific inquiry[40] is closed only to be repeated as theory is elaborated and refined in relation to more sophisticated data. "The old theories, the classical theories of science, provided models of limited aspects of nature," comments C. Truesdell.

> *The example set by the rational mechanics of Euler and Lagrange . . .*

> *illustrates the status of a "Law" . . .: a clear, precise concept of ideal*
> *behavior, embracing an enormous variety of precisely specifiable*
> *cases. . . . Any discrepancy between data of experiment and . . . an*
> *outcome of theory we attribute first and usually finally to our own*
> *failure to apply the "Law" well, not to the "Law" itself.*

The models generally used in classical science, Truesdell concludes, "teach us to find structure in experience, not merely to imitate one or another detail."[41]

Truesdell's last comment points toward a new kind of model that systems theory ushers onto the scientific stage. Post calls it a "floating model." A floating model is "neither deductive (because there is no overriding theory or because such theory is ignored) nor is it inductive, for scientists find interesting mismatches between the model and observation."[42] A floating model is imitative only. It floats free of the two traditional scientific anchors of data and theory. "The first step in modeling is to generate a model that creates the symptom," says Jay Forrester. Systems modeling is not based on theoretical knowledge but on "an intimate working knowledge of the actual systems." Nor is systems modeling based principally on data, for "the barrier to progress in systems is not the lack of data[;] we have vastly more information than we can use in an orderly and organized way." A systems model is a structure of relationships among parameters. A good model incorporates all those relationships that a systems designer thinks may be important in order to get the system model "to behave as the real system would." A systems designer/modeler fails if he allows a felt need for data or for information to stand in his way:

> *Much of the behavior of systems rests on relationships and interactions*
> *that are believed, and probably correctly so, to be important but that for*
> *a long time will evade quantitative measure. . . . It is far more serious*
> *to omit a relationship that is believed to be important than to include it*
> *at a low level of accuracy that fits within the probable range of*
> *uncertainty.*[43]

A systems theoretical model floats on the *beliefs* of the model's designers and needs find no ground except the ground (which was utterly infirm ground under the rules of analytical thinking) of imitation. "Does the output of the model look more or less like we believe actual systems behave?" is the grounding question for a systems model.

One should recall how systems designers build their imitative floating models. The designer's job is to assemble the best experts from the many fields encompassed by the model. The experts' job is to provide the best statement, based on the best available analyses, of the relationships between variables included in the model. This is precisely what Forrester did when he built his Urban Dynamics and, later, his World Dynamics models. If the experts do not have good knowledge of a particular relationship in a particular loop, the system designer solicits a best guess in the sure knowledge that one (or a dozen) "incorrect" relationships in the model are unlikely to have much effect on the outcome of a complex model. Besides, once a relationship is built into a model, it can always be adjusted to accommodate competing experts' ideas on the truth of the relationship. Unlike the experts themselves, who are often ready to go to war over the truth, system designers must be invitational to competing sources of knowledge and accommodative of conflicting ideas. To those who complain, for example, that Forrester's models can be reduced to only a few basic, debatable assumptions, the well-groomed system designer would respond, "Please, complicate it for me. Just how do you believe the system operates?" One might go to war over truth; imitation is not something worth battling over. Imitation as a scientific goal permits the systems scientist to be solicitous of competing ideas and completely open to criticism. With imitation, there is nothing to defend.

Of course, being accommodative, invitational and accepting of competing knowledges within frames provided by floating models leaves the systems expert in a position different from that occupied by traditional scientists and gives rise to a different goal for scientific work. A model is only a model and can never be the thing itself. It can only be a close approximation, a good estimation of what, in general, happens or may happen to the thing itself. "To be human ecologists," remarks Ophuls,

> *it appears that* we must integrate the better part of all human knowledge, *clearly an impossible goal. Yet it must be attempted. We must hope that, although any individual work in human ecology will*

fall well short of the ideal, there will emerge a body of works that
complement each other and give us the global understanding we need.[44]

The first part of Ophuls's hope is the acknowledgment that systems thinkers are relegated only to estimates of the behavior of particular, natural, complex systems. The second part shows that the dream for the totalization of knowledge is alive but, as sometimes happens with dreams, in a somewhat altered form. A disciplinary approach to knowledge left gaps, Holmesian ignorances, that one might dream of filling. A systems view of the world sees human knowledge as perhaps sufficient already but of secondary concern to the task of articulating "all human knowledge" into a seamless web of "global understanding" managed, likely, by a team of system managers. After all, no one person knows how a true system works whether the system is a Boeing airplane, Life, or the atomic system writ large, discussed next.

We can look to the practices of another Victorian character to get some sense of the tasks of the (new) expert who works with floating models and whose emphasis is necessarily on the particular. Sigmund Freud protested often that he was a scientist and that psychoanalysis was, first, a formidable science. He claimed to work with "data" and he claimed to be developing a "theory" and he claimed to be open to competing "hypotheses," but as he warned his students and himself, the case—the *particular* case—was what mattered in the end. As in other complex systems, the psychical problems Freud's patients presented were incomprehensible at the outset. The outward signs of the problems—symptoms, dreams, slips—were always confused and confusing "leaks" through the defensive structures of the psyche. The problem in its complexity lay buried in the structure of the individual's psyche, the structure of which remained more-or-less unknown, even after analysis. The analyst's task was to begin to tickle away at the surface ("What does that make you think of?" "What does that recall?") in the hope of creating some observable movement elsewhere that might give a clue to the labyrinthine structure and dynamics that were creating the presenting dysfunctions that brought the patient to analysis. To do this, the analyst developed a model, a floating model, that "(re)creates the problem." Gradually, the model would be elaborated and would, ideally, come to approximate the working of the underlying psychological system. Out of this model would come the interpretations that the analyst was to offer the patient more in the spirit of continuing to tickle the system than in the name of "knowing" the truth of the patient's problems. But the model was always only an approximation (and that is why the interpretation has to await confirmation from the patient herself). As Freud noted late in his life, there was always a bedrock to the psychic structure that analysis could not penetrate, a navel to every dream that acted as an ultimate block to any interpretations that one's models might suggest.[45]

Freud's work also suggests a way of thinking about the goal of expert work under this new way of thinking. The goal cannot be "mastery and control" of the old sort, since complex systems tend to be resilient and refuse to operate according to the old rules. No analyst, for example, would ever think in terms of an intervention that would represent a "cure" for a patient. But there is a goal in systems thinking that parallels the old goal of intervenient control. Following Freud, we might say that the systems expert seeks to *enable the system to realize itself, to realize its potential.* The new expert does this by "restructur[ing] the system so that internal processes lead in a different direction."[46] Freud's patients were leading problematic and always, in some sense, dysfunctional lives. Freud's task was not to intervene and solve the problem but to enable his patient to become the person he or she was (always, of course, recognizing that the resistances would lead to repetition and "cure" would remain an impossibility). Freud did this by restructuring the psyche, by making conscious some of the material that repression had pushed into the unconscious. If the analyst actually does anything, he creates a "challenge from the environment" in response to which the natural system of the mind recreates itself in order to realize the potential resident there.

The theme of enabling a system to realize itself is inherent in the work of all systems thinkers. Ophuls's book, with its cover picture of the earth seen from space, is a paean to the beautiful harmony resident, from a systems perspective, in the ecosystem of the planet, if only, as the ecologists tell us, people would stop exploiting "nature's economy" which is "generous and plentiful for those who would live modestly within its circle of interdependence." The task of the ecologist is to design systems of human participation in the natural systems of the earth so that "the desired result [of frugality, of diversity, of valuing stewardship] will occur more or less automatically without further human intervention."[47] In other words, the goal is to see to it that the earth might be enabled to realize its potential.

Parenthetically, we might note here the first suggestions of a necrophilic character of systems thinking. Out of the tradition of analytical thought that sought mastery and domination came the notion that the world is essentially a place for human beings, a place to be made into whatever they desired for themselves. Humans were here to make nature serve them. The systems world may be for humans, *but* it may not be. Just how much management of the human household will be necessary to achieve optimal systems of human participation in nature's economy is not specified by the systems thinkers. Systems create a certain equivalence between humans and other subsystems of the global system and lead directly to the concept of substitutability among sub-systems. There is no priority of human living over any other sub-system within the global system. The sub-system of "living human beings" is, from a systems perspective, conceptually equivalent to the "waste management" sub-system, for example. But to say this now is to anticipate what is best understood in the specific context of the atomic system.

Where in all of this complexity is the simplicity that is presumably being pursued? Paul Dirac, the mathematical physicist, argued in 1939 that modern thought had transcended the possibility of using a "principle of simplicity" in its researches as, for example, Newton and his immediate successors had done in formulating classical mechanics. The principle of simplicity, the pursuit of the complex via the article of faith that the world is simple, applies only in the realm of "fundamental laws of motion" and "not to natural phenomena in general," Dirac said. But if modern thought could not use a principle of simplicity as its ground, it could set up a "principle of mathematical beauty" as a goal.

> The research worker, in his efforts to express the fundamental laws of nature in mathematical form, should strive for mathematical beauty. He should still take simplicity into consideration in a subordinate way to beauty. . . . It often happens that the requirements of simplicity and beauty are the same, but where they clash the latter must take precedence.[48]

Instead of pursuing the messy precision of knowledge under a criterion of "correctness," a new criterion—an aesthetic criterion—is installed as that by which the utility of a contribution is to be judged. Human participation in nature's economy ought now to be hygienic and should leave no human trace on the face of what used to be a human dwelling place, that blue marble, an Earth floating in the void of space.

Edward Teller gave a series of lectures at Pepperdine University in 1978 which appeared later as a book called *The Pursuit of Simplicity*. He begins by noting that the modern complaint is, often as not, about the unbelievable and unapproachable complexity of the world and that, often as not, science is blamed for contributing to this complexity if not causing it outright. With Dirac, however, Teller sees modern science as engaged in a "pursuit of simplicity" whose principle criterion is aesthetic.

> *Simplicity, for me, is best characterized in a story from the art traditionally the favorite of mathematicians and scientists: music. When Mozart was fourteen years old, he listened to a secret mass in Rome, Allegri's* Miserere. *The composition had been guarded as a mystery; the singers were not allowed to transcribe it on pain of excommunication. Mozart heard it only once. He was then able to reproduce the entire score. Let no one think that this was exclusively a feat of prodigious memory. The mass was a piece of art and, as such, had threads of simplicity. The structure is the essence of art. [Mozart] could identify the threads, remember them and reinvent the details having listened once with consummate attention. The threads are not easily discovered in music or science. Indeed, they usually can be discerned only with effort and training. Yet the underlying simplicity exists and once found makes new and more powerful relationships possible.*[49]

The simple "beauty" achieved through complexity seems to be the object of admiration of all good systems thinkers. "Nature, in the systems view, is a sphere of complex and delicate organization," begins Laslo. And yet, he says, "The systems view of nature is one of harmony and dynamic balance."[50] Ophuls closes his book, which is putatively about politics, with a quote from Carlos Castaneda:

> *Don Juan . . . caressed the ground gently. "This is the predilection of two warriors," he said, "This earth, this world. For a warrior there can be no greater love. . . . This lovely being, which is alive to its last recesses and understands every feeling, soothed me, it cured me of my*

pains, and finally when I had finally understood my love for it, it taught me freedom."[51]

Forrester seems to enjoy the thought of his complex systems having a dynamic, even a life of their own. His urban model presents the city "as a living, self-regulating system which generates its own evolution through time."[52] Freud, when pressed to say something about the goals of psychoanalysis, answered somewhat cryptically, "love and work." Given the exegesis on love as a *symptom* in the papers on transference and on the culpability of love and work for civilization's discontents in Freud's later work, these three words are readily recognized as aesthetic guideposts and not objective categories by which the success of psychoanalysis might be measured. As for the airplane builders with whom this section began, we can imagine them watching the first take-off of their million and more parts and uttering an awe-struck phrase like, "It flies." Dirac's "principle of beauty" has no objective status. It is something like Prisig's notion of "Quality"—you know it when you see it. It becomes a guiding principle: never quite to be hoped for, always sought, sometimes—usually surprisingly—achieved.

But we must try not to be caught by this pervasive rhetoric. We should pause to note that, just as with Prisig's Quality, there is something "outrageously megalomaniacal"[53] in this pursuit of simplicity as conceived by Teller and others. Indeed, Teller ponders what he calls "The Ultimate Dream: Simplification Completed." It is not entirely clear what he has in mind, but it has something to do with big questions about the nature of the world like, "What is life? What is consciousness? What are human beings?," and it has a lot to do with science actively striving to introduce "consistency and simplicity into a world that without them appears confused, random and even whimsical."[54] "The pursuit of simplicity in science leads to understanding and beauty," Teller concludes.[55]

Perhaps we shall be able to appreciate the meaning of this pursuit if we begin with the work of a relatively small group of modern thinkers whose scientific activity culminated in the Trinity test of the first atomic bomb just before 5:30 A.M., July 16, 1945, an event that many have understood as marking the "dawn of a new age." It was the unnatural first light of that dawn that lit the way to the mornings of August 6 over Hiroshima and August 9 over Nagasaki. Perhaps it is only in the aftermath of the beauty of that rolling, colorful cloud, the awe-inspiring light of those three "shots," and the engaging quiet of two cities laid low that we can begin to grasp the meaning—the human meaning—of these persistent appeals to the new aesthetics our modern systems offer to our senses.

The Atomic Bomb System

When the first atomic bomb exploded at the Trinity test site in the New Mexico desert,

> *Marvin Wilkening, then a young graduate student with Fermi's group, was fascinated with how relatively* simple *it all had been. Ernest O. Lawrence, watching from Compania Hill, felt the same way. What impressed him most was that the whole affair had gone off exactly as the scientists' calculations had predicted. It was, in the parlance of the time, "technically sweet."*[56]

The outcome may have been simple, but nothing leading up to that moment had been simple at all. Perhaps the most complex undertaking of the war, based on some of the most complicated, sophisticated human thought, led to this simple event.

It is time to recount something of the history of the making of the bomb as we know it. My purpose, recall, is not to write the history right or more fully. The history as we know it is valuable in so far as it shows us that the bomb emerges from a systems way of thinking, that it really was a matter of simplicity coming from complexity, that the experts who were party to this endeavor—and the rest of us by implication if not in consequence—really were and are living in a new age in which the principal question may be whether it is possible to live anymore.

THE MARK OF A NEW AGE:
THE SIMPLICITY OF MASS DEATH

Shortly after 7 A.M. on the morning of August 6, 1945, a single B-29 came into view over Hiroshima, Japan. Air sirens sounded. Twenty minutes later, the plane was gone. Nothing had happened.

At this point in the war, the Japanese knew to fear the drone of the scores, sometimes hundreds of B-29s that rained fire on their cities. Incendiary bombing killed as many as a hundred thousand people in six hours in Tokyo. The Japanese military threw all of its meager defenses against these massive attacks. As August 6 approached, the United States' general staff in the Pacific decided to "condition," as modern psychologists put it, certain cities to overflights by single B-29s so that the Japanese military would not deploy any of its resources against single planes. The U.S. Air Force sent the bombers unloaded, one at a time over a select set of targets and, as was to be the case with that first B-29 over Hiroshima on August 6, nothing happened. No bombs were dropped. No anti-aircraft guns were fired. No fighter intercepts were attempted. Nothing.

One hour after the first B-29 flew over Hiroshima on August 6, three more B-29s approached the city. One plane carried one bomb. The other planes were along to make a movie and to monitor what happened next. Many people looked up. At 8:16, the first atomic bomb used in combat exploded over the courtyard of Shima Hospital.

Tens of thousands of people were killed. Some were incinerated. Some were disemboweled as their viscera, super-heated in the first fractions of a second following the blast, expanded and burst through the skin. Others were killed by falling or flying debris. Others died days, weeks, months, or years later of a new pathogen, radiation.

What is striking about the bombing of Hiroshima and, three days later, the destruction of Nagasaki, is not the number of deaths or even the short length of time in which so many deaths occurred. What is striking about these events is the simplicity with which so much death and destruction was achieved.

The fire bombings on the Japanese mainland and, earlier, the fire bombings of German cities, were complex operations. The early assaults on Japan required that advanced staging areas in the Pacific be won at the cost of many lives. Airports—at the time, the largest in the world—had to be built quickly. The newest in aviation technology had to be imported from thousands of miles away. Ordnance on a massive scale had to be assembled. The round-trip flights of hundreds of aircraft manned by thousands of carefully trained military crews had to be charted. The right mixture of incendiary and high explosive weaponry had to be delivered to set the maximum number of small, densely located Japanese homes on fire. And all of this took place against the statistical backdrop of known rates of airplane engine failure, aerial defense efforts, "missing in action" figures, and the other uncertainties on which one can count in war.

The killing of millions on another continent had been similarly complex. The objections of high-ranking officials like Himmler and Goering to the brutishness and sloppy violence of the *Kristalnacht* led in a straight line to the machinery of the camps. But the camps were still a hellishly complicated machine that depended on the assembly of material enough to build new cities, albeit cities of the dead, that needed military discipline and bureaucratic planning on a scale not seen before, and that required an international railroad system that worked well during a war.

In contrast to the killing that occurred before August 6, 1945, the killing at Hiroshima was simple. One advance plane at 7 A.M. to check the weather. One plane—plus its redundant observation and photographic escorts—with one bomb at 8 A.M. Even the bomb itself was simple if, at four tons, big. Named "Little Boy" (in contrast to the Nagasaki bomb, "Fat Man"), the first deliverable atomic bomb was basically a one-use-only gun barrel that fired a uranium bullet into a uranium target. The scientists were so confident this bomb would work that they had not even field-tested it. Once the gun fired its bullet into the target, atomic fission set off a chain reaction that caused a flash, a blast equivalent to twelve thousand tons of TNT, and the death of a city. It was so simple that in his journal chronicling the flight of the Enola Gay, co-pilot Robert Lewis wrote, "There will be a short intermission while we bomb our target."[57] Paul Tibbets, the pilot, would recall later, "It was all impersonal."[58]

The simplicity, the impersonality of the bombing of Hiroshima is the marker for a new age, a new approach to life as well as a new approach to death. Hiroshima, and Trinity before that, were expressions of simplicity formulated from the enormous complexity of what we might call the atomic bomb system. This system is encompassing. It extends from the sub-atomic level up through globally interlinked systems of communication, intelligence and military operations. The atomic system is, in a real sense, the first spectacular success of a systems approach to knowledge.

THE ATOMIC SYSTEM ENGENDERS A
NEW WAY OF THINKING

The atomic physicists were the inheritors of the most ancient of problems of the classical analytical tradition: What are the constituent parts of matter? What are the simplest components that, when assembled in all their variations and permutations, lead to the obvious complexity of the world as they knew it? While the problem was a classical one framed in the most analytical of terms, its solution would derive from new ways of thinking. In some respects, the modern solution to this ancient problem would form the ground for our new way of thinking.

Democritus had said that matter consists of "atoms and void." Atoms were, for him, the basic constituent part of matter. But this kind of thinking would not become popular until Isaac Newton imagined atoms to be "solid, massy, hard, impenetrable, movable particles."[59] Newton's "billiard ball" model of the atom satisfied the new analytical mind as an answer to the question of what was the simplest, irreducible constituent part of matter.

The Newtonian model served well until late in the nineteenth century when it began to unravel. Clerk Maxwell in 1873 proffered the idea that instead of just "atoms and void" there were also electromagnetic fields. Although Maxwell continued to believe in a Newtonian atom, his idea that electricity, magnetism, and ultimately light were best conceived as waves would become an important factor in the shift that would occur over the next few decades away from the billiard ball model.

Around the same time Walter Gibbs developed the Laws of Thermodynamics which included the well-known Second Law. The Second Law said, in one version, that systems always tend to move from a state of relative order to a state of relative disorder, from less probable to more probable (i.e., more random) configurations. Observed order was, accordingly, an artifact of how one conceived of a "system." Orderliness and ordering are illusions facilitated by visions of what constitutes a "system" narrowed by an analytical mentality. If one ignores apparent boundaries and considers the wider picture, entropy is the ruling principle.

Thermodynamics was either the first or the second nail in the coffin of a Newtonian universe firmly grounded in analysis and boundary-based thought. It had two related effects on classical, mechanical thinking. First, a Newtonian world operates without regard to time. Mechanical processes are, in principle, reversible. Billiard balls that strike one another and follow their respective paths across the table could, in principle, precisely retrace their paths if the forces acting on them were simply reversed. And there is nothing inherent in the essential concept of a "force" to prevent forces from being reversed. The Second Law of Thermodynamics voided such in-principle thinking and installed time as an essential factor in any system. Circumscribed systems give up energy in the form of heat when work is done (as when billiard balls are moved) and nothing could force that energy or "heat" back into the system. System behavior was no longer reversible, not even in principle. The machine metaphor gave way to the dynamic, directional metaphor of "time's arrow." Time flowed in one direction and what was done could not be undone.

Second, thermodynamics forced people, for the first time, to think beyond boundaries that gave definition to all things and their constituent parts. Newton's world permitted attention to be circumscribed. The working system, with all of its forces and counterforces neatly contained, was all that one needed to consider to understand a phenomenon. The Second Law forced scientists to look beyond a working system's boundaries and consider all the "heat sinks" into which dissipated energy flowed. The environment, "outside" the walls of the working system, became an essential part of the system itself. The Second Law was the first formulation of the premise of systems theory, now a cliche, that everything is connected, nothing is irrelevant.

The 1890s was the decade in which classical physics finally lost its grip on the atom. Because of the discoveries of that decade, the "solid, massy, hard, impenetrable" atom of Newton's world was found to be mostly empty, not solid, massy only in one very small part, fractionable, even in some instances almost fluid instead of hard, and, finally and fatefully, capable of being penetrated.

The fact that the atom was not the last constituent part of matter came from experimenters passing electrical currents through evacuated glass tubes. Joseph John (J. J.) Thomson in England and Philipp Lenard and Eugen Goldstein in Germany, among others, noted that "rays" appeared when an electric current was passed between two electrical poles mounted inside a vacuum tube. The fact that Goldstein would call the beam in his tubes a "ray" betrayed a belief that he was observing a form of light. J. J. Thomson showed in 1897 the beam could be deflected or bent by electric or magnetic fields. That meant the "rays" were, in fact, beams of particle. He calculated the weight of the particles in the beam to be much less than the weight of the lightest atom. Because he got the same kind of beam from many different elements heated in his vacuum tubes, Thomson was convinced that his "negative corpuscle" was a *part* of the atoms of the various elements. This part of the atom would later be known as the electron.

Thomson's discovery led him to develop the first non-Newtonian model of the atom. His model is called the "plum pudding" model because it conceived of negatively charged electrons embedded like plums in a positively charged batch of other stuff whose nature remained unknown. Heating these plum pudding atoms on the negatively charged cathodes in evacuated tubes caused the electrons to be ejected from the mush and form into beams.

The cathode ray experiments led directly to the other set of experiments that caused one person to make the initial discoveries concerning radioactivity, the spontaneous decay of atoms. The particle beams Thomson was generating caused some bodies they encountered to fluoresce. Wilhelm Roentgen studied the phenomenon in detail and called the highly energetic radiation that emanated from the point where the electron beam struck a substance "X-rays." Henri Becquerel melded Roentgen's discovery of X-rays with his own thorough knowledge of fluorescence of naturally occurring substances. His famous experiments with uranium salts on photographic plates showed that some substances gave off penetrating radiation even when they were not stimulated by energetic particle beams. Becquerel had discovered what Marie Sklodovska, later Madame Curie, would call "radioactivity," the spontaneous decay of elements that led to chemical changes and the emission of various kinds of radiation. The Newtonian atom could not withstand the assault of this discovery. Not only was the atom not hard and not solid, it was fractionable and, worse, some of them tended to fly apart of their own accord.

Ernest Rutherford, Thomson's successor at Cambridge, put all the pieces of the atomic puzzle together into a new model. Rutherford first identified two types of radiation from decaying atoms, "alpha" and "beta" radiation. Beta radiation consisted of highly energetic electrons. Alpha radiation consisted of particles much heavier than electrons. Rutherford experimentally demonstrated that alpha particles were identical to the nucleus of a helium atom and, with Hans Geiger, he developed methods for visualizing and counting individual alpha particles.

Rutherford and his assistants started using alpha radiation as an atomic probe. Rutherford fired his particles through thin foils of various metals to see what would happen. If the foils consisted of plum-pudding balls, some of the alpha particles should hit some of the atoms in the foil's atomic lattice and scatter slightly. In fact, almost all of them were scattered within a two degree range, about what was expected using Thomson's atomic model that imagined small atoms and much void.

There was something, however, in Rutherford's experiments for which Thomson's plum-pudding model of the atom could not account. Some of the alpha particles strayed outside the predicted two-degree range of deflection. In fact, Geiger's detector, positioned on the same side of the foil as the alpha source, showed that some alpha particles bounced back from the thin metal foils instead of passing straight through as Thomson's model said they must. As one famous description of that result puts it, it was like firing cannon shells at tissue paper and having some of the shells bounce back toward the gun.

Rutherford used this experiment to argue that the atom is not a spherical mass of positively charged stuff with electrons embedded in it, but instead consists of a tiny, very heavy nucleus with electrons orbiting at a very great distance from that nucleus. Some alpha particles came back toward the gun, Rutherford reasoned, because they had, in a sense, "collided" directly with the metal atoms. But Thomson's model would not permit the number of direct, head-on collisions Rutherford's students observed. Rutherford argued that, instead of a billiard-ball collisions, the alpha particles that passed very near an atom's nucleus were attracted to the nucleus, swung around the nucleus, and traversed a return path. For this type of interaction between metal atoms and alpha particles to occur, Rutherford said, the atom must have a small, massive nucleus, which accounted for the gravitational force, around which electrons had to orbit. This was the first step toward the modern view of the atom.

However, the first step was not a complete step away from Newtonian thinking. Classical physics and analytical procedures still were carrying the weight of explanation. After all, these experiments only showed that the atom was not the last, irreducible constituent part of nature. They showed merely that the atom itself could be subjected to "decompositional procedures," the ground of the analytical method. Indeed, Rutherford's deductions about the size and mass of the nucleus from the data on alpha particle bounce back followed strict Newtonian reasoning.

But to the degree that classical mechanics was involved with Rutherford's atom consisting of a central nucleus and orbiting electrons, that atom had a problem. The problem was that this atom simply could not exist. Maxwell's electromagnetic theory said that any electrically charged particle had to radiate when it deviated from a straight-line path. Rutherford's said that electrons were *orbiting* the nucleus, and therefore, were deviating from a straight-line path all the time. According to Maxwell's theory, that meant they had to be radiating energy all the time. If Rutherford's electrons were radiating energy constantly, they would eventually lose all the energy that was keeping them in motion and fall into the atomic nucleus. Rutherford's atoms would collapse on themselves. Put somewhat differently, something had to collapse: Rutherford's atoms or classical physical theory.

Enter Niels Bohr, the man who dreamed of great interrelationships. Bohr had left Thomson's lab and gone in 1912 to work with Rutherford while the latter was still at Manchester. As Richard Rhodes has shown, Bohr was temperamentally and philosophically amenable to thinking in non-classical ways. Notions of continuity of processes and classical cause-and-effect held no privileged position in Bohr's mental landscape. As Bohr wrote in his doctoral dissertation, "One must assume that there are forces in nature of a kind completely different from the usual mechanical sort."[60] This openness to the possibility of different kinds of forces and to new ways of thinking about ancient problems permitted Bohr to solve the problems from which Rutherford's atomic model suffered.

And Bohr solved them in a masterstroke. He simply *asserted* that electrons did not need to radiate as they constantly changed direction in their orbits about the nucleus. They just orbited in stable orbits. They did not gain or lose energy, he said. Bohr was not contradicting classical thought. He simply declared it inoperative, as they say, in this instance.

One does not rupture a system of thought without paying a price. Bohr's declaration left him with another problem. For a long time physicists and chemists had known that atoms of the various elements gave off identifying spectra of light when heated. That is, atoms *did* radiate under certain circumstances. The radiation of atoms was a discontinuous phenomenon, since the spectra consisted of sets of discrete lines of light, light of different, distinct and, for each element, characteristic wavelengths. After an intense study of what was known about atomic spectra, Bohr realized that he could use his model of the atom, with its electrons in stable, distinct orbits, to explain this well-known, little understood phenomenon.

Bohr, of course, knew of Max Planck's work on the elementary quantum of action which said that energy was exerted in discrete packets, or quanta. And he knew of Einstein's application of Planck's elementary quantum of action to the understanding of light. Einstein had argued that light, since Maxwell's time believed to be a wavelike phenomenon, behaved as if it consisted of particles or photons. Bohr put these ideas together with his view of the atom and argued that the electrons may change instantaneously from one stable orbit to another stable orbit. The change is made discontinuously and is always accompanied by some type of electromagnetic activity. If an atom is excited, it absorbs a quantum of light and an electron jumps, discontinuously, to a stable orbit of higher energy farther from the nucleus of the atom than it had been in before excitation. When an atom enters a less excited state its electrons fall to a stable orbit of lower energy, and—and this was the missing element for understanding spectra—the electron gives off a quantum of light of a particular energy/wavelength. Those quanta of light of a particular wavelength form one line of the characteristic spectrum of an element. Bohr used his theory to determine the orbits of the electrons in a hydrogen atom and then calculated the wavelengths of light that would be radiated if the hydrogen atom's single electron jumped from one possible orbit to another. The calculated wavelengths matched the experimentally observed spectrum for hydrogen exactly. Einstein reportedly said, when he heard the news of the match between Bohr's atomic theory and the experimental data, "Then this is one of the greatest discoveries."[61]

Bohr's model of the atom was an advance over Rutherford's on two counts. First, Bohr's model did not suffer the fatal flaw that classical mechanics handed Rutherford's because Bohr just announced that classical thinking did not apply at the atomic level. But second, Bohr's model accounted for an important phenomenon no one had been able to explain before, the radiation of a characteristic spectrum of light from each element. Bohr's atomic model shared with Rutherford's a central, massive, tiny, positively charged nucleus, but Bohr's electrons orbited in stable specifiable orbits.

What is important for our purposes is not so much that Bohr's atomic model was better than Rutherford's; what is important is that Bohr's model was possible only by thinking in new ways. Bohr's thinking dismissed classical thought and introduced the analytically discomforting notion of discontinuity. Discontinuous shifts in system states was an inadmissible concept before Bohr. Prior to this point analysis (and its representative mathematics of the limit situation in analytical thought, the calculus) insisted that between any two states of a system there was an identifiable trajectory that could be known if one had access to ever finer analytical instruments. Bohr blithely, or so it seems from our vantage point, revolutionized the form of thought available to the western mind.

From this point other thinkers would not feel bound by the constraints of classical thought. For example, to solve the problem of how to account for spectra more complicated than that of hydrogen, Werner Heisenberg said, in effect, why worry about the nature of each electron's orbit when one cannot see them anyway? Why not just develop a mathematical representation that accounted for the observed facts? Why not, in other words, develop a model that would float? As C. P. Snow put it,

> On this view, each type of atom would have a particular set of numbers associated with it. Then there would be rules to calculate its observable properties. For example, you want to know the wavelengths of sodium's spectral lines? Apply the "spectral lines" rule to a set of numbers corresponding to sodium, and the wavelengths will drop out. You can apply the same rule to the mathematical representation of sulfur, and out will come its spectral line wavelengths. To work out how sodium's spectral lines are split up by a magnetic field, apply another rule—the "Zeeman effect" rule—to the set of numbers describing sodium. An so on.[62]

So, in concept, was born quantum mechanics. Heisenberg and his Gottingen colleague Max Born set down a systematic method for linking the model of the atom in which electrons orbited in distinct, stable orbits (and hence were amenable to simple numerical representation) with the enormous range of curious experimental data that had accumulated in the first decades of the twentieth century.

As another example of the willingness to think outside old rules, consider the work of Louis de Broglie who, in 1925, suggested that all atomic particles might be equally well understood if they were thought of as waves. He worked through the corpus of atomic theory, conceived of all the particles as waves, and found that all of the results accounted for by the Bohr/Heisenberg/Born scheme were accounted for by the de Broglie wave scheme as well. And furthermore, de Broglie asserted, there were some phenomena that the particulate conception of the electron could not account for that the wave conception could. In particular, the interference pattern caused by firing an electron beam through an atomic lattice could only be explained if electrons were waves, not particles.

Erwin Schrodinger linked de Broglie's wave conception of an electron to Bohr's view of the electron as existing in stable orbits. Schrodinger showed that an electron's orbit could have a circumference equal only to a whole number of electron wavelengths, where wavelength is given by de Broglie's work. Once again, C. P. Snow provides a useful, visual interpretation:

> Schrodinger thought of the electron in its orbit not as a miniature planet, but as a wave—like the wiggles in a rope when you jerk it up and down. But the electron rope is tied right around the nucleus. It has no end. To think of it another way, the two ends are tied together, so as it vibrates the two "ends" must move with one another.[63]

A standing wave in the rope has a non-fractional number of crests in it and the distance around the middle of that wave-infested circle of "rope" was exactly equal, Schrodinger showed, to the size of Bohr's electron orbits.

All of this is easy to understand if one thought of an electron as simply a wave. But the fact that electrons behaved as a wave in some respects did not dismiss the previously established fact that they behaved as particles in other respects. For example, a beam of electrons could be bent by a magnetic field so electrons must, therefore, have a mass and be particulate. The electron, it seemed in the wake of de Broglie and Schrodinger's elaboration, was best conceived of as *both* a particle *and* a wave. The electron acquired a "wave-particle duality," as it came to be called. One had to use both ways of understanding the electron if one was to have a meaningful description of it. The two ways of (simultaneously) understanding the electron were complementary to one another. Without one or the other description, one's understanding was incomplete. Duality required complementarity for an electron to be appreciated in all of its empirical details. The pot of analytical thought was, it seemed, spilled and a new approach to thought was beginning to thicken nicely.

The wave-particle duality of all matter including the electron was one of J. Robert Oppenheimer's favorite ways for introducing lay audiences to the new ways of thinking on which modern physics insists. "Try for a moment to describe this," Oppenheimer writes in *Science and the Common Understanding* of wave interference patterns of electromagnetic radiation,

> in terms of the passage of particles of quanta. If one of those quanta
> which characterize both the emission of light at the source and its
> detection—let us say, by the eye or the photoelectric plate or photo-cell
> on the far side of the screen—if the quantum passes through one of the
> holes, how can the presence of the other hole through which it did not
> pass affect its destiny?

The pattern of light or electrons at the point of detection shows that there are more quanta or electrons at some points (the points where the wave crests join, if one were to invoke a wave-based explanation) and fewer at others (the points where crests and troughs cancel each other) *only* when there are two holes in the screen through which the particle beam passes. But the second "hole" in the atomic lattice would be, from the perspective of the quantum passing through the first "hole," staggeringly far away. "How can there be any science or any prediction if the state of affairs remote from the trajectory of the quantum can determine its behavior?" asks Oppenheimer.[64] For Oppenheimer, the question is a rhetorical one. The old science that had the principle of local causality as its guide and the enumeration of forces and the description of trajectories as its goals was not available to those whose field of observation was the small world of the atom.

Heisenberg, once again, put the lid on the problem of finding and following the electron. He said, again simply, it cannot be done. "Don't let the old questions worry you, because they cannot be answered," Heisenberg seemed to say in his uncertainty principle. And the notion that some questions "cannot be answered" had to be understood, according to Heisenberg's principle, in the strongest possible sense. Not being able to find and follow an the electron was not just a problem of the imprecision of measurement. It was a problem of the *fact* of measurement. The very act of locating an electron makes it impossible to ascertain its velocity and the very act of assessing an electron's velocity makes it impossible to locate, with certainty, the object in flight. The new scientific outlook would bring probability to the fore. Using the new scientific mindset one could predict average behavior of a large batch of particle-waves and one could state, within specifiable ranges, the likely outcome of experiments. But the hopes of ever discerning with certitude the exact nature of nature were dashed in the early decades of the twentieth century when studies of the smallest known constituent parts of nature made it clear that the common questions should no longer be asked, much less answered.

It was, of course, on this realization that the famous break between Niels Bohr and Albert Einstein occurred. Einstein retained his faith—for that is what it must be called given the passion with which he pursued it and the lengths to which he would go on the basis of his commitment—that at its root the universe is ultimately predictable for "God does not play dice." Bohr, who saw things with new eyes, saw chance at the root of process and being, and he saw complementarity and uncertainty as the necessary bases for a new understanding of nature.[65]

Revolutions in science occur when the basic questions one might ask of nature are declared to be invalid questions. Newton had changed the basic scientific question from, "Why do objects move?" to, "Why do objects ever change direction or stop?" In their turn, the early physicists tried to apply Newton's questions to the atom and, in particular, to the electrons. They found that Newton's questions could not be answered in a way that makes sense, common sense. As Oppenheimer put it,

> what are we to think of the transitions [of electrons from one orbit to another] themselves? Do they take place suddenly? Are they very quick motions, executed in going from one orbit to another? Are they causally determined? Can we say, that is, when an atom will pass from one of its states to another as we disturb it; and can we find what it is that determines that time?

All of these questions received a simple "no" in answer from modern physics.

> *We learned to ask . . . what determined not the moment of transition but the probability of the transition. What we needed to understand was not the state of affairs during the transition but the impossibility of visualizing the transition—an even more radical impossibility than the states themselves—in terms of the motion of matter.*[66]

The atomic system required a new kind of understanding. Indeed, it required a new *approach to understanding* that admitted non-material descriptions of matter and that permitted nature to behave discontinuously rather than according to the processural notions supplied by the calculus. The conception of "the atomic system" had to be expanded to include not just the atomic nucleus and its electrons but also the experimental apparatus, including the experimenter himself, designed to investigate the system. There was no "outside" from which to gain an independent perspective on the system. All boundaries had to be dissolved. Old understandings had to be forsaken. The system bound everything together in such a way that the usual expectations about the pursuit of knowledge and understanding were undermined.

THE NUCLEUS: TAKING IT APART,
PUTTING IT TOGETHER, BREAKING IT OPEN

The decade of the 1930s was as critical for atomic physics as it was fateful for the rest of the world. It was the decade in which the atomic nucleus would take shape in the minds of the researchers only to be broken apart in their labs. The decade began with Bohr's electrons firmly ensconced in stable but indeterminate orbits, but the nature of the nucleus still was mostly a mystery. Nuclear size, mass and charge were known but little else. The 1930s would mark the transition to a new set of practices based in the new way of thinking that had emerged over the preceding several decades.

Atomic fission, in the sense that we now understand it, would not be accomplished until 1938. But the hard, impenetrable atom was actually being "split" some twenty years or so before. Rutherford fired his alpha particles at non-metallic atoms. When his little energetic research devices hit nitrogen atoms, hydrogen nuclei, which Rutherford would call the "proton," were chipped off the nitrogen nucleus. Actually, the alpha particle, with an atomic weight of 4, combined with the nucleus of a nitrogen atom, atomic weight 14, and yielded an isotope of oxygen plus a single proton. With typical experimental zeal, Rutherford tried the same trick with other elements and roughly the same results obtained.* As a result of Rutherford's assaults on the nucleus, the existence of the proton was confirmed by 1919. One year later, Rutherford was speculating about the existence of another constituent of the nucleus, the neutron, a particle similar in size to the proton but without an electrical charge.

The actual search for the neutron began with some odd results from the laboratory of Walther Bothe in Germany. When Bothe bombarded beryllium with alpha particles, the element gave off a tremendous amount of radiation. The emitted radiation was greater in quantity and much more energetic than it should have been given the energy imparted by the impact of the positively charged alpha bullets. James Chadwick, one of Rutherford's co-workers, suspected that the radiation might be the electrically neutral neutron that might escape easily from the electrical trap of the atomic nucleus once it was knocked loose. Building on some results from Irene Curie, Chadwick confirmed the existence of the neutron in the nucleus.

The discovery of the neutron solved two problems that the emerging model of the atom had left unaddressed. First, the neutron bridged the gap between atomic number and atomic weight. The difference between weight and number, which increased with number, was an anomaly that had fired Rutherford's speculations about the neutron. The second problem solved by the existence of the neutron was the problem of the isotopes, those unstable, often radioactive forms of an element that are chemically identical to the element itself. Neutrons could change the nuclear behavior of an element without changing its chemistry, since chemistry is principally dependent on the elec-

---

* As he worked his way through the periodic table, Rutherford and his colleagues could see a problem looming on the chemical horizon. As the atomic nucleus got bigger, the electronic charge of the nucleus increased and so did the force with which the positively charged nucleus repelled the positively charged alpha particles. Some of Rutherford's colleagues talked of building a particle accelerator that would increase the energy of the alpha particle so they might break through the formidable electrical barriers of the heavier elements but Rutherford would not have it.

trons. All of this post-experimental reconceptualization of the atom around the neutron occurred in 1932.

It was also in 1932 that atoms were actually "split" under the total control of researchers for the first time. John Cockcroft developed the method of accelerating protons from hydrogen gas through an electrical field. The protons developed enough energy to split the nuclei of light elements like lithium. That same eventful year saw the discovery of yet another atomic particle. The existence of the "positron" had been predicted by the mathematical synthesis of quantum mechanics, the de Broglie-Schrodinger wave theory, and Einstein's theory of relativity provided by Dirac in 1928. Dirac's equations implied a natural, aesthetically acceptable symmetry that required the existence of a particle like the electron but with a positive charge. Carl Anderson found such a particle in cosmic rays and received the 1936 Nobel prize. The game of building the atomic system continued as the scientists used their new tools, mathematical and material, to explore a world they could not see or even visualize fully.

A decisive finding issued from the laboratory of Irene and Frederic Joliot-Curie in 1934. They found that bombarding some elements with alpha particles created highly unstable isotopes that decayed spontaneously and gave off radiation. Theirs were the first artificially created radioactive isotopes.

When Enrico Fermi learned of the Joliot-Curie results he immediately set about the task of trying to make radioisotopes. He planned to work his way through the entire periodic table. But instead of using alpha particles as his atomic probes, Fermi decided to use neutrons as his nuclear bullets. A neutron could penetrate the electrical barrier that would rebuff Rutherford's alpha particle. Fermi fired neutrons at atoms hoping that the neutrons would "stick" to the atomic nuclei and make them into heavier isotopes. Because the neutron was quite energetic and passed unimpeded through the electrical field of the nucleus, Fermi slowed down his neutrons by forcing them to pass through paraffin before they hit the target.

The results Fermi obtained when he eventually used uranium as a target were curious, to say the least, and Fermi failed to grasp their meaning. When Fermi's neutrons, slowed by their passage through paraffin, hit a uranium nucleus, a large amount of radiation was emitted. Fermi eventually came to think he had created nuclei that were heavier than any naturally occurring nuclei. He assumed that the radiation was the result of the spontaneous radioactive decay of these so-called "trans-uranic elements." That was in 1934.

For four years and across several countries other physicists and chemists would follow the false leads offered by their own replications of Fermi's experiments. Some tended to believe like Fermi that the results indicated the existence of trans-uranic elements. Others, like the Joliot-Curies, believed they were dealing with unusual isotopes of elements lighter than uranium, like radium.

Otto Hahn, Lise Meitner, and later Fritz Strassmann at the Kaiser Wilhelm Institute also undertook the bombardment of elements with neutrons. Lise Meitner was Jewish and as the events of the late thirties unfolded in Germany she went into exile in Sweden. She left behind not just her unfinished research but also her mutually vitalizing collaboration with Hahn. Late in 1938, Hahn and Strassmann conducted a long series of chemical analyses that showed the result of firing neutrons at uranium was not radium and not some element heavier than uranium but was a much, much lighter element. In particular, they detected barium in their results. Barium is element 56 on the periodic table and has an atomic weight of 137. Uranium is element 92 and has a weight, in its most commonly occurring form, of 238. Obtaining barium from the bombardment of uranium was another impossible result for the physicists. But Hahn and Strassmann were chemists. They reported these chemical analyses in a paper that appeared in January 1939. They also sent their results, prior to publication, to Lise Meitner in hopes that she might provide a physical explanation for their physically odd chemical results.

Meitner, in her exile, was more closely associated with Bohr than she had been in the past. She knew well of Bohr's speculative efforts to visualize the nature of the atomic nucleus some two years earlier. Bohr, repeating a common pattern in science, had relied on some of his earliest research to develop a working model of the atomic nucleus that accounted for some of the results observed when a nucleus captures a neutron on bombardment. While he was still in his teens, Bohr had earned a prize for an essay on the surface tension of water. Now, decades later, Bohr applied the concept of surface tension, the cohesion among the molecules in a liquid that causes drops to tend toward a spheroidal shape, to the atomic nucleus. There must be an attractive force among the nuclear particles, Bohr reasoned, that tended to hold the nucleus together as a globule. When a neutron is absorbed by the nucleus, the globule is disturbed and becomes more energetic, much as a drop of water is disturbed and becomes more energetic when tiny, sub-drop amounts of water are added to it. The atomic nucleus tries to return to a spheroidal state of equilibrium by dissipating some of its energy. This model accounted for some of the radiation released by bombarded nuclei. It also accounted for the fact that there are no naturally occurring elements heavier than uranium. Add more particles to a huge uranium nucleus and the nucleus, like its water-drop counterpart, tends to fly apart because the repulsive forces are greater than the cohesive forces of its "surface tension." It was an elegant model that helped physicists understand some of the science that was being done, but beyond that, the model was not terribly helpful. It was not helpful, that is, until Meitner received notice of her colleagues' barium results during the Christmas season of 1938.

Meitner and her associate Otto Frisch reportedly went for a walk in the snow to puzzle over Hahn and Strassmann's results. It finally dawned on Meitner that the added slow neutron that struck the uranium nucleus did not set up a "vibration" or a general excitation that was relieved by a short burst of radiation. Instead, the energy added by the encroaching neutron set the giant nucleus wobbling. This motion could overcome the effects of the "surface tension" that was holding the thing together. The uranium nucleus probably developed a harmonic vibration, Meitner speculated, much like cables or poorly designed suspension bridges do when struck by just the right wind. The harmonic vibration could be sufficient to break the nucleus apart— split it roughly in two parts. The electrical charge of the two parts would repel one another at the same time the cohesive forces in the two new parts tried to pull themselves into spheres. The resultant spheres would be new nuclei. The energy with which the two new nuclei would fly apart would be very great. The two parts would probably be barium, the presence of which Hahn and Strassmann had demonstrated, and krypton, but exactly what they would be in any given nuclear instance would depend on chance.

Frisch later drew a picture of the likely physical splitting of the atom for a friend of his, the biologist William Arnold. Looking at the picture, Frisch to asked Arnold the biological term for the splitting of a bacterium. "Binary fission," was Arnold's reply. From that encounter came the well-known and emotionally loaded term of "fission" for the splitting of the atomic nucleus. As Richard Rhodes says of this conversation, "Thereby the name for a multiplication of life became the name for a violent process of destruction. 'I wrote home to my mother,' says Frisch, 'that I felt like someone who had caught an elephant by the tail.'"[67] Frisch's elephant would later be termed a "dragon" by Richard Feynman at Los Alamos, and a man named Louis Slotin would die from conducting an experiment called "tickling the tail of the dragon."

The images of immense power and uncontrolled violence contained in Frisch's "elephant" or Feynman's "dragon" were apt, for Meitner had developed, along with her model of the likely physical behavior of the atomic nucleus undergoing fission, an estimate of the energy that would be released by atomic fission. The mass of the two daughter nuclei that resulted from the fissioning of a single uranium nucleus was less than the mass of the parent uranium atom. This much could be read from the periodic table once the elements that resulted from the split were identified. Meitner had committed the atomic weights to memory so that even out in the snow where she and Frisch were working through their ideas, she knew that the "lost mass" in a single atomic fission was equal to about one-fifth of a proton. But mass is never just lost. Instead, as Einstein had shown earlier, there is an equivalence between mass and energy expressed in the formulation $E = mc^2$. The mass "lost" during atomic fission was converted to energy and that energy matched the energy with which the two products of the fission ought to repel one another. Only a few weeks later Frisch would experimentally confirm the energy release that Meitner's calculations had predicted. The energy release was of a spectacular order.

A number of people had earlier speculated that the fissioning of an atom might release a tremendous amount of energy. Rutherford had co-authored a paper in 1903 that contained the assertion that the energy associated with radioactive changes was very great, in fact, many orders of magnitude greater than the energy release associated with any known chemical change. Frederick Soddy, Rutherford's associate, wrote, "It is probable that all heavy matter possesses—latent and bound up with the structure of the atom—a similar quantity of energy to that possessed by radium [a radioactive substance]. If it could be tapped and controlled what an agent it would be in shaping the world's destiny."[68] Francis Ashton, inventor of the mass spectrograph that, among other things, permitted the separation of isotopes, realized that there was tremendous energy located inside the atomic nucleus. His realization was based on Einstein's mass-energy equivalence. Anticipating some of the so-called ethical debates that would take place later, Ashton, in 1936, rehearsed the arguments for stopping all research on atomic nuclei and atomic energy because of the inherent danger. He concluded his own version of Oppenheimer's "a peril and a hope" speech by saying, "Personally I think there is no doubt that sub-atomic energy is available all around us, and that one day man will release and control its almost infinite power. We cannot prevent him from doing so and can only hope that he will not use it exclusively in blowing up his next door neighbor."[69] On the basis of the Joliot-Curie research on transmutations, Joliot anticipated that science might "[build up or shatter] elements at will" and "will be able to bring about transmutations of an explosive type." Joliot even imagined the possibility that such explosions would set off chain reactions that could spread across the whole planet in one great, doomsday reaction.[70] Leo Szilard, a fellow who was until the late 1930s a marginal but prescient figure in nuclear physics and chemistry, envisioned the possibility of a nuclear chain reaction, atomic fission set in motion by one set of reactions giving off not only the daughter elements of the first fission but also enough spare neutrons to fission other uranium nuclei that would give off more neutrons, and so on in a self-sustaining, extraordinarily energetic sequence of events. Szilard patented the idea several years before Meitner and Frisch developed the common understanding of the experiments originally reported by Fermi. Those who knew chemistry and the new physics in the late 1930s knew they were getting very close to a very big dragon.

Bohr went off to the United States and the news of atomic fission leaked from his entourage before the experimental results were published some days later. The news sent American physicists scurrying to their labs to confirm and extend the Hahn-Strassmann results. Quickly experiments showed only uranium-235, the isotope of uranium that had three fewer neutrons than the common form of uranium with 92 protons and 146 neutrons (uranium-238), was able to undergo nuclear fission. Szilard had already worked out the concept of a "critical mass," the amount of fissionable material that would be necessary to sustain a chain reaction. The implication of all this work was that if one put enough uranium-235 together in a proper form, it would explode. Virtually every physicist who heard these experimental results realized that a bomb of enormous proportions was possible. A short time after the discovery of fission was announced, Robert Oppenheimer had a rough sketch of an atomic bomb on his office blackboard.

"There the pure science finished," C. P. Snow says.[71] The atomic system was well enough understood that the implications of that knowledge were sufficiently compelling to set the work of most scientists onto a new tack. The atomic system would now be linked with another system, the bomb building system.

THE BOMB BUILDING SYSTEM

"Action at a distance" had enchanted the physicists from Volta to Marconi. Electrical and magnetic forces seemed a gigantic step from the local causality of the analytic tradition even though they were embedded in it. With the interference experiments involving the dispersal of electrons through atomic lattices (and, more generally, with De Broglie's wave conception of particles), however, this little enchantment of the eighteenth and nineteenth centuries took on monstrous proportions. Admittedly, the absolute scale of actions was, for the traditionally trained analytical mind, inconceivably microscopic. But for those who could imagine the previously unimaginable quantum scale of action, the distance between the "holes" in the lattices was, to echo the systems thinkers of our time, gigantic. What is more, the action that occurred over this gigantic distance was enabled by a new way to conceive of the constituent parts of matter, by a way of thinking that admitted (no, required) two fundamentally different conceptions of the parts in question. A new way of thinking had to bridge the vast distance over which action was, obviously now, taking place for nothing under the old ways of thinking could do that job. "Action at a distance" became utterly dependent on a new way of "thinking across distance."

It was only a small step from this new way of thinking at the subatomic level that enabled the construction of the modern atom to a new way of thinking at the level of social organization that would enable the potential resident in the atom to realize itself. The systems thinking that conceived the atom would now enable the bomb on Oppenheimer's blackboard.

Nuel Pharr Davis opens the joint biography of Ernest O. Lawrence and J. Robert Oppenheimer by saying, "The quarter century of their association was an age of personality in physics, as distinguished from the present, which is an age of organization."[72] Between the two men there was one of those passes that mark an irreversible transition. Lawrence would be left in the background and Oppenheimer would become an exemplar of the new form of expert.

Oppenheimer was, during the war, the scientific director of the laboratory at Los Alamos, New Mexico, the place to which the products of the rest of the Manhattan Engineering District would be sent to be assembled into this country's first complement of atomic bombs. But to use the title "director" casually would be wrong. He was a part of the system, a remarkably vast system. To try to make Oppenheimer a more important or more responsible part of the system than any other part would be to undertake the same sort of effort Einstein put into preserving the old questions against Bohr's new mode of developing answers. Trying to make Oppenheimer into "the father of the atomic bomb" or to put him into some equivalent position is to try to preserve the old ideas that organize themselves around "agency" and "responsibility." Such thinking cannot be sustained now because our situation is different. Consideration of the enormity of the system alone suggests that new understandings are necessary.

Bohr was one of several early skeptics about the prospects of being able to make a bomb. His doubts were practical. He suspected that a single country would not have the industrial capacity to produce sufficient quantities of fissionable material. The bomb could not be built, Bohr thought, "unless you turn the United States into one huge factory."[73] Under the guidance of General Leslie Groves, an organizational feat of just about that magnitude was accomplished. Action over vast distances was necessary to permit the bomb to be built. Facilities were built at Oak Ridge in Tennessee and at Hanford in Washington. The resources of several major universities across the country were augmented and enlisted to the task. Los Alamos rose out of the mesa that had been the site of the Los Alamos Ranch School for Boys. Some of the nation's largest companies participated in the project. At least one corporation's board of directors, that of the du Pont Company, agreed to its company's participation without knowing what they were being asked to take part in. Groves himself wrote of the accomplishments of science that led to the accomplishments of the Manhattan Engineering District, "no single stroke of genius

delivered up the finished product." Groves understood the importance of organization above personality and wrote his memoir of the
project, in part, he says, "to emphasize the cohesive entity that was
the Manhattan Project, a factor in its success that has been largely
overlooked."[74] The Manhattan Project was an exemplary system.

Systems may have architects and even "builders," but once set in
motion, they run independently of those who appear to be "in charge."
And they quash personality. Systems make it proper to speak of
expertise separate from experts. The accomplishments of the system
built during the Second World War that enabled the atomic bomb to
realize itself renders such a jarringly odd construction meaningful.

The final pieces of the bomb puzzle were put in place in 1939. Leo
Szilard confirmed by a series of experiments that neutrons were produced when uranium nuclei underwent fission. That finding confirmed Szilard's long-held suspicion that a chain reaction was possible
and, indeed, likely.

Szilard chose not to publish his results and he urged other researchers to do the same. His efforts were not successful. Research
on fission from France and Germany soon appeared in the literature.

Szilard enlisted Albert Einstein's assistance in doing something to
thwart likely Nazi efforts to develop their own bomb. He eventually
helped Einstein draft a letter to the President of the United States to
let the President know the practical implications of the science that
had been done in the first part of the twentieth century and to try
to impress on Roosevelt the gravity of the situation should Germany
be the first country to develop an atomic bomb. In that famous letter
Einstein informed the President of the prospects of developing a bomb,
issued a rather oblique warning about the possibility that the Germans
might be at work on a bomb, and urged the President to develop a
liaison with a group of scientists in order to keep up on experimental
work and, reciprocally, to be able to mobilize the government to assist
the scientists. The President, sensing the Nazi threat that Einstein
only alluded to, ordered immediate action.

Committees were formed, but little happened beyond that. The
"Uranium Committee," as the first organizational effort was called,
had no clear mandate, few funds, and not very strong leadership.
Only in response to a Pascal-like wager, put to E. O. Lawrence by
Marcus Oliphant of a visiting delegation from Britain, viz., that the

threat posed by the Germans' likely progress on a bomb was infinitely grave, did Lawrence try to invigorate the efforts of the Committee.

In September 1941, two years after the President's order for action, Lawrence took the case to the chief scientist on the Uranium Committee, James Conant. As a result of the Lawrence-Conant meeting, which took place in the home of Arthur Compton, Lawrence had a mandate to develop fissionable materials and Compton, the University of Chicago's Dean of Physics, was to work on bomb design. The link between the two was to be provided by J. Robert Oppenheimer, a theoretical physicist whom Lawrence respected and who came to provide some speculative answers to the questions Compton's work would necessarily raise in the absence of a test of a bomb. The Uranium Committee was eventually disbanded in favor of a more intensive, more carefully coordinated and pointedly directed effort to build the bomb.

Oppenheimer's mode of thought was to be crucial for what followed. That mode of thought started to become clear in his first clash with Gregory Breit, whom Compton retained from the Uranium Committee. At first, Oppenheimer worked under Breit. Samuel Allison observed, "Breit was always frightened that something would be revealed in the seminars" that were held to coordinate the disparate activities of the contractors. In contrast, "Oppenheimer was frightened something would not" be revealed.[75] Oppenheimer believed strongly in openness. As systems thinking requires boundaries to be opened conceptually, Oppenheimer wanted boundaries around thought opened practically. He was opposed to the bureaucratic tendency to impose barriers and create boundaries even where they might not otherwise exist. Breit, being nominally in charge, won the battle but not the war. Oppenheimer was the embodiment of the new kind of expert. With Breit's resignation from the project in June 1942, Oppenheimer was elevated to an influential and visible position in the ranks of the bomb builders. Oppenheimer called a group of physicists to Berkeley to formulate the scientific response that would be needed from that point.

Oppenheimer's group had available to them not only the theoretical and experimental knowledge generally available to the world of physics but also the practical report of two German physicists then working in Birmingham, England. They were Rudolph Peierls and Otto Frisch. Their 1940 memorandum outlined all the essential elements of an atomic bomb and pointed out the remaining technical difficulties including the separation of the fissionable U-235 isotope, the problem of assembling a super-critical mass of fissionable material, and the problem of realizing the full potential of a bomb, which meant not having the critical mass of material blow itself apart and "fizzle."

Under Oppenheimer's leadership, the group of fewer than ten theoretical physicists meeting in Berkeley proceeded quickly to outline the problems that remained: the problem of the behavior of neutrons under the extreme conditions that fission would create; the problem of determining how pure their fissionable material had to be to provide an explosive reaction; the problem of assembling the bomb core rapidly enough that the core would not expand, blow itself apart, and explode while remaining atomically a dud; and the problem of delivery—putting everything together into a package that an airplane could carry to a target. They realized that the task was to mobilize expertise in all these areas.

A small diversion from the rapid progress of Oppenheimer's group occurred when some calculations by Edward Teller potentially upped the ante of the wager they might be undertaking by pursuing bomb research. Out of interest in using a fission bomb to ignite a fusion bomb (or "hydrogen bomb"), Teller fiddled with the information on the heat that a fission explosion might generate. His calculations suggested that a fission bomb could conceivably ignite not only the light elements that comprise the distinctive component of the hydrogen bomb, but also the slightly heavier elements, like nitrogen, that make up major parts of the atmosphere. An atomic bomb might set fire to the air and the oceans. Oppenheimer took Teller's conclusions to his boss, Arthur Compton. Compton's reaction was: "This would be the ultimate catastrophe. Better to accept the slavery of the Nazis than to run a chance of drawing the final curtain on mankind!" Oppenheimer's group was ordered to check Teller's calculations. Compton concluded, "Unless they came up with a firm and reliable conclusion that our atomic bombs could not explode the air or the sea, these bombs must never be made."[76] As it turned out, Teller had made an error in his calculations and work could proceed. But the concern would not go away. Each new wave of recruits to the bomb project would "discover" the problem and raise it. The wager would see a final new life in the hours before the Trinity test in the summer of 1945.

Things began to move quickly in 1942. In May, the German scientists in Heisenberg's lab had demonstrated that more neutrons were given off from a "pile" of uranium, as a large mass of refined uranium would come to be called, than were injected into it to begin the nuclear reaction. At the University of Chicago, under Compton's authorization, Enrico Fermi conducted the same experiment. In addition to showing that a controlled nuclear reaction was possible, Fermi's pile produced plutonium, the second trans-uranic element, whose name came from "Pluto," the lord of the lower world, the source of fertility and the holding tank of the dead. Fermi's experimental pile went critical in early December 1942, and paved the way for the development of the reactors at the Hanford reservation.

In the wake of Fermi's experiment, everything was ready for the building of the bombs. The project was, however, still arrayed across the country with only the coordination that collegial contacts among scientists, working across the barriers of imposed secrecy, could provide. Action across such distances required a gigantic organizational effort. Vannevar Bush solicited the support of Lieutenant General Brehon Somervell, Commanding General of the Army Services of Supply, who had already thought of bringing the project under the direction and control of the Army Corps of Engineers. In fact, he had already thought of a person to assume command responsibility on behalf of the Army. That person was then-Colonel Leslie Groves. Groves's most recent assignment had been to oversee the building of the Pentagon. He knew his way around and through the problems of procurement and he had proven he could handle the difficulties posed by large construction projects. He would handle the truly gigantic construction "project" that the Manhattan Project was quickly to become.

Groves waited for his promotion to General and then started a cross-country journey to all research facilities connected with the "uranium project." He was not encouraged. In Pittsburgh, he saw the hopelessness of the Westinghouse Corporation's efforts to separate U-235 by a centrifugal method. At Columbia University, Groves met John Dunning and was shown the gaseous diffusion method for separating U-235 from U-238 developed by Harold Urey's team. This filtration process was effective but slow and would need a tremendously large filtration system if it was to work. That realization by Groves led to the gigantic buildings at Oak Ridge. From New York Groves went to Chicago where Compton was overseeing the work of more than one thousand research staff members and where Fermi was building his piles. Groves realized that Fermi's pile was a crucial experiment for the bomb program, but even it did not offer the General the assurances he so desperately wanted. He recalled,

> I was en route east from the Pacific Coast at [the time Fermi's pile went critical], so Compton could not even inform me of their success. He did telephone Conant at Harvard to pass on the now famous message, "The Italian navigator [Fermi] has just landed in the new world. The natives are friendly." The December 2 test proved that a controlled chain reaction could be achieved, but it gave no assurance that it could be used to produce plutonium on a large scale. Neither did it give us any assurance that a bomb using plutonium or U-235 would explode.[77]

Even successes were not unequivocally encouraging for this practically oriented man.

From Chicago Groves had traveled to California to meet with Ernest Lawrence to see if any hope for the project's success could be garnered from Berkeley's cyclotrons. Lawrence, the personality scientist, was a superior salesman of big science. He had just finished building the Calutron, a cyclotron with a 184-inch magnet at its heart and he was anxious to show Groves how his electromagnetic processes might be used to separate the precious U-235 isotope. Lawrence eventually had to tell Groves that his process was "still experimental" (for which Groves read, "probably not practical") and Lawrence fell from the emerging system's favor.

After his meetings with Lawrence, Groves had a fairly clear idea about the scope of his construction program. He planned to move on several fronts, since no single technique for the collection of fissionable material could be guaranteed to work. His plan called for massive, secret construction projects at Hanford and Oak Ridge, projects that employed over a hundred thousand people. What Groves did not have was a scientific leader to receive the products of his plants and put them together to make a bomb.

Groves met Oppenheimer during his visit to Berkeley. For reasons not clear to anyone, probably including Groves and Oppenheimer themselves, the two hit it off. Oppenheimer, a dedicated theoretician, was not bogged down in the it's-still-experimentals. His mind was unfettered by the disconcerting facts to which Groves had been exposed on his cross-country trip and he was able to engage in sweeping, comprehensive assessments of the prospects of bombs of various sorts, including Teller's Super. Groves was refreshed by Oppenheimer's openness and frankness and by the scale and mode of his thoughts. When Groves asked Oppenheimer for a recommendation for a project director, Oppenheimer made his disarming comment, "There are no experts." Groves, after having just met all of the experts in the field, each of whom had his technique and territory to defend, probably appreciated this comment more that anyone else could.

Groves had leaned toward the appointment of Lawrence, Compton or Urey as the project's scientific director. All were experts critical to the development of their piece of the project. Groves considered others but he concluded, "none of those suggested appeared to be the equal of Oppenheimer." Groves wanted Oppenheimer but, as he put it later,

> Oppenheimer had two major disadvantages—he had almost no administrative experience of any kind, and he was not a Nobel Prize winner. . . . Because of the prevailing sentiment at that time [that accorded high respect to Nobel laureates], coupled with the feeling of a number of people that Oppenheimer would not succeed, there was considerable opposition to my naming him. Nor was he unanimously favored when I first brought the question before the Military Policy Committee. After much discussion I asked each member to give me the name of a man who would be a better choice. In a few weeks it became apparent that we would not find a better man; so Oppenheimer was asked to undertake the task.[78]

Groves even overrode the concerns of security personnel to have Oppenheimer granted his security clearance. This was the birth of a new approach to practice. The common sentiment still bowed to traditional experts and their expertise and Groves was inclined to respect this tradition. His ultimate, uncommon appointment of Oppenheimer was emblematic of what was now necessary.

Oppenheimer had all that was necessary to bring the project to a successful end. He was an exemplary specialist in the general. He had a mind that could synthesize brilliantly. He had uncanny organizational and managerial talent. Both supporters and later detractors commented favorably, if sometimes enviously, on Oppenheimer's ability to facilitate the work of people on teams or in committees. Edward Teller summarized the views of most of Oppenheimer's colleagues when he reflected, at Oppenheimer's 1954 security clearance hearing, on Oppenheimer's demonstrated administrative ability at Los Alamos: Oppenheimer's direction was

> *a very outstanding achievement due mainly to the fact that with his very quick mind he found out very promptly what was going on in every part of the lab, made right judgments about things, supported work when work had to be supported, and also I think with his very remarkable insight in psychological matters, made just a wonderful and excellent director.*[79]

Louis Alvarez seemed dazzled by Oppenheimer's managerial acumen. In his testimony at the security hearing, Alvarez was hard put to explain why he had signed a report that Teller later told him was used to slow work on his Super bomb when Alvarez had been put on the committee precisely because he was known to favor a crash program for its development. Through pages of testimony Alvarez stumbles through a variety of explanations that boil down to the assessment that Oppenheimer was just a remarkable people handler, organizer, and administrative operative.[80]

One of Oppenheimer's earliest suggestions to Groves struck a resonant chord after all that Groves had seen in the disparate research efforts being conducted across the country. Oppenheimer urged the General to collect all the scientists in one laboratory. The idea appealed immediately and the search for a site began. Quickly the decision was made to locate the laboratory on the mesas of New Mexico, at Los Alamos. A town was built and its new citizens immigrated there from all over the country. The name "Los Alamos" became equivalent to the notion of mobilizing expertise.

After Los Alamos was under way, Oppenheimer's second organizational suggestion probably cut across Groves's military grain, but eventually Groves came to accept its wisdom. Oppenheimer told Groves that science could not succeed when knowledge is, as bureaucratic, military jargon puts it, compartmentalized. Groves, with his penchant for security, wanted to keep all knowledge, even at Los Alamos, on a need-to-know basis. Oppenheimer argued that everyone needed to know everything because in science one never knows from whom or from what odd concatenation of ideas the next breakthrough might come. The official historian of Project Y, David Hawkins, writes,

> The need for collaboration was emphasized by the fact that the bomb had to be ready for production as soon as usable quantities of nuclear explosive became available. Success would require the highest integration and, therefore, decentralization and mutual confidence. To this end, free communication within the Laboratory was indispensable.[81]

No boundaries, disciplinary or otherwise, could be allowed to interfere with the development of a team ethic.

Oppenheimer instituted the weekly colloquium, to which all of the scientific staff were invited and where the assessment of value was made not on the basis of prestige, seniority, or prizes, but on the basis of contributions in the moment. Oppenheimer said later that before the laboratory and before the colloquium,

> there was good compartmentalization and the result was that people would not know what was going on anywhere else. Work was duplicated, and there was almost no sense of hope or direction in it. . . . This did not seem sound. It seemed to me and knowledgeable people, it was one package, ordnance, chemistry, physics theory, effects, all had to be understood together or the job would not get done.[82]

Groves, in his memoirs, called the colloquium "another means of stimulating interest and progress." But as if to justify his original concerns about its value and its threat to security, he added,

> In the final analysis, though, the colloquium existed not so much to provide information as to maintain morale and a feeling of common purpose and responsibility. From the standpoint of security, it presented a major hazard, and it was one of the reasons why the treachery of Fuchs was so disastrous to the free world.[83]

Oppenheimer's belief in openness carried the day, but the General had to have the final say.

At the first assembly of the "bunch of eggheads"—Groves's term—on April 15, 1943, at Los Alamos, Robert Serber presented an "indoctrination course" on everything that was known about the still-potential bomb. This lecture, which became in note form the introductory manual for new recruits to the Hill, showed just how much was already known. It also showed that the task of these experts was to let a nuclear explosion, which Meitner's calculations had shown was inherent in nature, to become itself.

Serber discussed the amount of energy liberated in each fission and the theoretical output of a mass of fissionable material. He covered Bohr's old ground about the dynamics of fission, the release of neutrons, and the concept of a chain reaction. Then he went on to the dimensions of the problem that would occupy many of the scientists for two more years: how to manage the neutron release. He reviewed one of Szilard's ideas of using a "tamper" to reflect neutrons back into the mass. He discussed one method of assembling the subcritical pieces of a bomb into a super-critical mass. The method that would eventually be used in Hiroshima's "Little Boy" bomb was to use a high velocity gun barrel to fire a uranium bullet at a uranium target. When the two pieces—each subcritical when separate from the other—came together, they would form a super-critical mass and explode, Serber explained. Another idea came from the audience. Seth Neddermeyer proposed surrounding a hollow sphere of fissionable material with high explosives, detonating the explosive charges simultaneously, and compressing the sphere into a solid, super-critical mass. This was the "implosion" method of effecting a nuclear explosion.

Since Project Y stood on completely untested ground, Groves's and Oppenheimer's shared approach was to pursue any idea that had any merit. Some ideas led to dead ends like the building of a water deionization plant at Hanford that proved unnecessary. Others, like Neddermeyer's implosion idea, proved to be not only fruitful and necessary but essential. As it turned out, plutonium, like uranium, consisted of a primary element, Pu-239, and several isotopes of the element. One isotope, Pu-240 with one extra neutron, proved to be a neutron emitter. It supplied neutrons that would pre-detonate a bomb and lead to a large but inefficient explosion—a fizzle—if the material was fashioned in any configuration other than a hollow sphere. Neddermeyer was sent off, with resources, to work on his ideas as was anyone else who seemed to have a promising notion.

Also discussed at that first April conference was Edward Teller's Super, the hydrogen bomb. Everyone knew that the Super would require a fission bomb as its ignition device, but it was yet another promising path and so was opened for discussion and was funded.

Oppenheimer originally imagined that thirty or so of the nation's top scientists might be able to bring the bomb into being in relatively short order if they were able to work under the right conditions. By the time plans for the Los Alamos Laboratory were formulated in late 1942 or early 1943, Oppenheimer envisioned having to recruit "more than 100 highly qualified and trained scientists" and having to assemble with them "the technicians, staff, and mechanics who would be required for their support" together with "the equipment that we would have to beg and borrow since there would be no time to build it from scratch."[84] Even this was a serious underestimation of what would eventually come together on top of the Hill. The working population at Los Alamos doubled about every nine months, David Hawkins says.[85] The lab became "a walled city of 6,000. The cost escalated to $56 million. Seven divisions: theoretical physics, experimental physics, ordnance, explosives, bomb physics, chemistry, and metallurgy."[86] Near the end of the war, before high speed electronic computers came to Los Alamos, rows of soldiers were enlisted to do the mindless calculations of adding one column of numbers to another column of numbers and returning a third column of sums. Organizationally and administratively, Los Alamos was an extraordinarily complex place that put most of its demands on a new category of person, the "scientific administrator,"[87] a person schooled in the sciences who could be equally concerned with shaped explosives, the health problems posed by new chemical elements, and the city manager's problems of water supply, garbage disposal, and so on.

Los Alamos became a world unto itself even though it was only one component of the bomb building system. Out of sparse accommodations and few resources came major social events and entertainments of every size. Over two hundred babies were born at Los Alamos during the war years, too many for General Groves's taste. (He is reported to have ordered an officer to "do something" about the baby boom.) Humor is always local and Los Alamos developed its own brand. Richard Feynman enjoyed breaking into secure areas and leaving notice of his entry for security staff. (His pranks were not discouraged. The military authorities felt that Feynman helped keep the security guards of their toes.) Contact with the world outside Los Alamos was discouraged. After some scientists suspected their mail was being censored during the early months, Groves obliged their suspicions by instituting a censorship program. (One person wrote to the Russian philatelic society requesting information just to observe the reaction of the censors to an envelope covered with Russian stamps.[88]) Many of the memoirs of the Los Alamos alumni speak of their experience as essentially vitalizing. They worked harder than most of them had before. They worked more collaboratively than ever before. And, "In that heady new freedom, they seldom noticed the barbed wire."[89]

The work of the scientists proceeded with an eye to the particular. All of the keen management of a tremendous group effort—Oppenheimer called it "the very opposite of a one-man show"[90]—was dedicated to making a particular product as quickly as possible, with no detours for general knowledge of universal laws. Hans Bethe recalled Oppenheimer's transformation from the mumbling would-be expert to the systems designer-manager: "It is a very different attitude, if you want to find out the deepest secrets of nature—which is what he had wanted to do before—and on the other hand, if you want to produce something, to produce a mechanism that works. It was a very different problem, different attitude, and he completely changed to fit the new role."[91]

One experiment conducted at Los Alamos illustrates the way in which the work on the Hill focused attention on the particular. That experiment came to be called "tickling the tail of the dragon." Appropriately enough, it was conducted at "Omega site," a building at the farther reaches of the laboratory.

Since 1939, physicists had understood the general concept of a critical mass. However, general concepts are not sufficient for those who had to enable a *particular* critical mass of fissionable material to realize the destructive potential that it alone contained. They needed knowledge of the behavior of *particular* lumps of plutonium or U-235. The subcritical, not yet assembled pieces of plutonium or uranium were the scientists' dragon. One tickled the tail of the dragon by bringing pieces of subcritical material into proximity of one another so that the assembly became momentarily critical and a chain reaction started. The trick was to end the experiment soon enough—before the chain reaction could progress through too many iterations—that it would not give off significant doses of radiation. One might tickle the tail of a dragon, but one should stop before the dragon notices, one might say.

This was a completely new kind of experiment in several respects.

No one knew the best way to assess criticality. No one knew even what constituted a "significant dose of radiation." But scientifically it was new as well. This was not an experiment designed to discriminate between two competing hypotheses about the workings of nature. This was an experiment that had to be conducted over and over again to assess the potential of every particular instance of a category of entities, subcritical bomb cores.

> There were and are ways of calculating theoretically the amount of fissionable material required to form a critical mass. But such calculations can never be wholly precise. Moreover, in order to achieve "optimum efficiency"—for which read killing power—in an atomic bomb, the size of the crit [critical mass] had to be determined—and still must—under various conditions. . . . The idea was to shove together lumps of fissionable material in such quantities, and in such a geometric relationship [that a] chain reaction was permitted to begin—thus establishing the crit.[92]

In the early form of the dragon experiment, a uranium hydride slug was mounted on a vertical track and allowed to slide down through a uranium ring. As the slug passed through the middle of the ring the assembly—the ring with the slug in the middle—went critical, the chain reaction started, the assembly heated almost instantaneously, it gave off a burst of neutrons, and the researchers could gather the data they needed. All of this occurred in the instant when the slug was just in the middle of the ring, for as the slug passed through the ring the assembly was "disassembled" and the reaction stopped. During one such experiment, the slug landed on the ring and stuck there or paused momentarily in its passage. The assembly seriously but not fatally irradiated four people. Hawkins writes of these experiments, "the Health Group had no responsibility except to be sure the men were aware of the dangers involved. These experiments were especially dangerous because there was no absolute way of anticipating the dangers."[93] When one is dealing with dragons, anticipation is one thing one cannot count on.

In its later version, tickling the tail of the dragon involved pieces of actual bomb cores—the hemispheres of plutonium, for example—and various forms of tampers used to manage neutron emission. These experiments were conducted by a serious researcher, thirty-one-year-old Louis Slotin. Slotin would set up his Geiger counters and his neutron counters and place two parts of a bomb core on a table. Sometimes with a tamper in place, sometimes without, Slotin would push the pieces of fissionable material together. Or Slotin would use his screwdriver as a wedge between two pieces of tamper and wiggle the screwdriver out to close the gap between the pieces of reflective material wrapped around a bomb core. All the time he would watch the recorded line of the neutron counter arch away from the horizontal toward the vertical. "The task was dangerous, suitable for a bachelor leading a crew of a half dozen other bachelors who leaned over his desk in utter silent fascination. . . . [Slotin] seldom spoke with much animation except about the Dragon and about his other interest, the extrapolation of blast and radiation casualties."[94]

Omega site was one of the places to which Oppenheimer would repair when he needed spiritual nourishment and the quiet that Slotin's research team had established as their hallmark. Nuel Pharr Davis suggests there was a certain sympathy between Oppenheimer and Slotin. "One of humanity's most ungrateful instincts is to dread not only the frontier but also the frontier guard," and in Davis's view, Oppenheimer and Slotin worked that post together. Both knew the nature of their task. As we shall see, Oppenheimer never tried to hide behind glib rhetoric and he urged others to face what they had created, to understand things as they are, as Lenny Bruce might put it. Davis makes a similar comment about Slotin: "In its frustration at having become the physicist's test animal, the human race should find a certain comfort in the thought that Slotin knew what he was doing."[95] Slotin was temperamentally suited to the tasks he performed. "'Slotin had a positive hankering for danger,' [one] of those who knew him says. 'He seemed to be suffering from some sort of inner tension, and he was always very quiet. But he was downright gay when he was doing something dangerous.'"[96] In a similar vein, Fermi, who shared the Omega laboratory with Slotin, told one of his friends, "'There's something about the man that outrages me.'. . . What it was, Fermi said, he did not know, except that he found it anarchical, reckless, disturbing."[97] Stewart Alsop and Ralph Lapp add a final stroke to this portrait of Slotin: "He was particularly proud of the fact that he had been chosen to test the criticality of the world's first atomic bomb—he cherished the receipt for this bomb he got when he returned it to be exploded at Alamogordo, after having tickled its tail."[98]

All of this personalizes Slotin to a degree not deserved by anyone at Los Alamos. His story illustrates that in some very deep sense, even Slotin understood himself to be just another component in the bomb-building system. The gap between being a collector of data and becoming a datum does not exist in the world of systems.

On May 21, 1946, Slotin tickled the tail of a dragon to show his subordinates how it was done (since he had been assigned to the Crossroads tests in the Pacific) and to put on a little show for a visiting VIP. An edited, declassified report on the accident says,

> The critical assembly decided upon consisted of a [word deleted] and a beryllium tamper. The active sphere was in the laboratory, along with two others, for their final checks before shipment to Operation Crossroads. . . . Slotin probably placed the upper [deleted] hemisphere onto one inch aluminum shims or blocks. . . . Slotin removed the blocks and lowered the shell until one edge touched the bottom hemisphere. The opposite edge was lowered onto a screw-driver. . . . The assembly was still not critical and Slotin . . . began to lower the [deleted] shell by moving the screw-driver handle back and forth horizontally apparently in order to inch it slowly outward. Suddenly at about 1520 hours there was an audible click made when the screw-driver slipped entirely out of the crack and the [deleted] shell came entirely down upon the rest of the assembly.[99]

After the click, everyone in the room facing the experiment saw a blue flash. Most experienced a metallic taste in the mouth and felt heat even through clothing.

Slotin knew exactly what had happened. The assembly had gone critical. Immediately he reached out, lifted part of the shell from the assembly and threw it to the floor. The other men left the room and ran to a guard station.

Slotin realized that he had just conducted a valuable experiment on the effects of radiation. After calling an ambulance, he "called back those who had run up the road and prepared a sketch showing the approximate positions of everyone present at the moment of the accident."[100] Slotin then tried to use some of the measuring devices in the room to assess the radioactivity of various objects. All of the equipment was, however, jammed off scale due to the radiation released from the assembly. Later assessments would show that Slotin probably received about eight hundred rems of radiation, far above

"LD/50," the amount of radiation that produces death in 50 percent of the people exposed to it. Slotin died nine days after the accident but not without contributing a significant amount of data to the bomb project.*

The work of the Los Alamos scientists would come together in July 1945, atop a platform built on the Jornada del Muerto, Spanish for "Journey of the Dead Man." The Jornada is a stretch of desert in southwestern New Mexico, so named for the number of Spanish explorers who died there on their treks from Mexico northward. The work would culminate in a test Oppenheimer decided to call Trinity. The symbolism could not have been more apt nor more pregnant.

The site for Trinity was selected in late 1944 as it became clear that Hanford would be able to supply sufficient plutonium for at least one bomb by the spring of the following year. The Trinity test site was spread across one corner of the Alamogordo bombing range. In the spirit of the age of systems, the site itself became an information conveying device. Bunkers were established ten thousand yards from Ground Zero. Roads linked vital points on the site and wires snaked everywhere across the desert. Robert Wilson sent his team from the Weapons Research unit across the desert to place and calibrate instruments that would collect data on the explosion.

Final assembly of the two hemispheres of plutonium and an initiator—a source of neutrons placed in the middle of the plutonium sphere that would boost the chain reaction on implosion—was done by Robert Bacher. He was to insert Slotin's uranium tamped plutonium sphere inside Kistiakowsky's high explosive implosion device. It was not a job for the faint of heart. Anxiety increased when the plutonium would not fit. Some people worried that Slotin had mismatched the hemisphere's in his lab and had brought with him an incompatible pair of parts of the Dragon. Oppenheimer, Bacher, and Kistiakowsky decided that adding the desert heat to the heat naturally generated by the plutonium may have caused the unit to expand. Once they got the bomb core's temperature equal to that of the firing

---

*Slotin was the second person to die from a radiation accident. Harry Daghlian dropped some bomb core parts into a pile of uranium bricks on August 12, 1945; he died on September 15. He had worked with Slotin. Slotin reportedly stayed near Daghlian's bed for long periods between August 12 and September 15, 1945.

device, the whole deadly thing fit together nicely and it was hoisted to the top of a firing tower.

In the spirit of the probabilistic reasoning that the age of the system engenders, all the physicists at Los Alamos had entered a pool: each put one dollar on the explosive yield that would result from Trinity. Enrico Fermi put a side bet before those assembled on the Jornada. As Davis tells it,

> One of Fermi's traits that caused his colleagues to rank him in the genius class was his knack of extrapolating problem solutions that hid just beyond the range of mathematical proof. On . . . Sunday, July 15, he gave a chilling demonstration. It began with a graceful complement to Oppenheimer. If the bomb failed to go off, Fermi said, no one else could ever do better to make it go off, so Oppenheimer and the laboratory would have proved implosion impossible, and this would be the best of good news for mankind. Less obvious and more interesting, he went on, was a point about atmospheric ignition: long study of the possibility had put him in a position to handicap the odds of two contingencies. "I invite bets," he said, "against first the destruction of all human life and second just that of human life in New Mexico."[101]

Many people present knew Fermi well enough to realize his reconstruction of Teller's speculation was not entirely a joke. Groves, listening to Fermi, was a man who liked to be prepared, even in the era of multiple and wildly different contingencies. He had drafted press releases for several possible outcomes in hopes that the media would be put off the trail of the atom bomb by reports of an explosion at an ammunition dump. He was, he says, "a bit annoyed with Fermi" for bringing up these possibilities at such a late date (so that, one might infer, there was no chance to prepare press releases for *those* outcomes). He put Fermi's comments off to a conscious effort "to smooth down the frayed nerves and ease the tension of the people at the camp."[102]

In the pre-dawn hours of July 16, with an electrical storm raging about them, Joseph McKibben and two armed military guards waited at the tower to close some safety switches after the storm passed. As the weather settled and with the bomb armed, McKibben returned to the control bunker and assumed his place at the firing panel while Samuel Allison began the countdown over loud speakers. At forty-five seconds, McKibben started an automatic timing device. At ten seconds, he threw the final switch. At zero, Allison shouted, "Now!" McKibben saw the light.

In the many descriptions of the Trinity test that we have, the light given off by the bomb seems its most memorable characteristic. It came before the noise, the heat, the blast, and the mushroom cloud. It was so bright that a blind woman miles away from the site asked her companion what had happened when the flash occurred. Brigadier General Thomas F. Farrell was not at his most militarily objective as he reported,

> The lighting effects beggared description. The whole country was lighted by a searing light with the intensity many times that of the midday sun. It was golden, purple, violet, gray and blue. It lighted every peak, crevasse and ridge of the nearby mountain range with a clarity and beauty that cannot be described but must be seen to be imagined.[103]

Several observers compared the fireball to the rising sun. The historian Ferenc Szasz would call his book *The Day the Sun Rose Twice.* "'You felt the morning had come,' Philip Morrison was ten miles from Point Zero, 'although it was still night, because there your face felt the glow of this daylight—this desert sun in the midst of the night.'"[104]

Scientists had always thought of themselves as casting a bright light on the face of nature so that she might be made to yield her secrets. In 1803, in the early years of the first new age, George Ticknor composed a poem that reflected this attitude of inquiry:

> Where late the Savage roam'd in search of prey
> Fair science spreads her all enlivening ray
> The ancient forest fall'n; its inmates fled
> See Seats and Sons of learning in the stead
> 'Tis scenes like these, that freedom's power disclose
> She makes the desert blossom like a rose.[105]

Trinity turned the tables on science just as systems thinking turned analysis on its head. Rabi recalls that Trinity produced "the brightest light I have ever seen or that I think anyone has ever seen. It blasted; it pounced; it bored its way right through you. . . . You would wish it would stop." And then, instead of a rose springing from the desert, a fireball: "there was this enormous ball of fire which grew and grew and it rolled as it grew; it went up into the air, in yellow flashes and into scarlet and green. It looked menacing. It seemed to come toward one."[106]

Instead of the brightness beaming a sign of fertility, potential, and growth, it left nothing. The tower was vaporized. Groves records, "A crater from which all vegetation had vanished, with a diameter of 1200 feet and a slight slope toward the center, was formed."[107] Davis notes, "Better than anyone besides Slotin, Oppenheimer knew the light was death."[108] Instead of science assaulting nature, the reverse seemed to occur in the S-10,000 bunker over six miles south of the blast and in the hills where observers watched from more than twenty miles away.

It was, indeed, the beginning of a new age. The *New York Times* observer-reporter wrote,

> The Atomic Age began at exactly 5:30 Mountain War Time on the morning of July 16, 1945, on a stretch of semi-desert land about 50 airline miles from Alamogordo, N.M., just a few minutes before the dawn of a new day on that part of the earth. Just at that instant there rose from the bowels of the earth a light not of this world. . . . Up it went, a great ball of fire about a mile in diameter, changing colors as it kept shooting upward, from deep purple to orange, expanding, growing bigger, rising as it was expanding, an elemental force freed from its bounds after being chained for billions of years.[109]

General Farrell wrote in a similar vein, "All seemed to feel that they had been present at the birth of a new age . . . and felt their profound responsibility to help in guiding into right channels the tremendous forces which had been unlocked for the first time in history."[110] Norris Bradbury put it in more social-psychological terms: "Most experiences in life can be comprehended by prior experiences, but the bomb did not fit into any preconceptions possessed by anyone."[111]

For all of its destructive power, there was a certain beauty about the simplicity of the explosion and a certain satisfaction that the blast caused among the scientists who had enabled the energy resident in the atom's nucleus to be realized. That is to say, the bomb met aesthetic as well as technical criteria for success. Farrell's description contained the following on the esthetics of the explosion: "The effects could well be called unprecedented, magnificent, beautiful, stupendous and terrifying. . . . It was the beauty the great poets dream about but describe most poorly and inadequately."[112] In an interview with Carl Sagan, George Kistiakowsky said he felt "satisfaction" that the thing had worked:

Sagan: You had worked for some years on it. . . .

Kistiakowsky: Gee, that was hard work and I was satisfied.

Sagan: You weren't thinking about the military use of it.

Kistiakowsky: Not at the moment. And Oppenheimer rushed out as soon as the thing went off, joined me, and I said to him, "Oppie, congratulations. Remember, I won the bet."[113]

Kistiakowsky had bet Oppenheimer a month's salary against ten dollars that Kistiakowsky's explosive lenses would work. Oppenheimer paid off.

Oppenheimer seemed transformed by the success of the test. Several people noted that his face relaxed visibly when the light appeared. Rabi saw him as he stepped from the jeep that took him from the S-10,000 bunker to Base Camp. "His walk was like 'High Noon'—I think that's the best I could describe it—this kind of strut. He'd done it."[114]

Fermi, ever the expert, who would have lost his Sunday night wager had anyone taken his bet, was not so inspired that he was distracted from the opportunity of doing one more experiment. As the bomb went off, Fermi was tearing strips of paper into small pieces. Just before the blast wave arrived, he started dropping his papers. When the blast hit it carried the papers away from Fermi. They blew about eight feet downwind. From a chart relating paper displacement to blast size he had devised earlier Fermi offered the first estimate of the size of the explosion: about ten thousand tons of T.N.T. In fact, the blast was equal to more like nineteen thousand tons of T.N.T. Rabi had selected eighteen kilotons in the physicists' pool. He won *that* bet.

THE BOMB DELIVERY SYSTEM

Between July 16 and August 9, 1945, the United States emptied its nuclear arsenal. Trinity used one plutonium core. Hiroshima received the gun-assembly uranium bomb in Little Boy. The other plutonium core devastated Nagasaki in Fat Man. The issue of delivery was moot for the moment. Special squadrons of B-29 pilots had trained for months in their specially modified planes to deliver their cargo and safely escape the blast area. In very short order, their job was completed and there were no more bombs to drop.

The bomb-building system continued to operate. Bombs became cheaper[115] and better designed.[116]

As the new arsenal grew, the systems concept took hold with a vengeance around the issue of delivery. If questions of agency had been pushed to the background in the mobilization of expertise that occurred thorough the middle of 1945, such questions would virtually disappear as the problem of how best to deploy and use the nation's nuclear stockpile became paramount. Professor Falcon's admonishment to the general at NORAD in the film *War Games*—"General, you are relating to a machine. Please don't act like one."—would come to seem like a bit of romantic nostalgia as the notion of "system" achieved a spectacular incarnation in the bomb delivery system.

Early in the nuclear age, the United States was the only country with the new bombs. For a variety of political reasons, the decision of precisely how our nuclear arsenal would be used rested with Curtis LeMay, the general in charge of the Strategic Air Command. Throughout the early 1950s his plans were simple. Once the President said "Go," SAC bombers would fly toward the Soviet Union loaded with all the U.S. bombs that were available. They would approach the Soviet Union from various directions and unload their bombs as they crossed each target on the SAC hit-list. If they had any bombs left by the time they got to Moscow, they were to unload the rest there. LeMay did not plan for retaliation against the aggressions of an enemy. His plan was for a preemptive strike:

> It was always the first punch that mattered. The last war had ended with the United States having the capability to inflict total destruction and that, as far as LeMay was concerned, was how the next one would begin. Such thoughts prompted almost no dissent in the immediate post-war period: Strategic bombing was an accepted doctrine at the Pentagon, which is the reason the spearhead of the post-war air force was named the Strategic Air Command.[117]

The U.S. military had acquired a "nuclear capability" and planned to use all of its "capability" if circumstances warranted.

A change in thinking was prompted by two circumstances, one material the other conceptual.

In the immediate postwar period, most scientists had predicted that the U.S.S.R. would be without its own bombs for eight years or more. In the fall of 1949, planes flying along the eastern border of the Soviet Union sampled the air and found radioisotopes that had to have come from an atomic bomb. The Soviet Union had acquired its own nuclear capability and the situation of the U.S. war planners changed materially.

The second impetus for a change in thinking had occurred somewhat earlier. Sometime in the middle of the Second World War, the concept of "national defense" had been replaced by the now-common concept of "national security." The former idea rested on the notion that our interests were limited by and protected by boundaries—if not actual national boundaries then at least conceptual boundaries, such as those implied by notions like "spheres of influence," that had a specifiable location and shape. "National defense" thinking promoted an analogous notion of "containing" an opponent within its borders. In fact, this idea of containment was a ground on which LeMay's view of his mission rested. His task, as he saw it, was to deploy forces around the U.S.S.R. so that when the "Go" order was received, his planes would cross Soviet borders and destroy everything inside them.

"National security" thinking recognizes no boundaries, not ours, not theirs, not anywhere. Anything might conceivably be caught in the national security net. "National security" interests extend worldwide. Theodore Draper links the development of the concept of "national security" to the proclamation of the Truman Doctrine that extended the interests of the United States to all parts of the globe. He writes that this doctrine began "to live a life of its own, undisturbed by specific, practical, complex circumstances, such as those that had called it forth [in Greece in 1947 following the British withdrawal]." The policy has been used by all the administrations since Truman's through the invocation of phrases like "'vital interest,' 'national security,' 'free world,' 'peace is at stake,' and, above all, some version of 'Soviet threat.'"[118] "National security" thinking calls for management plans that contain options for many contingencies and for flexibility in war-fighting capability. Just how old-fashioned was the notion of "national defense" was emphasized symbolically and materially as Sputnik beeped across skies not respecting any boundaries. Borders, boundaries, divisions of any sort were recognized now as artificial. They could be breached by fairly simple technologies.

There is a link between the existence of "boundaries" and the development of "capabilities." Boundaries give definition to entities that can formulate goals. They also contain resources that can be organized into capabilities that might be developed to achieve those goals. When boundaries collapse or become irrelevant, "entities" become more or less meaningless, goals lose their importance for their is nothing "outside" for which to strive, and capabilities, in turn, lose their importance. When boundaries collapse, a shift in interest must occur from "developing capabilities" to "processing information," one of the hallmarks of systems thinking.

In the nuclear arena, the task shifted from developing nuclear capabilities to developing means for gathering intelligence about Soviet intentions and actions. By 1953, the U.S. had in place a radar line extending from Alaska to Iceland that was designed to detect incoming Soviet planes or, later, missiles. The information from this radar system was routed, from 1957 onward, to the North American Aerospace Defense Command in Colorado Springs where their SAGE (Semi-Automatic Ground Environment) computer processed the data and sounded the alarms. "The Pentagon said [SAGE] was an 'automatic brain,' something that would be safe and efficient because it *'removed the human element by replacing man with automatic equipment.'*" The technological loop was closing and circumventing the human components of the "early warning system"[119] very early in the new age. The information gathering capacities of the U.S. government would later be supplemented by reconnaissance flights over Soviet territory by the fast, high-flying U-2 and SR-71 planes and, later still, by satellites capable of high-resolution photography and of detecting missiles as they left their pads or silos.

Once a system has information and processes it, the system must be designed to act on that information. That is, it must be able to send out information in response to the conclusions drawn from the processing in a way that the responsive information will initiate some activity. The activity might be either more information collection or the activation of another part of the system. The early warning, information-gathering system was, of course, connected to the nation's evolving war-making system. In theory, information on a Soviet attack on the U.S. national security interests would go the president. He would make the decision to release nuclear forces. In systems terms, which were quickly becoming the military's terms after 1950, the problem was to achieve and maintain "connectivity."

The military felt it had sufficient connectivity in the system. They had built the intelligence-gathering and early warning apparatuses and they had built the weapons-delivery, war-making systems. They had their act together.

It was precisely the extent of the military's connectivity that worried the first president who tried to take a serious interest in what it would mean to wage a nuclear war, Dwight Eisenhower. He sent his science advisor, George Kistiakowsky, to SAC headquarters to find out what would happen if he ever decided to say "Go." He did not get a satisfactory answer. "Despite his military background Eisenhower had never had a full picture of what was happening at Offit [Air Base, Omaha, SAC headquarters]. He had only outline briefings on SAC's operational nuclear plans. . . . That is not to say that he was as remote from the planning process as Truman had been."[120]

In fact, Eisenhower spent the last part of his presidency trying to reformulate the military's "total retaliation" scheme for bombing the Soviet Union back to the stone age, as the cliche had it. Eisenhower became, in a sense, the system's first major critic. As happens with well-functioning systems, his criticisms were used by the system to refine and improve itself. Criticism rarely reformulates a system.

Eisenhower demanded, for example, that the Joint Chiefs explain their reasons for the choice of each target. (He was especially bothered that SAC targeting called for the destruction of all major Soviet cities.) The Joint Chiefs altered the targeting plan slightly, but from that point on they made a point of offering a "rationale" for every target choice, including the cities that would gradually be put back on the list. Systems are able to use criticism to their advantage: Behind Eisenhower's call for an explanation of targeting plans lay an implicit call that the system be altered in a fundamental way. The result was a refined system—one that included the "rationalization" of all plans—that was harder to criticize, and much, much harder to alter.

President Kennedy and his brain trust headed by Robert McNamara came into office with only the weak links between the military and political systems that had been established, more by default than design, during the Truman and Eisenhower administrations. The early crises of the Kennedy administration left the president and his advisers to create a clearer link between the civilian commander-in-chief and his military operations. "More direct political control of military actions seemed essential, along with a technically competent staff loyal to the president and equipped with the information and management tools necessary to support such high-level intervention" in the military's early warning/massive retaliation loop. To this end, Kennedy established the National Military Command System in the Pentagon with direct links to the White House. The National Military Command System, which in its modern form has a duplicate site inside Raven Rock Mountain in Pennsylvania and airborne command centers aboard Boeing E-4Bs (the "Doomsday Planes"), became the point of articulation for information gathering and order issuing, and the point at which political leaders were to insert themselves in the loop. "Capabilities" had given way completely to "communication" as the principal concern of those involved in the war-making system.

The extent to which our nuclear forces had come under the full sway of a systems approach is illustrated by the appearance of a new form of "war games" in the 1980s. It used to be that war games were designed to assess the readiness and effectiveness of the war-fighting materiel. War games traditionally tested capabilities. How many planes might deliver how many bombs when faced with the defenses they might be expected to encounter, how many tanks would start, how quickly could troops be mobilized, were the kinds of questions that guided the games that warriors used to play. Credibility of deterrent forces was assured by demonstrating the strength—the overwhelming brute force—of those forces. The war planners of the Reagan administration played a different kind of game in May 1982. The game was code named "Ivy League." This war game, as one set of commentators put it, was principally about the *communication* of information that would allow war managers to receive and send information: it was "about the telephones, the radio links, the satellites, and the computers that would be used to transmit orders to fight the big war." The modern war games, say Pringle and Arkin,

> test whether the president is able to communicate with his nuclear forces during and after an attack and, most important, they examine the ability of the president and his generals to survive long enough in their command bunkers to continue ordering the nuclear forces into action during an extended nuclear war.[121]

Modern credibility is assured by demonstrating the so-called C^3-I (command, control, communication, intelligence) system will survive an enemy attack or will at least "degrade gracefully."[122] Bombs, planes, rockets, and submarines are important components of the war-making system, but the capacity to keep information moving is the modern cornerstone of deterrence. It must be so, since this is, after all, the age of systems.

The appearance of intercontinental ballistic missiles drastically reduced the time available for executing the loop from receiving information on hostile intentions to the point of issuing orders of battle. When the sole threat to the U.S. came from the Soviet bomber fleet, the president had between three and eight hours to make decisions and issue orders. Now with submarine based missiles in the Atlantic, the decision-making time is reduced to a matter of ten minutes or so. The response to this new order of threat was natural: the system had to be more tightly integrated to decrease the time needed to execute the loop. Paul Bracken notes that this integration occurred across two dimensions:

> The development of standard operating procedures, correlation methods in fusion centers [military centers to which intelligence data are routed], communication linkages, and organizational routines all had to be carefully worked out over many years for this vertical integration [from raw data to interpretive assessments of national intent] to work effectively and smoothly. Moreover, all of these had to be specified as functions of tension and alert levels, so that the vast organizational resources of the American warning and intelligence system could be directed to the most urgent priorities. The vertical nature of this integration meant that warning and intelligence were fused and interrelated to the control of nuclear weapons themselves. A corresponding horizontal integration of nuclear forces, in which the war plans of the different unified and specified commands were coordinated one with the other, was also being developed at the same time as vertical integration. The two forms of integration constituted the maturation of the American nuclear force.[123]

This total integration created a system that, like Boeing's new airplanes, no one fully understood, but that, in a sense, no one had to understand. Bracken says,

> The overload of information and the proliferation of fusion centers . . . had a fragmenting effect of the national security establishment, as the number of individuals with a broad overview of the functions of the entire establishment declined. It was common in the 1950s and 1960s to

find project engineers or particularly knowledgeable generals with a
grasp of the entire defense establishment's activities. By all accounts this
kind of individual began to disappear in the late 1960s and 1970s.[124]

The system had become in its maturity a classical complex system that no longer needed knowledgeable people to run it.

As Bracken goes to considerable effort to show, it is not correct to think of our nuclear forces as a complex C³-I and war-making system that operates in isolation. Our system is, in fact, coupled with an equally complex system of communication, intelligence, and war-making capabilities operated by the Soviet Union. It is much more appropriate to think of the nuclear forces of the world as constituting a single complex system in which humans play only minor roles. To illustrate this notion, Bracken offers two anecdotes.

The first shows how a complex system reacts to events that are, in true fact, minor. In the early hours of June 2, 1980, the tracks of two Soviet submarine launched missiles appeared on the computer screens at NORAD and in the National Military Command Centers. Computers calculated impact points and "time to impact" estimates. SAC bomber crews were ordered to board their planes and start their engines. Missile crews were alerted. In Hawaii, a flying command post was ordered to take off. More missiles appeared on the screens even though early warning radar had no missiles in sight. The operators of the system decided that the pictures of the missiles had to be due to a faulty computer relay. Indeed, a forty-six-cent computer chip had gone bad and was causing the alert. The alarm was shut down and the system was put back to its normal readiness state. It is arguable that this anecdote shows that complex systems have several levels of protection built into them so that errors can be detected and their effects counteracted. In this case, just that happened. It also shows, however, the way "relatively small stimuli in one part of the system produce vast reverberations throughout the rest of the system."[125] A small computer chip inside a hollowed-out mountain in central Colorado caused dramatic actions across the U.S. mainland and in Hawaii. The system is very "tightly coupled," as systems planners put it, and "it tries to 'manage' every small threat in detail by centralized direction, reliance on near real-time warning, and dependence on pre-arranged reactions."[126]

The second anecdote suggests the extent of the coupling between the Soviet and American systems that has evolved. At the height of the Suez conflict in 1956, four independent, individually benign events happened in a short period of time. Radar picked up a flight of jet aircraft over Turkey and the Turkish air force was put on alert. One hundred Soviet MiGs were reported over Syria and a British Canberra bomber was downed in that area. At the same time, the Soviet fleet sailed through the Dardanelles. This set of events caused one general to worry that the NATO plan to unleash a nuclear attack might be set in motion. The four events each had their own independent explanation. The "jets" over Turkey were in fact swans. The MiGs were less numerous than reported and were escorting the president of Syria back from a state visit to Moscow. The bomber went down with mechanical problems. And the Soviet fleet was beginning a long-planned exercise. Bracken suggests that our complex early warning system may be set up to handle and properly interpret one or two such events. But when a complex system detects four coincident events, it may not be able to attribute the simultaneity to "mere coincidence." At least, such an occurrence, if it happened today, would probably push our modern system to a higher level of alert. Then, Bracken argues, the major modules of the world-wide nuclear system—one "ours," the other "theirs"—could begin to feed on each other. Because the Soviets monitor, among many things, our levels of alert, they might raise their system's level of alert.

> Once warning and intelligence systems are stimulated beyond a certain threshold, or once a certain level of alert has been ordered by political or military authorities, the situation may alter dramatically. . . . The overall effect of both Soviet and American actions might be to aggravate the crisis, forcing alert levels to ratchet upward worldwide. Although each side might believe it was taking necessary precautionary moves, the other side might see precaution as a threat. This would in turn click the alert level up another notch.[127]

Whether the system could ever rachet itself into a war is not clear. Probably no one knows. John von Neumann thought it *would* and so wrote in 1951,

> The preliminaries of war are to some extent a mutually self-excitatory process, where the actions of either side stimulate the actions of the other side. . . . After several rounds of amplification, [this process]

> *finally leads to "total" conflict. . . . I think, in particular, that the*
> *U.S.A.-U.S.S.R. conflict will probably lead to an armed "total"*
> *collision, and that a maximum rate of armament is therefore*
> *imperative.*[128]

This "'total' collision" has not happened yet, but that is small comfort. As a reviewer of Bracken's book summarized the image Bracken draws, "The war system [Bracken] describes is a kind of great microchip beast which is preternaturally sensitive and alert, with one overriding primitive impulse hard-wired into its cerebral cortex—to strike out and destroy the only other beast of its kind."[129]

The world-wide nuclear force system is a beast of enormous complexity. It is technologically sophisticated, multi-faceted, and all encompassing. For all its complexity, it is also, we should not forget, quite simple. Everyone has experienced the ratcheting up of "squeals" over loudspeakers. That is the simplicity with which the system will work when the fail-safe threshold is crossed and a "Go" order issued.

Oppenheimer, even without knowing the kinds of technology that would be available to the bomb delivery system, anticipated its essential character immediately after World War II. He said,

> *The pattern of the use of atomic weapons was set at Hiroshima. They*
> *are weapons of aggression, of surprise, and of terror. If they are ever*
> *used again it may well be by the thousands, or perhaps by tens of*
> *thousands; their method of delivery may well be different and may*
> *reflect new possibilities of interception, and the strategy of their use may*
> *well be different from what it was against an essentially defeated enemy.*
> *But it is a weapon for aggressors, and the elements of surprise and of*
> *terror are as intrinsic to it as are the fissionable nuclei.*[130]

The bomb-delivery system includes not only bombs, planes, radar, and so on; it also covers and leaves its traces on the psychologies of nations.

The bomb was for Oppenheimer something that ought to focus the attention of the peoples of the world on what were, for Oppenheimer, common interests. Following Bohr, Oppenheimer believed that the existence of the bomb would force nations and diverse peoples to come together in a "common bond," recognizing a "common responsibility" and showing a "common confidence that in a world thus united the things that we cherish—learning and freedom and humanity—will not be lost."[131] Defense was out; security, and security based on a recognition of absolute interdependence and linkage through common interests, was in. Oppenheimer said, "We knew how dim and inadequate the prospects were of defense" against the bomb. "The people of the United States, and the government that represents them . . . have seen that their security in this age is inseparably linked to that of other peoples of the world. They have understood that purely national methods of protecting that security would be woefully inadequate."[132] The bomb, like the systems that enabled it to realize its potential, would tie together everything that exists, whether it was used or not. Its existence would be sufficient to unify the whole across which the systems it engendered extend. A kind of unity, not without an aesthetic appeal similar to the aesthetic appeal of Trinity itself, is the gleam in the eye that sees from a systems perspective.

The Pursuit of Simplicity (Reprise)

Descartes's dream has not been realized. It was abandoned, but not forgotten, in the transition from analytical thinking to systems thinking. Knowledge is not unified. The world is complex. The physicists tell us that nature gets "curiouser and curiouser," the deeper its secrets are probed. No matter. We know that dreams fulfill wishes. In an odd and perverse way, which is the way dreams often operate, the *wish* for the totalization of knowledge has been fulfilled by a systems perspective on the world. Models of urban systems like Forrester's are a commonplace. Models of the "world system"[133] are used alike by undergraduates in policy studies courses as they have their go at "solving the population problem" and by fiction writers in stories about nipping total international conflict in the bud.[134] Such models link all aspects of the world in principle. Only one step farther up the ladder of perversity, if Oppenheimer is correct, the bomb and its attendant systems link the world in fact. But the linkage of all knowledge in theory and of all aspects of living in fact is only one sense in which Descartes's dream fulfills a wish. Sometimes with dreams it pays to dig a bit deeper.

To achieve the linkage of knowledge and the aggregation of life under the umbrella of the bomb, there has been a dissolution of the boundaries that used to make possible arguments in which we used to find some comfort for the distance they provide from the illuminating light of the violent events with which our new age began. Albert Borgmann, for example, begins his philosophical inquiry into the place of technology in modern life by outlining the philosophical positions on technology that seem to be contending for prominence. He aims to expertly establish the boundaries of the philosophical thinking that grounds thought about technology.

> Is technology a powerful instrument in the service of our values, a force in its own right that threatens our essential welfare, or is there perhaps no clear problem of technology at all, merely an interplay of numerous and variable tendencies? The three parts of this question are answered affirmatively by the instrumentalist, the substantive, and the pluralist schools of thought. That they cannot all be right at once is readily apparent.[135]

Into which category, this expert asks, can technology be expertly placed? Or should we, perhaps, not invent yet another category that transcends previous categorizations so that the object of our analytical inquiry—technology in this case—fits in a neater, less forced way into the world as we have it? Borgmann's own goal is to develop a "theory of technology" that respects the best in each of these categories and rejects their less desirable features. His work ends only with a hope, a sustaining hope he calls it, for a better balance between technology and other social institutions. His desire is to recover the "promise of technology" which "was one of liberty and prosperity."[136]

But in his rush to construct a theory that will harmonize the world with its technological advances, Borgmann, like many others, overlooks the possibility that modern technology may not respect the mischievous distinctions of all expert, boundary-placing categorizers. It may not be subject to the technical interventions envisioned by expert philosophers of technology. The instrumentalist, the substantivist, and the pluralist *may* all be right at once. At least one can find in the bomb project the essential elements of precisely the argument that technology is all things to all philosophical positions: at once an instrument in service of our most cherished values *and* a force that threatens *and* not essentially problematic. And that argument enlightens us on one of the darker implications of the work in which we have been collectively engaged as we set up, admire, and refine the Atomic Bomb System.

In a speech given to the staff at Los Alamos just after he left the post of director, Robert Oppenheimer reviewed all of the reasons he had heard (and had used himself, he tells us) for people having involved themselves in the creation of a new weapon. But then he dismissed all statements of motivation with the view that, "when you come right down to it the reason we did this job is because *it was an organic necessity*. If you are a scientist you cannot stop such a thing."[137] Science and technology have a dynamic, an organic necessity of their own. They are not essentially problematic. The modern scientist is not a creator, not even a "discoverer." He is more like an agent of necessity, an executive of the inevitable. There is an irresistibility to the rationality that says it is but one's job to help something realize its potential. ("If you don't, someone else will, of course," and other stock phrases can be added here.)

The individual scientist at Los Alamos was a consummate team member at once vitalized by the work and submerged in it. The media made Oppenheimer into the "father of the atomic bomb," but that is because, culturally, we wish to think that some *one*, some *body* is in charge and, ultimately, responsible. When something has been made to happen, some one had to have made it so. There had to have been people whose ambitions led them to their accomplishments that may subsequently be judged mad.

To draw an example from another theater of violence, one review of Yitzhak Arad's account of the camps at Belzec, Sorbibor, and Treblinka concludes that the book is not the "definitive" work on this portion of the Nazi machine because it leaves the reader "a long way from understanding the *sources* of the Nazi's monstrous *ambitions*."[138] It is unacceptable to modern sensibility simply to describe, as Arad does so well, the systems that make people their agents as well as their objects. We find a measure of comfort in the notion that humans—human ambitions, urges, ideas, desires—must necessarily lie behind deeds.

Oppenheimer not only understood that such was not the case with the bomb but also, and more acutely, he understood that what people *thought* they were doing as they did what they did—their motivations, the orientations of character—*did not matter* in the end. As he tried to explain in a portion of an interview that was edited from its final television presentation in Britain, "I think that irrespective of what was done with [the bomb], irrespective of what was to come of it, it was clear that this was a very major change in the human situation, and the people who were involved in it had a sense that they were playing a part in history."[139] The people with whom Oppenheimer worked were not making history or moving it. They were each playing their parts. Fermi took his group on hikes through the mesas far from Omega while Slotin tickled dragons' tails. Neddermeyer took his pipes and wrapped charges to the canyons around the mesa. Kistiakowsky ground his explosive lenses into final shape with old dental tools. Teller sulked as he schemed for bigger bombs. Each person had his laboratory or his place in the laboratory of another. Each did his own work. Individual contributions counted for much and also for little. The whole, finally, mattered. Each person played his part and the whole issued from the team.

If one can not find a problem with the ambitions and plans of people, perhaps there is a problem in the threatening essence of technology itself as the philosophical "substantivist" would argue. For Oppenheimer, technology, and the knowledge on which it is based, is not essentially problematic and it constitutes a force in its own right. But to say this is Oppenheimer's position is *not* to say that he believed technology is, therefore, evil. Borgmann says that people often make such an equivalence. In fact, as the scientists contributed to the team effort at Los Alamos, there was rarely a morally quibbling eyebrow raised about the fact that a bomb would be built. From the moment of the discovery of fission in 1938–39, a test like Trinity was a foregone conclusion. Japanese scientists knew a bomb would be built.[140] The German scientists knew a bomb could be built.[141] The only question was, who would build it (first)? The bomb was the natural next step for the knowledge machine.

Louis Alvarez has recently described how Oppenheimer himself came, so simply it seems, to the inevitable conclusion about the possibility and likely inevitability of the bomb. When Alvarez, early in 1939 after the news of fission had leaked from Bohr's entourage when it arrived in the United States, sought out Oppenheimer to tell him of the discovery of fission, "He instantly pronounced the reaction impossible and proceeded to prove mathematically to everyone in the room that someone must have made a mistake." The next day Alvarez and his associate Ken Green set up the Hahn-Strassman experiment and brought Oppenheimer to see the results. "In less than fifteen minutes he not only agreed that the reaction was authentic but also speculated that in the process extra neutrons would boil off that could be used to split more uranium atoms and thereby generate power or make bombs."[142] That was the afternoon Oppenheimer had the drawing of a bomb on his blackboard. Technology is not villainous in this view but it does have an autonomy that is irresistible. It carries the scientist/technologist along with it.

Alvarez's representation of Oppenheimer's view that the atom might "generate power *or* make bombs" is sometimes seen as the value-conundrum of modern technology. A technology might be used for good or for evil, so we say. Then such dichotomies get subjected to philosophical arguments, and then we worry about how responsible people might be when the products of the knowledge machine are in their hands. This is a common way to proceed with a "values problem," but it is just another way of invoking the desire that there be a responsible party for what happens to occur. Scientists think differently. Teller, for example, says that the responsibility of scientists is to make science. They cannot know, he says, whether it will be used for good or evil.[143] John Kemeny, chair of the presidential commission on Three Mile Island, respects the "non-responsibility" of the scientist, but wants to ensure that someone remains institutionally in charge. He believes that in every technologically or scientifically complex situation scientists ought to be called upon to present options along with considered reviews of the costs and consequences of each. Then it remains, in his view, for elected, political representatives to make choices among the options—and to assume responsibility for the side of the good-evil divide on which the results happen to fall.[144] Before Kemeny, Szilard had proposed just such a role for the scientist. A tribunal of scientists would advise governmental authorities not only on technological options but also on which parts of scientific knowledge should become public and which should not, according to Szilard's scheme.

But the "good *or* evil" concern, the "values issue," may be but a gloss on a deeper issue. If it were the case that technology and science can be used for good or for evil, the only remaining problem would be to follow Szilard's and Kemeny's lead and try to design social-technical mechanisms to ensure that it never gets used for evil. The prior problem, the deeper issue, is that the "or" on which such hopes rest may necessarily be an "and."

The bomb may be both the best *and* the worst of human creations.

It is a claim that Oppenheimer made implicitly in 1945. To the staff at Los Alamos he said, "If you are a scientist you believe it is good to find out how the world works; that it is good to find out what the realities are; that it is good to turn over to mankind at large the greatest possible power to control the world and to deal with it according to his lights and values." Two weeks later to a different audience: "[As scientists] it is our faith and commitment, seldom made explicit, even more seldom challenged, that knowledge is a good in itself, knowledge and such power as must come with it." Simultaneously, however, Oppenheimer realized that in the bomb, "we have made a thing, a most terrible weapon, that has altered abruptly and profoundly the nature of the world. We have made a thing that by all standards of the world we grew up in is an evil thing." It was not equivalent to the invention of dynamite, or the invention of the long range gun barrel, or the aerial bomb sight, he argued. "Atomic weapons are," Oppenheimer knew, "a peril which affects everyone in the world,"[145] not just the unlucky people who happen to reside in "enemy territory" because dichotomies like that between friend and foe built on the differences between good and evil are meaningless now in the seamless world of our new age.

To be told that a thing is both the best and the worst may appeal to the poetic imagination, but, again, common sense rebels. Our common sense, even our common philosophical arguments, would have it as good or evil, a peril or a hope, open to individual judgment, debate, and disposition according to the will and authority of those responsible.

It is helpful to remember that a systems perspective often makes a mockery of common sense. Oppenheimer reminds us of this when he says that all the developments in physics that led to the bomb "forced us to reconsider the relations between science and common sense."[146] Common sense flows from the analytic tradition and knows through a capacity to separate, categorize and simplify. But common sense is voided when the mind grasps a totality. Dichotomies become untenable. Arad sagely dubs Himmler's capacity to think of the Final Solution as a whole, a unity, a totality, "an unwritten and never to be written *page of glory*." The old distinction of good or evil carries little weight when there is such "stunning disregard of common sense"[147] as we witnessed over the first half of this century. It makes more sense to try to understand how technology transcends the dichotomy of being either "a powerful instrument in service of our values" or "a force . . . that threatens our essential welfare" and to examine the nature of the "glory" in which the bomb builders, their predecessors like Bohr, and their successors in *their* stunning disregard of common sense, reveled.

When Oppenheimer said that it was good to create knowledge that allowed people to control nature, that allowed people to make something happen around them, he was speaking a cultural truth. It may be more accurate, if more clumsy, to say he was *speaking culture.* "We recognize as cultural all activities and resources which are useful to men for making the earth serviceable to them."[148] People engaged in such cultural activities retrieve that sense of a center that Freud's list of iconoclasts stripped from us. They become the center of all events and everything seems to move around them. They know themselves to be human and vital, ironically perhaps, by their stillness relative to events that happen or that are made to happen around them. They become like one of Len Deighton's spies, "very still . . . always the onlooker no matter how involved [one] truly [feels]." Deighton says of "Stinnes," "He was always the sun; everything moved except him."[149] From this posture, we gain a sense of being alive by our capacity to "make something happen." Theory masters the vicissitudes of life by freezing each instant of a process in a concept, in an idea. And once each instant of a process is suspended in an idea, the idea guides intervention. Life lived in this freeze-frame manner seems to be recognized, for unfathomable reasons, as an exciting, vital life.

Sartre reflects on this approach to being alive in his *La Mort dans l'ame* in a brief scene where Mathieu is sniping at German soldiers from a tower: "For years he had tried, in vain, to act. One after the other his intended actions had been stolen from him: he had been no firmer that a pat of butter. But no one had stolen this! He had pressed the trigger, and, for once, something had happened, something definite." He had gotten a German soldier in his sight, fired, and caused a death to happen. Mathieu does not have the hubris to imagine himself a player in a historical drama. He becomes an overseer of life, even his own life, detached in his new-found vitality: "In the empty street lay four dead men: a little further on, two more. Nothing for it but to finish the job and get polished off. What difference had all this made to the Germans?—merely put their time-table out by ten minutes." And indeed, five minutes later Mathieu is dead because the Germans rolled in a large cannon that, in its turn, made something else happen.[150]

Through Sartre's Mathieu we can begin to appreciate the vitality and excitement the scientists experienced in their days at Los Alamos. Scientists have traditionally enjoyed a certain separation between the controller and the controlled, between the scientist and the object of inquiry. They have always been Stinnes-like, like the sun shining its inquiring light on knowable nature. It is a separation that has always permitted judgment to seep into the application of scientific works. The traditional scientist could ask, "Can we?" and then had the freedom to follow that with, "Ought we?" and could expect to receive separate answers.

The memoirs of the Los Alamos scientists recall their time on the Hill as the most vital period in their lives. They knew that the ambience, the colleagueship, the money, the sense of adventure and task, the satisfaction of unqualified accomplishment would never be duplicated. They were not only going to make *some*thing happen. They were on the verge of making everything happen. They could literally move mountains through their work. As the historian Spencer Weart puts it, they understood themselves to be unpeeling a cosmic mystery. Even though soon after the war, the scientists thought "a release of nuclear energy is cosmic only in the same sense that the burning of a match is," at the time, "not even scientists denied that there was something supremely mysterious, majestic, almost divine, in any manifestation of atomic energy."[151] The scientists were going to enter the *sanctum sanctorum* of nature and make nature yield. And when the whole thing, in its simplicity, worked, every millisecond of the event was captured by theories and equations on blackboards that shaped the minds of the scientists just as it was captured in the pictures of the high-speed cameras positioned around the Jornada del Muerto, pictures one still finds in Oppenheimer's personal papers in the Library of Congress. The capacity to make something happen to a degree not known before—and yet to be able to view the event as a series of stillnesses from a posture of stillness, every moment precisely captured in the freeze-frame of theory and equation—was thrilling, uniquely vitalizing.

Slotin tickled the tail of the dragon. He mobilized the power of nature and, but for one time, was able to arrest its mobility at a precise, pre-lethal moment. It was, certainly for Slotin given what we know of him, thrilling and vitalizing to be able to master the dynamics that would later mobilize everything into a truly "beautiful" explosion.

It is now time to confront the pernicious necrophilia that is the other side of one's participation in the achievement of beautiful simplicity out of enormous complexity. The management of complexity to achieve simplicity sometimes leads, simply, to deathly simplification. Taming life sometimes eliminates life, often in the name of an aesthetically pleasing harmony and hygienically acceptable beauty.

Consider, for example, a new product from Weyerhaueser. *Time* magazine began its review of this new product by saying, "Many plant lovers are also plant killers; they never quite find the right mix of light and water to keep their houseplants alive!" Weyerhaeuser solved this problem with a process that puts plants into "a kind of permanent 'sleep.'" The plants, *Time* says, "look, feel and even smell as they did before."[152] Stephen Barger, manager of Weyerhaeuser's division dedicated to marketing this product, told one newspaper, "They are not live, not artificial, but in between. It is a new category. Dead but real." The banner headline of the story read, "The Perfect Plant."[153] (The only problem with these perfect plants, reported Weyerhaeuser people, is that the owners insist on treating the plants *as if* they were alive. They water and fertilize them when all they need is the occasional dusting.) Like Mathieu, we enliven ourselves by creating an environment that is "dead but real" and, we should add, that has a certain unquestionable beauty to it.

The threat comes with a systems perspective, which makes the world seamless, that in our preoccupation with effecting beauty and the harmony we may fail to recognize that even would-be controllers are implicated in their acts of control, no longer as "responsible parties" but as objects of their own acts. They have to become dead to their own actions because that is the only way to find a place in this new world. The physicists shined their bright lights of inquiry on the atom in order to illuminate its nature. Reciprocally and fatefully, the atom shined its light on the scientists arrayed around the tower at Trinity. As the knowledge machine churned out its later inevitable products in the line extending on from Trinity, Little Boy and Fat Man, the light and the heat grew to unbelievable proportions, as Edward Teller knew from the first it could. After vaporizing the island of Elugelab, the fireball of the first hydrogen bomb "spread so far and so fast that it terrified observers who had seen many tests before. The explosion . . . 'was so large, so brutal—as if things had gone too far. When the heat reached the observers, it stayed and stayed and stayed, not for seconds but for minutes.'"[154] There is no privileged center from which an observer might now illuminate the dark mysteries of the world with an eye to taming them. The world may show its dragon's face and snap back with its own vicious illumination, because, as the chant goes, everything is connected to everything else.

The systems perspective of our new age links observer and observed in one complex system in which, as Slotin's accident suggests, the line between being a collector of data and being a datum no longer exists. The new perspective leaves no gaps in which questions of the rightness of actions may make their appearance. Robert Wilson, one of the young scientists at Los Alamos, said later in life,

> I would like to think now that at the time of the German defeat that I would have stopped, taken stock, thought it all over very carefully, and that I would have walked away from Los Alamos at that time. And I— in terms of my—everything that I believe in, before and during and after the war—I cannot understand that I did not take that [step], and make that act. On the other hand, it simply was not in the air. . . . Our life was directed to do one thing. It was as though we had been programmed to do that, and we as automatons were doing it.[155]

The scientists were something like "dead but real" executives of the inevitable.

Events in systems, to recall Oppenheimer's phrase, are "organic necessities" and have about them, as Einstein reportedly said of the bomb, a "weird inevitability" that drives them, without the interruption of a single "Ought we?" through a continuous trajectory from conception to enablement. There are no beginnings and endings from a systems point of view. There are no "natural" break points where questions of a moral sort might be voiced. Trinity—the metaphorically loaded name of the test site—is alpha and omega wrapped into one. The new expert whose job is to enable an event to realize itself does not have the space, the freedom, in which to ask certain questions. The modern expert is left only with a historically peculiar kind of freedom, the freedom to wager on the size of a particular event which he has helped enable to come to fruition. He has only the freedom to take up (or not, of course) Fermi's macabre bet or enter the pool Rabi eventually won.

Within such a understanding of the new science it is useful to reconsider Edward Teller's passionate "pursuit of simplicity." In his more studied moments, Teller imagines simplicity as a kind of muse. "The future will be influenced, hopefully," he writes,

> by all the billions of people on the planet. . . . Today, in an interconnected, interdependent world, it seems . . . self-evident that the importance of technology and science to mankind, both in the past and in the future, must be acknowledged. Each individual should hold evident that these human activities can work for the betterment of humanity. Each should hold evident that the power which people are rapidly acquiring over nature and potentially over one another must be subject to mutual understanding and agreements between nations.

The world, Teller admits, is a very complex place in which the vicissitudes of life and living threaten our collective future and one ought to begin to think about tempering the potential resident in our system to optimize, the line would go, the use of that potential. "In none of these discussions," Teller concludes his introduction to *The Pursuit of Simplicity*, "do I mean to imply that the world or life or the future can be simple. A more modest and realistic claim is made: to pursue simplicity in life, in the world, for the future, is a most valuable enterprise." He adds, "The pursuit of simplicity in science leads to understanding and beauty. In human affairs, it may fulfill our most desperate need: the survival of a civilized human society."[156] Teller's goal is modest. His studied, rational view keeps a firm grip on the traditional, common sense notion that people might stand separate from their affairs, deliberate on ends, contemplate the control that science offers them, and make their own futures.

In his more speculative moments, Teller has offered a less studied, less rational view of the situation in which we find ourselves. It is a view that aligns better with the view from a systems perspective, which we might, in our studied moments, fight not to adopt but in the grip of which we all seem to exist. It is a view that implicates those who would make something happen, perhaps more than those who are supposed to be in the sights. A documentary on Teller ends with the scientist reciting this poem by Eric Kästner, which he says he can never forget:

I never have dreams
That I can freely confess.
Once I'm in bed, I sleep deaf and dumb.
But recently, I have dreamt nevertheless.
It was of the war that will come.
From the trenches, millions of men have crawled,
volunteers all, I was assured by a voice.
They raised their rifles, just as a loud voice called.
Whom they should shoot, that was their choice.
They approached each other staring, without making a sound.
But then came a scream,
as of someone in pain.
As if on command, all rifles were turned around.
And by his own hand, each man was slain.
In unending rows, the dreadful slaughter was done.
Really, I never dream.
And I wish I could know who was the one.
The one who did scream.[157]

The emblematic event of our time may be a little-known side show that (probably) occurred when the Soviet Union exploded a very large hydrogen bomb in the early 1960s. Published estimates of the yield range between fifty-eight and a hundred megatons—between six and ten times larger than the first hydrogen bomb test that "terrified" seasoned U.S. observers and at least five thousand times larger than the Hiroshima bomb. Several of the top Soviet scientists have not been heard from since that "shot." As an American nuclear physicist put it to me, "We think they discovered a phenomenon [the so-called 'booster' phenomenon] and stood too close."[158]

Simplification need not remain merely an idealized guiding vision. We have the capacity to simplify the world and free it finally from the vicissitudes of life. Science has given us the capacity to realize a world where everything in it, including all the scientists and would-be experts, is "dead but real," where everywhere there is the eerie, green-glowing beauty of the slight depression around Ground Zero at Alamogordo. The wish is perverse but its attraction builds when even the staunchest defenders of the capacity of science to comprehend the complexity of the world, to bring some order to the apparent chaos, begin to say that the world is "too pluralistic for any mind [even of the omniscient sort] to form an adequate conception of it."[159]

The rational mind is repelled by the attraction and invents gentle rhetoric to cast this wish into the deep background. But even so rational a person as John von Neumann, who contributed no little share to our modern approach to knowledge, speculated that our passions for making something happen coupled with our new capabilities could lead us to "achieve togetherness" (and how many of us have entertained that beautiful hope?) through a grand, "cosmic suicide."[160] Teller's reluctant dream of total destruction is the modern corollary of Descartes' foundational dream of totalization of knowledge, control, and power. The dreams do not stand at odds with one another.

It is time to stop discussing the bomb in terms of good and evil. The bomb is simply nature having been enabled to realize its potential. It is, in its totality, one of our best efforts, an exemplary demonstration of our valued capacity to control nature and harness nature's forces. The fact that this nearly ultimate act of control sweeps back over those who our common sense tells us were "in control" in the first place, the fact that we are all implicated by the violent results of our rationality, the fact that our old forms of argument fail in our efforts to apprehend our own actions, none of this should surprise us anymore. We should be no more surprised than the Peter Sellers character in *Dr. Strangelove* who asks, *"You mean you built a doomsday machine and didn't tell anyone?"* How could any one know? Such is the nature of systems. Such is the nature of our new age on this side of the pass.

CHAPTER THREE:

Responsibility and "Life in This Kind of Life"

> *You are who you are.*
>> Army Colonel to Nuclear Weapons Scientist
>> *The Manhattan Project*

> *He was everything, and nothing.*
>> ARIEL DORFMAN,
>> on General Augusto Pinochet

In 1975, a slim volume issued "from one political conservative's attempt to reassess his views on politics and society in the aftermath of Watergate and the Nixon presidency."[1] In *The Cunning of History,* Richard L. Rubenstein concludes, "something happened in the twentieth century that made it morally and psychologically possible to realize dreams of destructiveness that had previously been confined to fantasy."[2] To inquire into the moral and psychological roots that grounded this modern age Rubenstein returned to the Holocaust. By adopting a Lenny Bruce-like posture of saying what is, by adopting "a mental attitude that excludes all feelings of sympathy or hostility towards both the victims and the perpetrators," Rubenstein finds himself concluding that "the Holocaust bears witness to *the advance of civilization*, I repeat," he writes, "to the advance of civilization, to the point at which large scale massacre is no longer a crime and the state's sovereign powers are such that millions can be stripped of their rights and condemned to the world of the living dead."[3] And, perhaps more shocking, this "political conservative" is forced to confront "one of the most difficult conclusions," viz., that "the Nazis

committed no crime at Auschwitz since no law or political order protected those who were first condemned to statelessness and then to
the camps."[4] Nuremberg was more an "exercise in national vengeance" than it was an advance in international law.[5] In order to find
any *one*, any *body* responsible, Rubenstein reminds us, new law had
to be invented, and furthermore, the law, once developed, was applied contingent on many "extralegal considerations."[6]

Let us try to be at least as open-eyed about Rubenstein's conclusions as he was. He returned to the Holocaust because the *advance* in
civilization it marked (recall Arad's "page of glory") was, for him, one
of the first steps toward *our* advanced civilization. The Holocaust
demonstrated the necrophilic capacity of the state to declare (part of)
its population to be "surplus population" and to dispose of that surplus however it saw fit. The state demonstrated its readiness to invalidate people's civic associations, to declare people to be socially
alone and without the protection that those associations had traditionally supplied. The Germans built, in Rubenstein's terms, "the
ultimate city of Western civilization, Necropolis, the new city of the
dead." He goes on to remind us that, "the world of the city, our world,
is the world of human invention and power; it is also the world of
artifice, dreams, charades, and the paper promises we call money.
But even the richest and most powerful city can only survive as long
as the umbilical cord to the countryside is not cut." When there is no
longer an "outside" to which the city can turn for sustenance and
revitalization, the city turns on itself, consumes itself, "feeds upon
its own ever-diminishing resources and finally collapses."[7]

The new city of the dead is not a historical aberration. It is the
logical conclusion of our rationality that would tie everything to
everything else and leave no "outside" which might sustain us and
provide a place to retreat to ask fundamental questions about what
is going on "inside." Since the new city is a logical conclusion, an
advance in civilization, one more turn of the crank, there is no responsible party to "blame" for what might be viewed, from some
moral stance (were one available to us), as excessive. No, as wrong.

I follow Rubenstein as far as he goes, but I am forced to go a little
farther. Rubenstein's argument is correlative with Primo Levi's. There
is in the camps a *difference* that counts for everything. Levi, for instance, knew that he did not commit murder in the camps and he
knew who did. The surplus population of which the Nazi machine
disposed consisted largely of people in certain categories. In the age

of systems, those differences that made all the difference in the machine of the camps does not exist. Systems do not create categorizable, disposable groups. Systems individualize. They recognize and foster the uniquely individual. But they use and feed upon everyone, regardless of categorical status. They can do this because in the individuation of individuals there is a snatching away of all bases for civic association, even among those traditionally privileged and protected. It is one thing for rationality to advance to the point of building a Necropolis out in the country at the end of a new railway spur; it is another for a rationality to be encompassingly necrophilic, for everything to be captured under the "new category" of "dead but real."

Under a systems theoretic logic, "man," even expert men and women, is reduced to a component of systems. All components invite thinking about substitutability. All components can be modeled and the models may suggest that one type of component is outmoded and can be "surplussed." Any person might find himself aptly characterized by Dorfman's phrase, "He was everything, and nothing."[8]

Consider this. Tom Wolfe wrote in *The Right Stuff* of the place of pilots, *expert* pilots, in the early space program:

> As late as the summer of 1960, at an Armed Forces-National Research Council conference at Woods Hole, Massachusetts, on the training of astronauts, various engineers and scientists from outside NASA thought nothing of describing the Mercury rocket-capsule as a fully automated system in which "the astronaut does not need to turn a hand." They would say, "The astronaut has been added to the system as a redundant component."[9]

Wolfe chronicles the astronauts' struggle to become something other than a human analogue of the monkeys or the collared dogs of the early space shots.

After the battle was won and the "human component" had proved its non-redundant, non-surplus value in events like the flight of Apollo 13,[10] it had to come to this: An article about the still-potential next generation of jet fighters discussed the place of expert pilots in the following terms:

> "At the current time, we have the airframe, engine and materials technology to build an aircraft that'll pull just about any kind of G that you can ask for," Dr. Robert E. Van Patten, chief of the acceleration

*effects branch of the Armstrong Aerospace Medical Research Laboratory
in Ohio, recently told the Aerospace Medicine Association.*

"Unfortunately, we're still working with the same model of
man that we've been working with for some years."

*And the problem is bound to get worse. Planes with super-
maneuverability—the ability to change their angle of attack by 90
degrees in a split second—are just beyond the horizon. "Frankly, I
haven't really thought too much about what we're going to do for
acceleration in that environment because it depresses me to think about
it," Van Patten said.*[11]

Human beings may continue to have a place in complex systems but,
at least in some instances, they are not well suited to the job. Given
that people, even experts, mostly conform to "the same model of
man" that has been in place for some years, what is the place of
experts in complex systems? How are we to understand the role of
the "human component" in closed-loop systems? Are terms like "responsibility" useful any more? Is there any place from which to ask
questions about moral action? And if the answer to these last two
questions is no, does it make sense to be concerned about moral
orders, from which notions of responsibility derive, and the like anymore? A practical, if frightening question: What will system components like Van Patten do to relieve their "depression"?

Material from sources distant from the making of the bomb will
help us appreciate the way systems create individuality while simultaneously stripping people of the traditional protections of civic association among individuals. It will also help us appreciate the fact
that systems have the capacity to surplus even those who are ostensibly "responsible" and "in charge." Material from several arenas will
permit us to adopt, eventually, an attitude "that excludes all feelings
of sympathy or hostility" so that we may appreciate the *logic* of Oppenheimer's disposal by the system he was so influential in creating.
There is a logic in the way systems make someone who was, in truth,
everything, into nothing.

The Place of Experts

IN *WALDEN TWO*

B. F. Skinner's account of his utopia ends, "Frazier was not in his
heaven. All was right with the world."[12] This system, this total system,
could be right only if its premier expert, its founder, was not in his
place on his "Throne."

Walden Two opens with two men, Rogers and Jannik, back from service in World War II, coming to see one of Rogers's college instructors, Professor Burris. They want to vitalize their lives; they want to make something happen. They want to build nothing less than "a social system somewhere that will really work." They have found fighting a war "easy," they say, because in war there is an enemy. There is a boundary around "us," bearers of the good, beyond which resides "them," evil incarnate. In such a situation one knows how to act. But a total system like the culture to which they are returning and in which they are now compelled to survive, if not live, is totally encompassing. There is no outside, no enemy, no one to fight against to give definition to life. In war, they say, "at least you know what you want and how to get it. But we don't even know how to begin to fight the mess we're in now"—the mess of not knowing what to do with lives that are, as they put it, "insane" in so many respects— "*Whom* are we fighting? What kind of war is it?"

There is to be no distancing objectivity for these young men. They disdain the distance of teachers, including Burris, in their "ivory towers." Not even the distance of the politician from the action of life is acceptable to them. Politics, they say, will not allow them to "find out what people really want, what they need in order to be happy." Only an experimental approach to living one's own life will satisfy this desire, they conclude. Rogers says to his old professor, "It's a job for research, but not the kind you can do in a university, or in a laboratory anywhere. I mean you've got to experiment, and *experiment with your own life!* Not just sit back . . . as if your own life weren't all mixed up in it."[13] The line between being a collector of data and becoming a datum must be erased for these young men if their lives are to have any meaning.

These young people feel compelled to build a total system that, if there is a place to repair for spiritual renewal and moral reflection, must be inside the system itself (and will probably be called something like "Omega site"). In the world of this novel there is already, it turns out, a total system which, once entered, becomes all there is, or more accurately, all that need be. This system is the utopian community of Walden Two, founded by Burris's schoolmate, T. E. Frazier.

In Walden Two, there is no problem of knowledge. As in all complex systems all necessary knowledge is resident in the system. The problem is to enable the potential of the system to realize itself, to mobilize expert knowledge and make it available for use. Walden Two does that, Frazier tells his visitors, by encouraging "our people to view every habit and custom with an eye to possible improvement. A constantly experimental attitude toward everything—that's all we need. Solutions to problems of every sort follow almost miraculously." A simple tea service provides the first introduction to such miracles. "Domestic engineers," we learn, invented tea cups that were large enough to hold two servings so that they did not have to be refilled, that were shaped so that they accentuated the odor of the tea, and that were structured so they could be carried easily without spilling. And these engineers "naturally hit on" this design as a solution to the problem of serving tea to all the community members who wished it. People "naturally hit on" solutions to problems because the knowledge needed for the solution is embedded in nature that acts as a constraint on the system.

When the visitors to this system are taken to see how infants are cared for during their first year, "Mrs. Nash" tells them why each infant is kept in a cubicle that looks to Castle "like an aquarium." "This is a much more efficient way of keeping a baby warm than the usual practice of keeping it in several layers of cloth," says Mrs. Nash. "The newborn baby needs moist air at about 88 or 90 degrees. At six months, 80 is about right." Asked how she knows, Mrs. Nash replies, "The baby tells us. . . . If the baby's too warm, it does turn rather pinkish, and it usually cries." And when the child is too cold, "The baby turns rather pale . . . and takes a curious posture with its arms along its sides or slightly curled up. With a little practice we can tell at a glance whether the temperature is right or not."[14] One comes to acquire necessary, specialized knowledge merely by watching, by paying attention, and by opening oneself to ways to improve a situation. If one adopts an experimental attitude, not only toward the world but also toward one's own life practices, one comes to see, occasionally, that it is the practices of the researcher that are part of the problem. "Improvement," in such a system, is always obvious to the unalienated participants in it. And, as with the conclusion that "blankets are bad for babies," improvement usually involves an adjustment of the behavior of those responsible for seeking improvement as much as it involves intervention by responsible parties in the system itself.

In Walden Two, as in other complex systems, no one has complete knowledge. But then no one needs complete knowledge. Needed expertise exists and comes to be located where it is required. On a tour of the dairy, Burris thinks, "I realized suddenly that Frazier, in a quite literal sense, seldom knew what he was talking about. He could not make a corn souffle or clear a pond, he probably did not know when peas were ready to be picked or how they should be stored, and I doubted whether he could tell wheat from barley." But such knowledge on the part of Walden Two's founder would be superfluous. Dairy experts were there to run the dairy and, Burris thinks, "the professional vigor of this young [dairy] expert was reassuring. While Frazier dreamt of economic structure and cultural design, he would get out the milk." Even Frazier admits, "Strange as it may seem . . . there are many things about Walden Two of which I am not competent to speak."[15] This is not the ignorance of a Holmes-like disciplinarian; this is the ignorance of one sure in his own absolute dependence on the system that, once enabled to realize itself, enables all those it supports to realize themselves. This ignorance derives from a sure knowledge of the ready availability of all necessary knowledge and engenders a willingness to sacrifice one's "authority" and "responsibility" to the system itself.

It *is* strange to most ears to hear that Frazier would not know everything there is to know about "his" community. We participate in a culture that places the burdens of responsibility on those who are responsible. Frazier is clearly responsible for Walden Two in the sense that he originated it. But for a system, responsibility for origination is a very limited responsibility. Frazier is in no way analogous to Brigham Young or any other *founder* of living cities. Frazier called the people together, sold them on his basic idea, and set the thing running. Since he is the responsible party, in this narrow sense, we tend to want to make him responsible in a broader sense. Through Burris and company, we look to Frazier to know how the community runs and why it behaves as it does. And we look to him to act responsibly on that knowledge. But we are in new territory now and we should not be surprised if Frazier can not live up to those old-fashioned expectations from an old order.

Frazier would like, to be sure, to satisfy the demand that he be the responsible party. He even involves himself in a little God-fantasy. Late in the book Frazier takes Burris up to his "Throne," a rock ledge overlooking all of Walden Two. Burris, Frazier's straight man, opens,

"It must be a great satisfaction. . . . A world of your own making."
"Yes," Frazer says, "I look upon my world and, behold, it is good."
When Burris challenges Frazier about implicitly comparing himself
to God, Frazier himself notes—somewhat disruptively, for Burris—
"There's a curious similarity." Frazier equates God's creation with his
own by saying, "All that happens is contained in an original plan,
yet at every stage the individual seems to be making choices and
determining the outcome." But there is a difference; Walden Two,
Burris and we are told, is "rather an improvement upon Genesis." "I
might claim," Frazier notes, "that I made a more explicit statement of
my plan [than did God]. I could claim more *deliberate* control. . . .
Walden Two was planned in advance pretty much as it turned out to
be,"[16] not unlike that first explosion at Trinity. Frazier *knows* himself
to be responsible, he *is* responsible, and he acts responsible because,
as he says almost to himself as he sits on the "Throne," he loves "his
children."

But Frazier *is not responsible.* And most of the book is devoted to
showing how he has come to be simply another component in the
system, no more and no less important than any other component
of the community. The community is "governed" by the Board of
Planners. The Board is a self-perpetuating body that selects its new
members from a slate supplied by the community's Managers. The
Managers are specialists who have worked their ways up skill levels
in the various divisions and service sectors of Walden Two. Walden
Two is a community that depends upon and values expertise. Experts
are everywhere. But there is no single Expert who is or who could
even hope to assume responsibility, for good or evil, for the system.
The Board of Planners is ever vigilant in its job of enabling Walden
Two to become what it is so that the people in it can become what
they are in their own, individual expertise. Their task is to create a
situation free of apparent force or the threat of force because, as
Frazier says, people "strike against jails and the police, or the threat
of them—against oppression. They never strike against forces which
make them act the way they do."[17] If there are walls, boundaries,
categories, people know how to act, how to resist, how to rebel. But
in Walden Two all the trappings of expertise—honorific titles, deference in the face of professionalism, inequality bolstered by symbol
systems—that would make a person into more (or less) than he or
she is are dropped. All boundaries and categories are gone. Good

government consists entirely of the experimental adjustment of the positive reinforcement schedules that more or less determine everyone's behavior so that people are happy and feel themselves free. Expertise is diffuse throughout the community and all experts disappear into the fabric of the system.*

The startling fact is that *no one* is responsible for Walden Two. The system ensures that. It is more accurate to say that the system is responsible for itself. It is a mechanism that monitors itself and uses its members to help make those improvements that the workings of the system reveal it is necessary to make. People do not come together in civic association in Walden Two; they come together around the technical problem of adjusting their own reinforcement schedules. And once one is involved in making such technical determinations, all other aspect of one's life, which used to be integral to the notion of "association," are held in abeyance.

Walden Two articulates Skinner's curious notion of "freedom." There is no such thing as freedom in the absolute but there is a socially useful *feeling* of freedom that a good government will nurture. A system that supplies everyone's needs, that uses no force, that rewards compliance to a code that is flexible and experimentally adjusted to enable everyone to do whatever he or she wishes so long as individual behavior contributes to community welfare, will engender a feeling of freedom. It will engender this feeling even though the system will, as a complex system like a social order always does, hold all the cards. "Each of us is engaged in a pitched battle with the rest of mankind," is Frazier's starting point. From there, the job of the social order is to effect harmony in place of the always-potential chaos. An essential aspect of harmony is a feeling of freedom. People who feel free are less likely to express openly their opposition to society where "in the last analysis . . . control always rests."[18] The measures of a total system's success are activity recognized as "productive" and development named "progressive." Such arbitrary notions are the only available standards, since a total system has no outside with which to compare itself in moral terms. It has no op-

---

*Remember that the Planners do not earn all of their "work credits" by serving on the Board. They must engage in some physical labor and other tasks around the community like everyone else. Nothing distinguishes them in a fundamental way from the others.

position to one's present "prison," the barbed wire fence that almost no one notices anymore, through the contemplation of which one might imagine a meaning for the term "truly free." The job of experts in complex systems is to keep the system running, to maintain *its* vitality, for it is from the vitality of the system that the system's components, including its human components, gain their vitality.

Walden Two is an exemplary complex system. It is a system that uses experts to embody expertise. It suggests that there is no place for the "universal intellectual," a person who might assume responsibility and exercise it through his expert, impassioned, general criticism. There is no place for an ultimate expert who "knows" a system completely—for that is impossible in a truly complex system—and who might be held responsible for its operation. In fact, the last line of *Walden Two*, about Frazier *not* being in his heaven, suggests that one requirement for ensuring the vitality of the system is that anyone who might presume to be an ultimate expert must be "disappeared" into the system itself. And we cannot invoke this new verb without hearing its echoes all the way down to the Strait of Magellan.

IN THE PSYCHOTHERAPEUTIC ENCOUNTER

It might be argued that a system such as Walden Two is simply too large for there to be an ultimate expert or responsible party. Expertise must reside in a classical sociological division of labor that is bureaucratically organized. We have known for over a century that people do not matter in a bureaucracy; offices do. Frazier's dream of being God-like is just a dream and bureaucratic structures accommodate such dreams by ignoring them for they are irrelevant to the operation of the order and bureaucracies only attend to the relevant. The disappearance of the person in social systems, it might be argued, has been a sociological commonplace since the beginnings of the discipline.

My argument about complex systems is different from this common argument about large social systems. There is something peculiar to *complex* systems, of whatever size, that makes the expert disappear and embeds expertise in a system where it is not accessible to people— experts—who might presume to use it to influence, dominate, and control the system. An examination of a system that is opposite in size to the thousand-person Walden Two reinforces the points made about expertise and the place of experts in complex systems. Systems create individuals, use expertise, and disappear the experts. Systems consume their own resources without respect for status. They effect mergers across traditional boundaries in the name of achieving smooth-functioning systems.

The psychotherapeutic encounter has been conceived since Freud as a complex system. It, like Walden Two, is a system in which experts do not exist as such, where all necessary knowledge is resident in the system, where knowledge uses people rather than the other way around, where freedom is illusory and exists only as a fiction associated in everyone's fantasies with vitality. But consideration of this very small yet complex system points to another important facet of this form of organization: far from being depersonalizing and impersonal like classical bureaucratic structures, the complex system is highly personal. A complex system makes problematic the character of the people and the nature of their associations. Complex systems demand knowledge of who their components are; they invalidate discretion, that single character trait that allowed people to respect differences, meet in civic association, and ask of one another that fundamental political question of how they might live together. Complex systems invite people to worry about who they are so that the system may make the people in them into just what they are. Whereas bureaucracies proscribe considerations of individuality, complex systems induce their participants to consider and to "work on" their individual characters and the natures of their personhood.

Freud's accomplishment was to recognize and to begin to describe the enormous complexity that lies behind the simple statement, "I am," that impenetrable mystery that Western people from Descartes through Freud would accept as the firm limit of their knowledge. The psyche, for Freud, was a system and, as Janet Malcolm puts it, "the most precious and inviolate of entities—personal relations—is actually a messy jangle of misapprehensions, at best an uneasy truce between powerful solitary fantasy systems. . . . We must grope around for each other through a dense thicket of absent others."[19] No one, not even the person herself, could ever know the full range and depth of the complexity that lies behind the "I am," but a floating model, not full knowledge, is the most systems thinkers ever hope to achieve. Freud developed a model of the complexity of the psyche that was constantly floating and never grounded.

Transference, the phenomenon in which we bring elements of

past relationships into present ones and engage in strategies aimed at getting the Other to conform to Model Others of our past, governs all relationships, according to Freud's theory. This phenomenon is the result of the complex relations among the components of the psyche whose contents have accumulated over the years. There is no master of the material that resides in the unconscious portions of the psyche, no person who knows all and can bring forth repressed, past material in ways that are useful in the present. Indeed, the Freudian aphorism, "What cannot be remembered is repeated in behavior," indicates that there is no ultimate "knowing subject" with regard to the unconscious material of the psyche at all. It is more accurate to say, in the passive voice of complex systems, that past material *is* used and, in a real sense, uses us as its agent.

While transference governs all personal relationships, it appears, Freud believed, in its most acute form and with the most intensity in the psychoanalytic encounter. There, after a few preliminaries in which the everyday defense mechanisms have tried to make themselves manifest in the encounter, a dramatic change occurs. Freud said the change occurs inevitably.

> No matter how amenable [the patient] has been up till then, she suddenly loses all understanding of the treatment and all interest in it, and will not speak or hear about anything but her love [for the analyst], which she demands to have returned. She gives up her symptoms or pays no attention to them; indeed, she declares that she is well.[20]

Jacques Lacan has called this the "closing off of the unconscious." It is as if a barrier has been erected over all the weak points of the ego through which unconscious material has, until this inevitable moment, escaped as symptoms, slips, and dreams. Like a laser, then, all the power of the unconscious is concentrated on a single object, the analyst. Freud makes it clear that the transference has a strategic intention: the patient's behavior seeks to "assure herself of her irresistibility [and] to destroy the doctor's authority by bringing him down to the level of a lover."[21]

Such language ("doctor's authority," "bring him down") tempts us to regard the analyst as the knowledgeable person in the encounter. Lacan makes it clear that this is precisely how the analyst is regarded— by the patient in the transference. The patient sees in the analyst a "subject who is supposed to know,"[22] or in another translation of Lacan's S.s.S. (*sujet suppose savoir*), a "supposed subject of knowing."[23] The patient's desire creates the analyst as a knowledgeable person and invests a certain responsibility in the analyst just as a would-be lover seeking the love of another often does. The patient tries to bring the analyst into the relationship as a person vested with expertise. This is an act that on the face of it is not an unreasonable thing to attempt, since the analyst is a trained, certified, psychological expert.

But what kind of expert is the psychoanalyst? If he or she follows Freud, then the analyst must become expert at disappearing from the relationship that the patient's strategies are trying to create. "It is quite out of the question for the analyst to give way," writes Freud. "However highly he may prize love [that his patient is offering him] he must prize even more highly the opportunity for helping his patient over a decisive stage in her life."[24] The analyst, by refusing to become present in the relationship, permits the patient to come to see the very real fiction her or his unconscious has created in the transference. The constructed and strategic aspects of the fictional, force-full reality stand a chance of being revealed only if the analyst does not become the person that the patient's psychical system is creating him to be. The system that tries to create the analyst as a person present to the patient comes to work "better," in some indeterminate sense, if the analyst can disappear as a person with regard to the system.

As with other complex systems, the knowledge that is required to effect such a change is already in the system. The task of the analyst is to create an environment for the patient's psychical system that enables the requisite knowledge to become available. In the systems idiom, the analyst presents a challenge from the environment and waits for the system to recreate itself.

The wait, of course, may be in vain. Accessing the knowledge resident in the patient's psychic system never guarantees a change in the patient. Complex systems are remarkably stable entities not given to easy manipulation and redirection. Janet Malcolm captures in two images the nature and extent of change that one might expect as the result of analysis. The first comes from her interviews with "Aaron Green," the pseudonymous orthodox analyst who was the subject of Malcolm's first report from the backstage of the profession. After saying how radical analysis is, since it attempts to rearrange psychical material ("making the unconscious conscious," etc.), Green notes, "the changes achieved are very small. . . . Analysis leaves the patient with more freedom of choice than he had before—but how much more? This much: instead of going straight down the meridian, he will go five degrees, ten degrees—maybe fifteen if you push very hard—to the left or right, but no more than that."[25] And of the effort required to achieve these small changes, Malcolm writes, "The crowning paradox of psychoanalysis is the near-uselessness of its insights. To 'make the unconscious conscious'—the program of psychoanalytic therapy—is to pour water into a sieve. The moisture that remains on the surface of the mesh is the benefit of analysis."[26] The point, of course, is that not even the *potentially* knowledgeable person (the patient) can be said to be a responsible party with respect to the functions of the system. She is the subject of a system that no one controls and for which it makes little sense to claim that anyone is responsible. Perhaps that is why Freud achieved some of his analytic breakthroughs by saying to the patient, in effect, "You are not responsible." For with respect to complex systems, of whatever size, it is difficult to say that anyone is.

The psychoanalytic encounter in which the patient is not in control, in which the analyst cannot be said to have decisive expert knowledge, in which the "I am" with which the encounter begins remains relatively stable throughout, and in which the analyst must disappear for there to be any effect at all, is the legacy with which subsequent generations of therapists and subsequent schools of therapy were left. Theories that followed psychoanalysis respected to one degree or another these elements of the encounter. A brief discussion of a few aspects of "client-centered therapy," Carl Rogers's refuge in his flight from psychoanalysis, permits one to see how someone who rejected the first psychotherapy retained the basic conceptual structure in which there is expertise without the necessity of there being experts. And it emphasizes how one's individual character and associations are made problematic by such systems.

Rogers retained Freud's notion of "conflict" as the basis for dysfunctional behavior but he did not retain Freud's idea that conflicts always involve repressed material that resides, relatively inaccessibly, in the unconscious. Rather, according to Rogers, people experience conflict between a "concept of self" that forms and changes over time and experiences that are not consistent with that concept of self.

Inconsistencies between the concept of self and one's experiences are threats. These threats to self cause one's concept of self to become more rigid. In its turn, rigidity of self concept increases the likelihood that subsequent experiences will not be assimilable into one's concept of self, will be inconsistent with the self, and will be, therefore, yet another threat.

Rogers's client-centered therapy aims to create an environment that contains no threat. The person in therapy should have, ideally, no experiences during therapy that are inconsistent with his or her concept of self. The therapist creates such an environment by trying to understand and appreciate, in a deep and profound way, her client's concept of self, his system of values which have become attached to all the patterns of relationships that have come to constitute his "I" or his "me." In such a situation, the client comes to see the nature of his self concept, experiences no judgments of any aspect of it, has no need to make that self concept more rigid, and can come to test the permissibility of changing the self concept so that previously threatening experiences might be assimilable. In short, a person comes to be able to live more easily with the situations his environment presents and his concept of self becomes more fluid, more flexible, more accommodating.

A therapist enables a person to become this flexible, accommodating entity, which Rogers believed everyone to be in essence, by disappearing in the therapeutic relationship. The client-centered therapist does not disappear behind a Freudian blank wall but instead disappears into the client's own concept of self and associated system of values. The goal for the therapist is that, "The therapist is able to participate completely in the patient's communication." And he or she is able to do so by making comments that are always "right in line with what the patient is trying to convey," by treating "the patient as an equal," by conveying "the complete ability to share the patient's feelings."[27] A client in a client-centered session will, ideally, experience nothing but a reflection of self. This approach enjoins the therapist "to assume, in so far as he is able, the internal frame of reference of the client, to perceive the world as the client sees it, to perceive the client as he is seen by himself, to lay aside all perceptions from the external frame of reference while doing so. . . ."[28] There should be no outside from which judgments based on external standards might be entered. The difference between the client's experienced reality and the reflection perceptible in the therapist is that the latter is the self without judgment, hence without threat, and therefore with all aspects of the self available for manipulation and alteration. As one client described the experience of therapy with a client-centered therapist, "we were *me*."[29] The boundary that marks even the difference between people—one "expert," the other "client"—disappears.

Again, the knowledge required to effect change resides not with the expert therapist but in the psychical system of the client. "The client is the only one who has the potentiality of knowing fully the dynamics of his perceptions and his behavior."[30] The expert therapist expertly disappears into a facsimile of the client's concept of self so that the client might be able to become what he or she already is, an organism capable of assimilating *all* experience presented by the varied, multifaceted, multidimensional environment into a consistent (albeit flexible and changeable) concept of self.[31]

What client-centered therapy makes more explicit than some therapeutic schools is that the character of the expert therapist is crucially important to the conduct of successful therapy. "It has become apparent," Rogers wrote in 1951 of his changing views on training therapists, "that the most important goal to be achieved is that the student should clarify and understand his own basic relationship to people, and the attitudinal and philosophical concomitants of that relationship." The proper attitude, the proper, necessary, "basic relationship to people" is not something one can be taught. "The basic attitude must be genuine." This view clearly makes the character of the expert, the would-be therapist, problematic. It is not every personality type that might aspire to become this kind of therapist for a person "who tries to use a 'method' is doomed to be unsuccessful unless this method is genuinely in line with his own attitudes."[32] An expert must examine the self—her own "concept of self"—and attempt to find an approach to therapy that is aligned with this concept. From that point it is a matter of constantly reexamining the self and its relationship to one's "technique" so that an optimal relationship can be carefully titrated. The person who might "naturally" begin to think of a client in evaluative terms or whose thoughts might wander to a concern for one's self is admonished to re-think his thinking. Both evaluative thoughts and thoughts of self-concern direct a person away from the deep respect and understanding that causes the expert therapist to disappear in the relationship and that effects the we-me merger this therapy requires. If one strays from the path of disappearing into the system, one must cause one's basic beliefs to reassert themselves and to reclaim dominion over the relationship.

The modern expert is one whose self is always in need of careful attention and constant refocusing, assuming he has the proper character to begin with. And if the therapist-expert himself or herself is not up to this task, the functions of self examination, titration of relationships, and character maintenance are institutionalized in supervision groups and other aspects of the training system.

Rogers, of course, believed that client-centered therapy was a good model on which to base all human relationships. "We have seen client-centered therapy develop from a model of counseling to an approach to human relationships."[33] Rogers wrote on how his ideas applied to education and administration, the other two Freudian "impossible professions" besides therapy. But this does not distinguish Rogers from other theorists. Skinner, too, felt that his behavioral theories were the handle on the mechanisms of the world and he was not reluctant to move easily from the training of pigeons to the big issues of freedom and right living. Similarly, Freud felt that therapy would come to be recognized as one of the least important contributions of psychoanalysis. His scheme was a way to understand the world as a whole. As Russell Jacoby described the second generation analysts who gathered around Freud, "They never viewed [psychoanalysis] as a medical theory or trade, but as a mission that would bring sense to a disjointed world."[34] All these people developed "floating models" of the way everything works. Each theory is comprehensive and totalizing. They must be, for that is the way we are enjoined to think in our new age.

IN MANAGEMENT

It is not surprising that this new way of thinking, a way of thinking based on complex systems in which experts disappear but leave their expertise behind as a useful residue, has penetrated approaches to management. And it is not surprising that it is in modern management manuals that this way of thinking receives its most articulate expression.

Herbert A. Simon was one of the first to write about "the integration of the human and electronic components of organizations into sophisticated man-machine systems."[35] His 1960 book on "the new science of management decision" was an early effort "to examine the changing job of the manager" as automation became a viable alternative not just to the labor of workers but also to human managers and executives as well. Simon wanted to "forecast the longer-run effects of change" that had started with the proliferation of automated computing machines and the development of managerial techniques that depended on computers. Simon's work was an extension of Norbert Wiener's work, published a decade earlier, which built on the idea that the new starting point for the study of social order ought to be *information* instead of relationships among parts of a social machine and the forces mediating among those parts. Wiener had eventually come to the view that "the [information-oriented] machine plays no favorites between manual labor and white collar labor."[36] The question Simon took up, in a way that was unashamedly normative and prescriptive, was, what was to be the place of expert managers in modern organizations reconceived around the concept of "information" that breached the one humanly crucial boundary in organizations, that between labor and management?

Simon's vision of well-integrated "man-machine systems" rests on a body of work that gave a new meaning to the man-as-machine metaphor. The idea that human beings are *like* machines had grounded scientific investigations from the late eighteenth century onward. But the metaphor was always a simplifying device that pushed one toward an analytic understanding of human beings. There remained an overlying belief that human beings were essentially incomprehensible because they were endowed with qualities, perhaps a soul, that distinguished them forever from made machines and also from non-human elements of the natural world. As Rousseau indicated, human beings were mysterious, since no one even knew if they were complex or simple beings. The man-as-machine metaphor, however, permitted analysis, the simplifying separation of certain aspects of the human from all other aspects (those that, as we say, make us human) so that some aspects might be studied, adjusted, eventually improved. The vessels and circulatory system might be conceived as a hydraulic machine that moved fluid and such a conception might guide intervention on behalf of someone experiencing "circulatory problems." The body as a whole might be conceived as a machine of machines and the complexity of the body might be comprehended more easily through the use of such a rhetorical/practical device. But never did these devices assume that one was thereby apprehending the thing itself—the human being—in and through mechanistic theories. There always remained something more, something of the essence, that was privileged from the grasp of theory.

The systems point of view reassembled human beings from the pieces left by two hundred years of analysis. They became not so mysterious anymore, since the concept of a system admits consideration of something at once complex and simple. The language of inquiry changed from speaking of man being *like* a machine to, simply, "man as machine." John Von Neumann, in a series of lectures at Princeton in the early 1950s, sought to show that there are no longer, in the age of systems, easy ways to distinguish between human beings and the new breed of information-oriented machines that were to evolve into what we call "computers." He outlined the functions that are sometimes thought to separate humans from machines and showed how machines might be built that could perform all these functions. Some of these machine functions that were revolutionary in the 1950s are commonplaces today. Can machines remember? Of course. Can they think? Well, they can unfailingly perform logical operations and they can make structured decisions after sorting through enormous amounts of relevant and irrelevant data. And, were Von Neumann alive today, he would no doubt wax eloquently about the generation of machines in which the documentation (or data) file is inseparable from the program (or execution) file and in which "artificial intelligence" seems to take place. Can machines reproduce? If supplied with a proper program and sufficient raw materials, yes. One early commentator on Von Neumann's work even asked, "Could such machines go through an evolutionary process?" and answered, a reproducing machine could have included in its reproductive process "a small number of random changes" on each reproductive cycle. "These would be like mutations," he wrote, and "if the machine could still produce offspring, it would pass the changes on. One could further arrange to limit the supply of raw materials so that the machines would have to compete for *Lebensraum*, even to the extent of killing one another." The implication of Von Neumann's efforts, with which we continue to struggle today, is "that there is no conclusive evidence for an essential gap between man and a machine. For every human activity we can conceive a mechanical counterpart."[37]

The research task that lay before the people who would effect the man-machine synthesis was to develop a better understanding of human thought processes. Simon wrote,

> *Human thinking is governed by programs that organize myriads of simple information processes—or symbol manipulating processes if you like—into orderly, complex sequences that are responsive to and adaptive to the task environment as the sequences unfold. Since programs of the same kind can be written for computers, these programs can be used to describe and simulate human thinking.*[38]

The expert has her expertise "captured," as the "expert-systems" experts of our day express it, by the system. The expert disappears to such a system, literally. Certainly, what a particular person knows is not crucial to such systems for "we must take a systems approach to knowledge instead of identifying 'what is known' with what is stored in local memories,"[39] "local memories" like the minds and memories of knowledgeable experts. The systems approach means that one might imagine going anywhere, well beyond the boundaries of local knowledge, to gain necessary information.

People can, in fact, become an encumbrance to machines and there is nothing in the new management to give people priority if they and not the machine becomes a hindrance to progress. While Simon acknowledges that "love, hate, pride, craftsmanship, jealousy, comradeship, ambition, pleasure" are "man's central concerns," he predicts that in the modern organization the person who used to derive some personal reward from working in, through, and around these human attributes will have to give way to the people who gain their rewards in different ways:

> *the manager will find himself dealing more than in the past with a well-structured system whose problems have to be diagnosed and corrected objectively and analytically, and less with unpredictable and recalcitrant people who have to be persuaded, prodded, rewarded, and cajoled. For some managers, important satisfactions derived in the past from certain kinds of interpersonal relations with others will be lost.*[40]

"Managing human resources" would soon become a technical course in higher education's programs in administration. Even though it would serve occasionally as evidence of a "humanistic" and "humanizing" element in management programs, "managing human resources" would quickly become true to its name. The "human element" would soon become so foreign to the new science of management that it would have to be reinserted through appeals to such barbarous phrases as "managing human resources."

The question in the age of the system is not whether human beings are more than machines. The question is, *does it matter* if they are? For the environment in which people find themselves will be one that is not conducive to the disorderlinesses of the passions. A person, Simon says, "works much better when he is teamed with his fellow men in coping with an objective, understandable, external environment. That will be more and more his situation as the new techniques of decision making come into wide use."[41] If we cannot develop a new model of man, at least "man" can be subjected to a new model of living.

This new model of living does not discourage individuality but instead makes problematic a person's individuality so that the systems that support a person might encourage and respect that individuality. This is a truth of a systems approach that is as evident in the management literature as it is in the arenas discussed earlier. To a modern, complex system, making individuality problematic in order to support it is not the paradox it sounds. Rosabeth Moss Kanter has become the most visible advocate of the "open system" approach to management, the approach in which organizations acknowledge that they need to be more tactical and responsive to their environments rather than presuming to be strategic and controlling. She articulates well the requisite philosophy of the individual in organizations.

> When it is the interests of the people involved, and they are given genuine opportunity and power, they can be committed to finding the time to contribute to solving organizational problems. . . . Employees can be energized—engaged in problem solving and mobilized for change—by their involvement in a participative structure that permits them to venture beyond their normal work roles to tackle meaningful issues.[42]

Any good organizational system contains the knowledge it needs to solve most of its problems. The agents of that knowledge are the people. And the management strategy best suited to the extraction of that knowledge so that it can be made available to the system is "to let [people] *alone* to use their knowledge."[43] Individuals have unique knowledge that can be made available for use if they are left alone long enough that they come to know what they know with respect to organizational problems.

In fact, in new organizations people must be forcibly individuated in their task-oriented contexts. They must be made to be "alone with others" in a task-oriented situation. If their togetherness ever threatens to become anything like civic association, where people begin to discuss not the technical problem of how best to complete a task but personal problems that have their locus in their lives as lived in institutions, disciplinary mechanisms come into play. It is not that traditional management techniques are no longer useful. The modern organization, according to Kanter, must establish parallel organizational efforts, one that involves a traditional "'mechanistic' production hierarchy" and one that is an "'organic' participative organization," the latter arranged, we might suspect, like a pentimento with respect to the former. The latter makes the whole organization "ultimately integrative" so that the individual knowledge that people have might be deployed and redeployed as necessary to meet the demands of the organization's changing environment, both internal and external.[44]

It is not helpful to understand modern organizations as either "depersonalizing" and ultimately abusive of individuality *or* as "empowering" and respectful of individuality. Modern organizations, like all complex systems, involve themselves in what, to common sense, are contradictions. "One person can't possibly manage alone in a complex changing system," said one of Kanter's informants in a modern corporate organization. "You need more specialists. . . . This new system saved the business." The "system" that saved this person's business was one that relied on individuals' specialized knowledge but that found "ways to connect specialists and help[ed] them to communicate."[45] Traditional specialists knew what they knew, wrote their reports, forwarded the reports to supervisors, and worried not at all about what happened after that. The integration of facts and opinions and the development of policy occurred elsewhere, higher up, in the organization. New, open-system organizations make the specialist's position in the organization an issue. The specialist has no fixed place in relation to other functions in the organization. His or her knowledge and the role it might play in the organization becomes a personal issue, not just an organizational one. The individual must begin to worry about those aspects of his organizational identity that make him an individual. The individual must work to make himself "fit" into the changing, fluid, dynamic, responsive organization for which he or she works, even as the organization uses its fluidity to be responsive to its people. Companies institutionalize "self-reflective discussions" that require corporate leaders "to examine their own and others' values." Rather than "going to work" in these organizations, one enters an arena in which "business life . . . may be seen not only as a necessity, but as interesting—a life through which people can express themselves."[46] In stark contrast to Weber's concept of bureaucracy, which placed a clear boundary between personal and professional life, modern management seeks to dissolve all such boundaries. Life is life, no matter where it is lived, or survived. Modern work organizations become yet another Foucauldian confessional mechanism in which people express themselves to themselves, to others, and to power so that individuals can become individuals.

Proclaimed criticisms of management technique often recapitulate the system they purport to criticize. Management—good management—thrives on criticism—good criticism. Criticism mirrors that which it criticizes. Kathy Ferguson's *Feminist Case Against Bureaucracy*, for example, extends the usual complaints about bureaucracy into realms not usually thought to be captured by bureaucratic discourse and practice. Thus Ferguson, following Foucault, shows how bureaucratization has collapsed the boundaries between bureaucrat and client (with both becoming members of the "second sex"). She shows how the dissolution of the personal-professional boundary permitted bureaucracy to invade the realm of sexuality, albeit unevenly and incompletely.[47] She makes an outstanding case *against* bureaucracy.

Given that Ferguson follows Foucault so closely in making her case, it is not surprising that she recognizes that theory, "even that theory rooted in a critical heritage," can be turned to the "cause of social control." What is surprising is that her proposed alternatives to bureaucratization follow almost blindly the path marked out by modern management specialists in the mode of Simon and Kanter.

Reacting against the naive, how-to-be-a-good-bureaucrat pamphleteering produced under a liberal feminist label, but ignoring Foucault's insight that power makes people its agent as they try to "gain power," Ferguson urges that "women need power to change society." She wants to restructure work so that there is both a "rejection of the hierarchical division of labor of bureaucratic capitalism and the reintegration of the planning and performance of tasks." This requires, she says, quoting Nancy Harstock, "creating a situation in which we can both develop ourselves and transform the external world." This leads her from her case against bureaucracy to a case for an "alternative vision" of expertise that reads like something directly from Kanter or even Simon. Ferguson says, "Feminist organizations do not need to dispense with expertise, but can wed it to a different form of power; the expertise possessed by particular individuals, in an environment that supports cooperation, can be shared with others so as to empower both the individual and the group. . . ."[48] Organizations need to accomplish their tasks and respect their people. Parallel organizations are necessary.

In feminist organizations, Ferguson says, power cannot become *too* personalized else a leader should emerge and become the center of an organization that must resist, according to this self-proclaimed case against bureaucracy, centralization. The actor in such an organization retains the identity with which she comes to the organization and certainly she can expect to have that individuality respected. But she must not become too identifiable in the group or become so individualized that she begins to make a personal appearance with respect to the organization. But this is just another way to state the seemingly contradictory dilemma of individuality and individualization that the modern organization qua complex system creates. The dilemma is resolved by recapitulating modern management schemes and legitimating them for the left by putting on them a "feminist" front.

Ferguson has, in my view, a valuable case against bureaucracy, but she may be simply another of Drucker's academics writing books against that which is past. The fact that she felt compelled to add a case *for* anything (new, feminist forms of organization, in her case) runs against the spirit of her Foucault-like, essentially destructive "case against" and—and this is crucial—puts her directly into the mainstream of constructionists attuned to the systems view. Writing books from an intention of "leav[ing] the extant world in ruins" is very hard. People like Ferguson, under the pressure of that most reasonable question that proceeds from our modern rationality—And so, what do *you* propose?—can only half succeed. She failed to laugh when asked such a serious question.

SUMMARY

Experts used to be people who could reason about their objects of inquiry and do it from a distance. They could develop a view from a particular perspective and be relatively uninvolved in the situation about which they had illuminating knowledge. This lack of involvement, as it were, saddled the expert with a measure of responsibility. Experts could not "see it all" and thus could enter a discussion of morality with other informed and thoughtful people who saw things from different, equally informative perspectives.

In complex systems, there is no "knowledge about. . . ," for all knowledge is within. Complex systems create "information rich environments," as Simon calls them. Since a specific, identified system is only a convenient fiction (because all systems are, in fact, open at their boundaries communicating more-or-less with all other systems, this approach says), there is no outside from which to attain any perspective on any issue. Experts are all within their systems. The modern expert is yet another component of the system whose identity is gained not from outside but from within the system. The expert is not one to be looked to for guidance because she cannot be seen, because she does not "stand out." It would be near foolishness to impute responsibility to one who can neither be seen clearly nor see well.

The modern expert's job is to enable the knowledge resident in the system to become manifest so that the system might use that knowledge so that, in turn, the system might do its job better, so that the system might realize its potential. To this end, the expert is obligated to examine carefully and to manipulate the nature of his or her associations. Proper links must be established and proper chains of relationships must be forged. To do this well, the expert must be of good character. That is to say, one must always hold one's own character in question. One must always question whether one is adequate to the task of managing the associations that the system needs to have in place.

In return for the constant monitoring, assessment, and adjustment of character and associations, the system grants its experts an opportunity to express themselves. It provides the ground on which people can stand to become what they are. Complex systems are among those modern mechanisms that *"foster* life or *disallow* it" (as opposed to old mechanisms that would *"take* life or *let* live"), and they will continue to foster life as long as life is usefully lived.[49] When usefulness to the system ends, means by which one has expressed one's self simply fail to continue to provide that arena anymore and one's life becomes disallowed. Systems may be stuck with the old model of man, but they can demand that new generic man live according to a new model of life, a model that includes the injunction that life be lived well ("ethically," "healthily," or whatever today's notion of "well" might entail).

In moving from this general discussion of the place of experts in complex systems to the specific case of a particular expert, it may be helpful to pass a comment on phrases like "in order that the system might do its work better" or "as long as life is lived well" that creep so naturally, it seems, into these elaborations. Such phrases bespeak a progressive faith. Systems can be improved; they can be completed, even if the "model of man" that constrains them must, eventually, be revised. If there are no external standards by which to judge "improvement," how is improvement to be judged? The answer from systems theory is, "through the study of errors." And errors are, to the systems theorist, always self-evident; an external standard of correct behavior is not necessary to spot errors anymore. There may be errors, but in complex systems, errors simply feed back to help the system function better next time. Pilot errors improve airplane design or pilot training. Errors in judgment about how much wiggling a screwdriver will take before slipping from between tamper halves improve the subsequent handling of radioactive material in experiments that remain, unquestionably to the atomic system, critical and necessary.

An obsession with error leaves no room for the tragic, for the sense of or the fact of limits in life. An obsession with error and a lack of attention to the limits of life leaves all limited beings behind as systems ruthlessly progress. So let's give the would-be critics their due. Even though Ferguson and others like her often succumb to the seductions of demands that they say how the world might be made better, they often have a starting point worth remembering. In Ferguson's case, there is the argument that women's experiences sometimes "uncover a tragic dimension of our existence." Those experiences allow us "to see ourselves as beings constantly seeking a completion that constantly eludes us."[50] Norbert Wiener expressed his own appreciation for the tragic in a common prose informed by the idiom of cybernetics. Life, for Wiener, is an "island of locally decreasing entropy," a "lucky accident," and people are "shipwrecked passengers on a doomed planet." Wiener believed, of course, that our situation was one in which human dignity might still inform our actions. But of standardless progress, the ground of the modern system-based faith, he said, "The best we can hope for the role of progress in a universe running downhill as a whole is that the vision of our attempts to progress in the face of necessity may have the purging terror of Greek tragedy."[51]

In quiet but decisive contrast to this ultimately humane understanding of our situation, complex systems use to their own benefits our constant seeking, our restless ambitions, and would have us think that in *this* activity, not in its inevitable frustration, lies the promise of what we are. And the purges that might occur are not of the self-cleansing sort but are effected in the name of order so that the world might be a more understandable, more smoothly functioning, perhaps more simple place.

It is very difficult for good, well-meaning critics like Ferguson to escape the sway of systems thinking because it is something like an *invisible source of axioms*, a basis for all thinking including critical thought. There used to be several modes of invisibility.[52] A thing could be invisible because it was *behind or beyond* (which includes "below," as in beyond the surface of the ground) another thing. The view from a systems "perspective" erases these two forms of invisibility by erasing boundaries beyond which something might exist and by enabling, for the first time in history, to utter seriously but without religious overtones such phrases as "everything is connected to everything else" and to begin imagining connections that extend behind and beyond. There is a third mode of invisibility, however, that systems thinking cannot erase. It is the invisibility of the medium in which everything is transmitted and carried. (We cannot see the "air" or the "light" that carries impulses to our senses.) My argument is that systems theory is our new medium for thought, and while systems thinking infuses everything, it remains invisible to us. We can talk about it (indeed, even know about it) as people in years past knew about the air and about light: through effects. We can resist the implications of systems thinking; we can even oppose its "presence" in our lives. But this activity is like battling the air or the light. One finds oneself striking at the invisible that makes everything else possible. It is time to move on to consider the *effects* of the atomic system, writ large, on a signal expert (not a model expert), J. Robert Oppenheimer.

Oppenheimer: Signal Expert

OPPENHEIMER: SYSTEMS ADMINISTRATOR
AND SPECIALIST IN THE GENERAL

Before his meeting with General Groves in Berkeley, Oppenheimer had not been an administrator of anything. He had not even served as department chair at a university. He may not have been a "natural" administrator, but he was to become a consummate systems expert after he was appointed Director of the project that would be housed at Los Alamos. Los Alamos become an accretion point for an assemblage of expertise from which would issue those first simple but very big bombs.

After his appointment, Oppenheimer immediately immersed himself in the complexities of administrative detail.

His first job was to recruit people to the project. He could be effusive and elegant or direct and abrupt with his potential recruits. He would titrate his pitch to convince each individual to put his career on the line and join the effort that would culminate on the Jornada del Muerto almost three years after the first invitations to Los Alamos were issued. "I am inclined not to take too seriously the absolute no's with which we shall be greeted," Oppenheimer wrote to James B. Conant on November 30, 1942. "The job we have to do will not be possible without personnel substantially greater than that which we now have available,"[53] he said in justification of upcoming raids on the nation's most prominent physics laboratories.

At the same time, and as a necessary corollary to his recruiting effort, Oppenheimer quickly familiarized himself with the military's plans for building the laboratory. He was familiar enough with the plans that at the end of December 1942, he could include details of likely living conditions at Los Alamos in a long letter to Hans and Rose Bethe. He wrote of the plan to build both a town—with a town manager, a city engineer, a recreation officer, schools, two hospitals, cafeterias, and a post exchange that would be "a combination of country store and mail order house"—and a laboratory. He was able to tell the Bethes the dimensions of the kitchens and living rooms in the two- and four-family housing units that would be constructed. Oppenheimer had insisted that the housing units each have a fireplace and told the Bethes of this amenity. In answer to a question about a garden he assured Rose Bethe that she would have one but, presciently, he added, "water limited in the Spring and Fall."[54] Problems of maintaining an adequate water supply would dog Director Oppenheimer throughout his tenure at the laboratory.

Problems of procuring needed material and scientific equipment would be handled by the University of California which would eventually open an office at Los Alamos. Oppenheimer personally involved himself in all the details of the early planning.

One of the administrative issues that was critical to the decisions of some of Oppenheimer's potential recruits was the question of whether the laboratory would be a military post and whether the scientists would necessarily become members of the armed forces. The military offered management by categories. Instructively—for this was a system—this approach was rejected. Categories are a blunt instrument in the world of systems. A group of scientists who had decided that they would probably join the Los Alamos effort—Isidor I. Rabi and Robert Bacher first among them—met with Oppenheimer in February 1943, to make it clear that they would not accept a military commission.[55] One scientist's letter of acceptance also included his resignation which was to become effective on the day that Los Alamos became a military post. Oppenheimer realized that he would not be able to attract sufficient talent if Los Alamos was a military base and if the scientists were categorized by military rank; he needed an assembly of uncategorizable "eggheads" in all of their eccentric individuality. He lobbied General Groves and extracted from him a promise that scientific work at Los Alamos would remain outside the direct control of the military, at least initially. Groves and Conant wrote to Oppenheimer to confirm that the Los Alamos site would be established as a military reservation but that the laboratory itself would be "built within an inner fenced and guarded area, called the 'Technical Area.'"[56]

Matters of security were placed in military hands although Oppenheimer played a significant role in setting up the security system in a way that was acceptable to the scientists. Under Oppenheimer's guidance Los Alamos became "a kind of privileged prison."[57]

The scientists who came to Los Alamos did, like contemporary experts must, disappear into their work. They left their university and laboratory posts, usually after a decent interval in which their work wound down, and boarded trains for Santa Fe. Once there, some were given pseudonyms and their new, common address became P.O. Box 1663, Santa Fe, New Mexico. Provisions were made for personal subscriptions to scientific journals to be sent to a Los Angeles address so that a publishers' paper trail did not point to northern New Mexico.

Oppenheimer tried once to cover for the literal disappearance of so many distinguished names from the public and professional scenes. He wrote to Wolfgang Pauli to ask if he might be able to publish a few papers under the names of some of the Los Alamos scientists so that the names would occasionally appear in print despite the fact that they were all engaged in classified, unpublishable research at an unmentionable place. Oppenheimer wrote to Pauli, "It would give you a chance to express in the most appropriate way your evaluation of their qualities and you would have the delicious opportunity to argue with yourself in the public press without any interference." Pauli refused the invitation to what Oppenheimer called this "burlesque" because he feared that his own funding agencies would not get the joke.[58] Those who disappeared into the anonymity of Los Alamos would have to remain disappeared from the physics journals and other public venues for the duration.

Work inside the Technical Area was organized so that it took maximum advantage of individual talents without ever permitting the issue of individual responsibility for the project as a whole to arise. After the militarization problem was set aside, "the colloquium" could convene. The colloquium was an arena where ideas, not people, were ascendant. Ideas got financial and material support until they failed to produce useful results. Above the colloquium Oppenheimer constituted a Governing Board, "which was established to counsel, plan, and conduct the technical effort and to act as a directorate for cooperative decision making. . . . The board served to expose all senior men to the progress and problems of each division." Collectively they dealt with problems as seemingly inconsequential to the bomb per se as water supplies and housing snags—issues that would later be turned over to a Laboratory Coordinating Council—to basic questions of how much support to give various projects and project directors.

Oppenheimer knew very early, like a good systems administrator does, that individual personalities and talents had to be respected and managed if the collective effort was to succeed. In rejecting one name suggested to him by Conant, Oppenheimer said, "in the tight isolated group such as we are now planning, some warmth and trust in personal relations is an indispensable prerequisite, and we are, of course, able to insure this only in the case of men whom we have known in the past."[59] For some, such sensitivity to individual concerns from Oppenheimer was odd, since he had something of a reputation for being abrupt and thoughtless of others. But Oppenheimer was one of the first "systems administrators" and, as such, he could be flexible and accommodative even with regard to his own seemingly inflexible personality structure. "Robert was a first class manipulator of the imagination and interpreter of it. It doesn't amaze me at all—it didn't at the time—that he should create this immense organization and have it run to his wishes, to his design,"[60] said one of his colleagues.

If all the scientists who came to Los Alamos effectively disappeared behind its inner fences and contributed their individual talents optimally to a collective endeavor, what of Oppenheimer? If the individual talents of individual scientists were not evident in that final amalgam of talent on the tower at Trinity, surely Oppenheimer can be distinguished from the rest and singled out as a responsible person for, or so the argument would go, the "immense organization [did] run to his wishes, his desires," didn't it? Indeed, after the war Hans Bethe singled out Oppenheimer this way:

> Los Alamos might have succeeded without him, but certainly only with much greater strain, less enthusiasm, and less speed. . . . I never observed in [any other laboratory] quite the spirit of belonging together, quite the urge to reminisce about the days of the laboratory, quite the feeling that this was really the great time of their lives. That this was true of Los Alamos was mainly due to Oppenheimer. He was a leader. It was clear to all of us, whenever he spoke, that he knew everything that was important to know about the technical problems of the laboratory, and he somehow had it well organized in his head. . . . He brought out the best in all of us, like a good host with his guests.[61]

But it would be incorrect to single Oppenheimer out from the rest of the assembled experts. He was the epitome of a "specialist in the general." "It seemed to me and knowledgeable people," Oppenheimer said at his security clearance hearing, "that it was one package, ordnance, chemistry, physics theory, effects, all had to be understood together or the job would not get done."[62] Oppenheimer himself said the bomb was "the very opposite of a one-man show." He would also say, at the height of activity at Los Alamos, "There is hardly a clear and qualified scientist in the country who is not available to Los Alamos for consultation or for such things as he is good for."[63]

We ought to take seriously the things serious people say seriously and not make people like Oppenheimer into more than they were or are. It is possible in the age of systems for someone to be everything and nothing. The scientists had their areas of expertise in the scientific divisions of the laboratory. Oppenheimer had his expertise in organization and the establishment of order out of the potential chaos of disparate knowledges. Oppenheimer had a hand in establishing the lab and, in particular, in creating the dynamics that would use the resident expertise, but even he disappeared into the complex of the laboratory. He could have been writing about himself when he wrote the chairman of the Physics Department at Berkeley of his concerns about the effects of working at the laboratory on the creativity of individual scientists:

> It is true that as far as men of graduate standing are concerned, projects like the one with which I am connected and many others are providing a real training, but the highly organized and highly integrated character of the work of these projects will probably fail to give men that deep and independent curiosity and vision on which the best research has in the past been based.[64]

In trying to decline an invitation to contribute to a festschrift for Bohr, he wrote that "for the last four years I have had only classified thoughts and anything I could write would be somewhat antiquated and somewhat trivial."[65] Even Oppenheimer's thoughts were fenced in by the organization of "his" laboratory.

After the conclusion of the war, the man who had disappeared into the bomb project was made into a celebrity. Just as *Time* magazine later personalized the women's movement by putting Betty Friedan on its cover against her suggestion of a picture of "lots of women," *Time* personalized the atomic bomb by putting Oppenheimer on a cover. He became the "father of the atomic bomb" and started on his speaking and consulting rounds.

Oppenheimer seemed to revel in the personalization of the bomb work accorded him by the press and other institutions. He set himself somewhat ahead and to the side of his ex-colleagues from Los Alamos as, in one incident that would be noted later as pivotal, he presented his own views as the views of the scientific community on the May-Johnson Bill, legislation designed to regularize control over atomic affairs. In fact, his views were quite different from most of those with whom he remained in contact. Some scientists first thought Oppenheimer had been deceived by the supporters of the May-Johnson Bill in order to enlist his support for it. Later, after these same scientists learned that Oppenheimer was an active and informed participant in the debates, many lost the faith in Oppenheimer that he had nurtured in them. Oppenheimer also helped burn some collegial bridges when he took a statement from the Association of Los Alamos Scientists on the future control of atomic policy to Washington and let the statement, which its authors had intended as an open, public document, become a "State document" that could not be released to the public. Despite all of his individuality, Oppenheimer was an integral part of the bomb system as it took shape immediately after the war.

It was at this point that Oppenheimer began to make the fatal mistake of any component of any system. Even though Oppenheimer was a component of the bomb system, he felt that there was still something called "responsibility" that individuals could take seriously. He thought part of his responsibility was to begin to implement Bohr's idea that the secrets of the atom ought to be open to everyone. Openness was the only possible route to sanity in the new world, according to Bohr. Oppenheimer first attempted to implement Bohr's ideas through the so-called Acheson-Lilienthal report.

Dean Acheson was the head of the committee that prepared the Acheson-Lilienthal report. David Lilienthal from the Tennessee Valley Authority headed the committee's advisory panel. General Groves, James Conant, and Vanevar Bush were the other members of the committee. The final report had as a premise that "our monopoly [over atomic energy] cannot last." It went on to propose that "a workable system of safeguards to remove from individual nations or their citizens the legal right to engage in certain well-defined activities in respect to atomic energy which we believe will be generally agreed to be intrinsically dangerous because they are or could be made steps in a production of atomic bombs."[66] The report argued that an international atomic authority be established as a subsidiary of the United Nations, that it assume responsibility for "the control of raw materials, the construction and operation of production plants, the conduct of research on explosives," and that the agency engage in active research and development so that any new findings in atomic energy would not be able to escape the agency's monitoring and control. Alice Kimball Smith says that even though "at the time scientists spoke of [the report] as Oppenheimer's work, recognizing, they thought, the stamp of his particular genius," the report was a collaborative effort.[67]

The course followed after that is well known and displays the cynicism of the system that stood opposed to the optimism of the scientists who believed in Bohr's "openness." Secretary of State James Byrnes appointed Bernard Baruch the U.S. representative to the United Nations' conference on the international control of atomic energy. Oppenheimer's response to the appointment was, "That was the day I gave up hope," for Baruch was staunchly conservative and not given to compromise in dealings with the Soviet Union. He was not an advocate of openness.

There was still a ray of hope for some as Baruch appointed Oppenheimer to his scientific advisory panel. Indeed, the scientists reached what Alice Smith called "the apogee of hope" when Baruch laid the U.S. plan, based finally on the Acheson-Lilienthal report, on the table at the United Nations' Atomic Energy Commission conference. "We are here to make a choice between the quick and the dead," Baruch began. "Behind the black portent of the new atomic age lies a hope which, seized upon with faith, can work our salvation. If we fail, then we have damned every man to be the slave of Fear. Let us not deceive ourselves: We must elect World Peace or World Destruction."[68] Baruch's plan for World Peace, expressed to him in a memorandum from President Truman,[69] echoed exactly the scientists' position, whose most obvious and articulate spokesperson had been Oppenheimer.

But as Oppenheimer watched the conference proceed his initial fears that hope would die quickly were realized. The Soviet and American sides came into conflict over a parliamentary issue. Would the Soviets have veto power or would the proposed international agency enact its decisions by majority vote? Baruch insisted that the Soviets should accept the dictates of the majority. The Soviets insisted on the veto. At this point Oppenheimer said to David Lilienthal in great discouragement, "I am ready to go anywhere and do anything, but I am bankrupt of further ideas. And I find that physics and the teaching of physics, which is my life, now seems irrelevant."[70] The conference ended and the early hopes for an international agreement were dashed.

Also dashed was the vision of openness and of responsible parties having responsibility that had grounded the effort from the start. The system, which had secrecy as a cornerstone and national interest as its edifice was, as systems are, stable and resilient against the critical efforts of the scientific experts.

Oppenheimer, bankrupt of ideas and with his life as he knew it seeming irrelevant to him, was entrenched in the atomic system. The civilian-controlled Atomic Energy Commission was established by the McMahon Bill. David Lilienthal became the first chairman of the AEC. He immediately appointed a General Advisory Committee (the GAC) to assist the AEC on scientific matters. Lilienthal named Oppenheimer to the GAC. Oppenheimer arrived late to the first meeting of the GAC to find that his colleagues had elected him its first chair.

Oppenheimer was allowed, for a while, to continue living a life that he thought was being lived in the national interest. The GAC became, in the eyes of many, Oppenheimer's personal vehicle for influencing national policy. John Manley, also a charter member of the GAC, would say that,

> In a sense the General Advisory Committee was his [Oppenheimer's] committee, though he never played boss to it, and the Atomic Energy Commission was the Committee's agency, though they never gave it orders. . . . There was a good deal of talk about how he swayed or hypnotized or improperly influenced the General Advisory Committee. I was there and I knew he didn't do any such thing. I can't imagine any nine people who'd be more insistent on each making up his own mind for himself. What happened was that he at all times had the national interest at heart and never did anything or wanted to do anything except in the national interest as he saw it.

Peter Goodchild describes this period in Oppenheimer's life under the title "The Man Who Would Be God." He notes, "Nobody was ever to disagree about the sincerity of Oppenheimer's actions, but there were to be many who would question his interpretation of the 'national interest.' Over the next few years Oppenheimer was going to learn the hard way the price of having an independent mind in the political world"[71] in the era of systems.

Indeed he would. In fact, Oppenheimer had become too independent, had personalized the issues too much, had gone beyond the bounds of the individuality accorded him by the system in which he served and whose agent he was. If he would not disappear into the political system as he had into the bomb building system at Los Alamos, if he dared assume some personal responsibility for the conduct of the system, the system would make him disappear.

The first glimpse of Oppenheimer's future problems came in early 1947 as the AEC commissioners received from J. Edgar Hoover a condensed version of the FBI's file on Robert Oppenheimer and his brother Frank. The file contained damaging information on Oppenheimer's past associations. The AEC commissioners huddled and requested a review of Oppenheimer's background by their own security staff before they would grant Oppenheimer the security clearance he needed to continue his work on the GAC. The security officers recommended that Oppenheimer be kept on the AEC staff. Even Hoover agreed that, with one exception, Oppenheimer's record was not problematic from the standpoint of security. Oppenheimer got the clearance and chaired the GAC through its most productive period, the period during which it recommended the construction of two new national laboratories (in addition to Los Alamos) and during which it oversaw the expansion of the nation's atomic arsenal.

The one exception in Oppenheimer's background that troubled Hoover was the so-called "Chevalier incident." The incident began during a dinner party at the Oppenheimers' Berkeley house in 1943 before their move to Los Alamos. Robert Oppenheimer had invited an old friend to the party, Professor of French Haakon Chevalier. At some point in the evening Oppenheimer went into the kitchen to mix drinks. Chevalier followed him. Chevalier told Oppenheimer that he had talked with George Eltenton, an engineer from Shell Corporation whom both Oppenheimer and Chevalier knew. Eltenton, Chevalier said, could pass technical information to the Russians and he wanted Oppenheimer to know this fact. Oppenheimer told Chevalier that he could not get involved in anything of that sort. That, as far as Oppenheimer and Chevalier both were concerned, was that. As far as

Oppenheimer's security problems were concerned, that was the beginning.

After Oppenheimer was named Director of Los Alamos, he had had to obtain a security clearance. Because of his past associations with left-wing organizations and because his brother and wife had been members of the Communist Party, security officers conducting background investigations were concerned about Oppenheimer. John Lansdale, General Groves's assistant for security, Boris Pash, the Army's head of counter-intelligence on the west coast, and Peer de Silva, security officer at Los Alamos, all had concerns about Oppenheimer. These concerns eventually led to the preparation of a memorandum in June 1943, from Pash to Groves that said Oppenheimer should be removed from the project completely. Groves needed Oppenheimer, and so on July 20, 1943, Groves issued a memo insisting that Oppenheimer be given his security clearance "without delay, irrespective of the information which you have concerning Mr. Oppenheimer."[72]

About five weeks later Oppenheimer was in Berkeley. Prior to his visit he had tried unsuccessfully to keep a student in Ernest Lawrence's laboratory, Rossi Lomanitz, from being drafted. Lomanitz was politically active and was suspected by security agents as being influential in organizing a group sympathetic to the Soviet Union. During his visit, Oppenheimer obtained permission from the local security officer, Lieutenant Lyall Johnson, to visit Lomanitz. Reluctantly, Johnson granted permission. Following the meeting, Oppenheimer volunteered to Johnson that he had heard that a British engineer named George Eltenton had contacted Berkeley faculty members to say that he could pass scientific information to Russia through a local consulate. The next day Boris Pash interviewed Oppenheimer and instead of talking about Oppenheimer's visit with Lomanitz, Pash quickly focused on the questions of who Eltenton's contacts might be and how Oppenheimer had learned of them. Oppenheimer told Pash that a member of the Berkeley faculty, not Eltenton, had approached two Los Alamos scientists and a person at Berkeley about Eltenton's capabilities. Oppenheimer refused to divulge any of the names.

The next month, in September 1943, John Lansdale interviewed Oppenheimer at Los Alamos about the "Chevalier incident." Again, Oppenheimer would not name names. Lansdale asked Oppenheimer to put himself in the position of a security officer and to imagine the difficulty he might have if—just as an example—he had to make a decision about "the case of Dr. J. R. Oppenheimer." This subject, Lansdale told Oppenheimer, was a person

> *whose wife was at one time a member of the Communist Party, who himself knows many prominent communists, associates with them, who belongs to a large number of so-called front organizations, and may perhaps have contributed to the Party himself, who became aware of an espionage attempt by the Party six months ago and doesn't mention it, and who still won't make a complete disclosure.*[73]

Oppenheimer did not give in to this pressure, and so that meeting too ended in a deadlock.

General Groves, under pressure from his security agents, personally asked Oppenheimer about the incident. Oppenheimer said that he would reveal the names only if Groves ordered him to do so. Another month or so passed before Groves decided to end the fencing by ordering Oppenheimer to speak. In mid-December Oppenheimer named Haakon Chevalier as the contact but he did not say that he, Oppenheimer, had been one of the three people Chevalier had told about Eltenton.

Oppenheimer created at least one other security-related problem for himself after his appointment to the directorship. During a working visit to Berkeley in June 1943, Oppenheimer made one of his occasional visits to his former fiancee, Jean Tatlock. Tatlock had been Oppenheimer's political tutor in the thirties, had awakened his political interests, and had gotten him involved with the "front organizations" mentioned by Lansdale in his quick summary of Oppenheimer's security file. The fact that Oppenheimer spent the night with Tatlock was duly recorded and reported by his security tails. It became another datum in the files that the complex system around Oppenheimer was accumulating. Even the fact that Oppenheimer took a solitary walk around the mesa at Los Alamos upon hearing of Tatlock's suicide in January 1944, became part of Oppenheimer's official, system-assembled "biography." The atomic system was creating, through its documentation and other support systems, the life that Oppenheimer was being allowed to live.

Lenny Bruce once said that he understood why he got "sent up" for his act. He performed, he said, while a cop in the audience took notes. Then the cop went before the grand jury and tried to do Bruce's act, from notes. Because the cop did the act so badly, Bruce got sent up. The atomic system's "cops" were noting down Oppenheimer's life. It is that life in the documents of the system that Oppenheimer would soon find himself answering to.

THE SECURITY HEARING

Oppenheimer's system-produced "life" was put on trial at his 1954 hearing before the Personnel Security Board of the Atomic Energy Commission. That was how the atomic system would disallow the life it had constructed for Oppenheimer to live to that point. I. I. Rabi, who was chairman of the General Advisory Committee at the time of Oppenheimer's hearing, testified midway through the hearing. After a long series of questions about Oppenheimer's activities, loyalty and character, the Board focused on the Chevalier incident. They asked Rabi what Oppenheimer might do in 1954 if confronted with a similar situation. They asked what he, Rabi, would have done in 1954. They asked if he would have told the whole truth. Finally, in exasperation, Rabi told Roger Robb, the Board's counsel and "state prosecutor," that he and the Board had to understand the Chevalier incident like any other incident in the full context of a person's life. "You have to take the whole story," Rabi said to Robb. "That is what novels are about. There is a dramatic moment in the history of the man, what made him act, what he did, and what sort of person he was. That is what you are really doing here. You are writing a man's life."[74] They were writing the life in order to find it no longer viable from the system's view.

The part of Oppenheimer's life that led to his hearing began in November 1950, when, unknown to Oppenheimer at the time, the young staff director of the Congressional Joint Committee on Atomic Energy, William Liscum Borden, requested copies of the security files on several AEC scientists and consultants. One of the files Borden requested was Oppenheimer's. Nothing formal would come of Borden's investigation for three years, but "the matter of J. Robert Oppenheimer" then started to take shape as Oppenheimer's loyalty, judgment, associations, and character came to be questioned. Complex systems, recall, make a person's character essentially problematic. It takes little to turn a problem into an issue. Complex systems are always poised to accuse, and usually have records at the ready on which to base potential accusations when provoked.

The provocation that would set the system into motion was Oppenheimer's personalization of matters of national atomic policy that antagonized influential people throughout the early fifties. His opposition to the Air Force's strategic doctrine of massive retaliation turned people in the Air Force, people up through Secretary of the Air Force Thomas K. Finletter, against him. Oppenheimer's decision not to advise an "all-out effort" to develop the super/thermonuclear/ hydrogen bomb, as expressed in the General Advisory Committee's report to the AEC in October 1949,[75] was the final blow on the wedge between him and Edward Teller. That decision also contributed to the Air Force's suspicions about Oppenheimer. Oppenheimer had alienated Lewis Strauss, the man who would become chairman of the Atomic Energy Commission six months after Eisenhower entered the White House, by making light before a Congressional committee of some of Strauss's decisions regarding the release of radioactive isotopes for research purposes.

Oppenheimer must have felt the wind begin to shift against him because he began to try to make his personal case for the internationalization, the limitation, and the control of atomic energy more publicly than he had before and with a somewhat stronger note of urgency. His efforts, for example, included a personal article in *Foreign Affairs* in 1953, the article that contained the famous simile of the two superpowers being like "two scorpions in a bottle, each capable of killing the other, but only at risk of its own life."[76] He also showed a greater willingness to use his contacts in the media to promote his views.

Eisenhower became President at the beginning of 1953. He appointed Lewis Strauss his advisor on atomic energy matters and, later, chair of the AEC. As Oppenheimer was going to England in November to deliver his Reith Lectures, later published as *Science and the Common Understanding*,[77] William Liscum Borden was delivering his commentary on Oppenheimer's file to his former employer, the Joint Committee on Atomic Energy, and to J. Edgar Hoover. Hoover wrote a response to Borden's letter and took it to Eisenhower on December 3. Eisenhower declared that a "blank wall" should be erected between Oppenheimer and the nation's atomic secrets until a hearing board could be convened to investigate Borden's allegations, now elevated to the status of FBI allegations. On December 7, Oppenheimer and his wife had dinner in Paris with Haakon Chevalier and his wife. It was the final moment in what Chevalier bitingly described later as "the story of a friendship."[78] Almost immediately on his return to the United States Oppenheimer would be faced with a series of charges that said, in effect, he had been in error to think he had lived his life in the nation's interest. The erroneousness of Oppenheimer's life was self-evident within the system, as all errors are.

Borden's letter was a well packaged review of Oppenheimer's life. It began by recounting his left-wing associations. It said that during the tenure of his directorship Oppenheimer had hired known communists to work at Los Alamos and was active in trying to help other known or suspected communists. The letter argued that Oppenheimer had deceived General Groves. It suggested that he had supported the Super bomb program until the day Hiroshima was destroyed and then he had turned against it. It said that Oppenheimer had urged that Los Alamos be disbanded after the war. And finally it presented a detailed commentary on Oppenheimer's post-war efforts to slow the development of the hydrogen bomb.

Borden's letter was quickly turned into a set of formal charges for presentation to the full AEC which would have to empower a hearing board. Kenneth Nichols, General Manager of the AEC, personally involved himself in the framing of the charges.

On December 21, 1953, Oppenheimer met with Strauss and Nichols at the AEC. Strauss and Nichols told Oppenheimer that there was a formal letter of charges against him. They showed him an unsigned copy of the letter in the hope that he would resign, in the hope, one might say, that Oppenheimer would see the self-evident error of his ways himself. After meetings with attorneys, one of whose offices was bugged by security agents, and with his wife, Oppenheimer went back to Strauss on the 23rd to tell him that he had decided not to resign. On the 24th, in Princeton, agents from the Atomic Energy Commission arrived to confiscate Oppenheimer's files.

The letter from General Nichols, dated December 23, was read into the record of the hearing before the Personnel Security Board as the Board's first order of business on April 12, 1954. The Board was chaired by Gordon Gray and had as its other members Ward Evans and Thomas Morgan. Roger Robb, counsel for the Board, had spent weeks reviewing with the Board the material on which he would base his "prosecution."

Oppenheimer selected Lloyd Garrison to head his defense team. Garrison not only did not have the benefit of the briefings that Robb conducted for the Board but he was positively barred from seeing much of the material, since action on Garrison's own application for a security clearance was delayed. Consequently, Oppenheimer's defense lawyers could not know the context of material read into the record by Robb from secret documents, nor could they have the documents before they became part of the record. And when secret material was discussed at the hearing, Oppenheimer's lawyers had to leave the room.

Chairman Gray began the first session by reading from Nichols's letter:

> As a result of . . . investigation as to your character, associations, and loyalty, and review of your personnel security file in light of the requirements of the Atomic Energy Act . . . , there has developed considerable question whether your continued employment on Atomic Energy Commission work will endanger the common defense and whether such continued employment is clearly consistent with the interests of national security.[79]

The invocation in a system-apt passive voice of that nebulous yet powerful and encompassing term, "national security," was followed by a series of passive voice accusations that paralleled Borden's letter.[80]

When Oppenheimer had first read the letter the previous December he had responded simply by saying that some of the charges were true, some false, and some were badly phrased. At the hearing he took a different tack, the only one that seemed responsive to the nature of the charges. His March 4 reply to the Commission, which was read into the record of the hearing next, began, "The items of so-called derogatory information set forth in your letter cannot be fairly understood except *in the context of my life and work*." He then offered "a summary account of relevant aspects of my life in more or less chronological order" that began with "I was born in New York in 1904" and that proceeded through the rest of his 50 years with breaks that must have seemed by now the "natural" breaks in his life, the beginning and ending of the war.[81] It was from this account of Oppenheimer's life that the Board would proceed to write its own account of Oppenheimer's life.

Oppenheimer made no attempt to revise the Board's account of his early association with members of the Communist Party or with fellow travelers. He did not disavow the label "fellow traveler" for himself. That part of his biography remained unchanged except for a few corrections of what everyone agreed were the facts about a meeting here or a discussion there. That left the Board with essentially two areas of concern, Oppenheimer's support, or lack of it, for the hydrogen bomb and his role in the Chevalier incident. The early part of the hearing focused on the latter.

On the third day of the hearing, April 14, Roger Robb engaged Oppenheimer in a rapid-fire exchange about the Chevalier incident. He inquired first about Oppenheimer's interviews with security officer Lieutenant Johnson:

> Q. *What did you tell Lieutenant Johnson about when you first mentioned Eltenton to him?*
> A. *I had two interviews, and therefore I am not clear as to which was which.*
> Q. *May I help you?*
> A. *Please.*
> Q. *I think your first interview with Johnson was quite brief, was it not?*
> A. *That is right. I think I said little more than that Eltenton was somebody to worry about.*
> Q. *Yes.*
> A. *Then I was asked why did I say this. Then I invented a cock-and-bull story.*

The exchange moved on to the next day's interview with Boris Pash and subsequent conversations with Groves and with FBI agents.

> Q. *Did you tell Pash the truth about this thing?*
> A. *No.*
> Q. *You lied to him?*
> A. *Yes.*
> Q. *What did you tell Pash that was not true?*
> A. *That Eltenton had attempted to approach members of the project—three members of the project—through intermediaries.*
> Q. *What else did you tell him that wasn't true?*
> A. *That is all I really remember.*
> Q. *That is all? Did you tell Pash that Eltenton had attempted to approach three members of the project—*
> A. *Through intermediaries.*

Q. *Intermediaries?*

A. *Through an intermediary.*

Q. *So that we may be clear, did you discuss with or disclose to Pash the identity of Chevalier?*

A. *No.*

Q. *Let us refer, then, for the time being to Chevalier as X.*

A. *All right.*

Q. *Did you tell Pash that X had approached three persons on the project?*

A. *I am not clear whether I said there were 3 X's or that X approached 3 people.*

Q. *Didn't you say that X had approached 3 people?*

A. *Probably.*

Q. *Why did you do that, Doctor?*

A. Because I was an idiot.

Q. *Is that your only explanation, Doctor?*

A. *I was reluctant to mention Chevalier.*

Q. *Yes.*

A. *No doubt I was somewhat reluctant to mention myself.*

Q. *Yes. But why would you tell him that Chevalier had gone to 3 people?*

A. *I have no explanation for that except the one already offered.*[82]

After a long exchange with Robb reading from transcripts of conversations that Oppenheimer could not recall and in which Robb led Oppenheimer to say, "the whole thing was pure fabrication,"[83] Robb asked,

Q. *[D]on't you think you told a story in great detail that was fabricated?*

A. *I certainly did.*

Q. *Why did you go into such great circumstantial detail about this thing if you were telling a cock and bull story?*

A. *I fear that this whole thing is a piece of idiocy. I am afraid I can't explain why there was a consul, why there was microfilm, why there were three people on the project, why two of them were at Los Alamos. All of them seem wholly false to me. . . .*

Q. *Isn't it a fair statement today, Dr. Oppenheimer, that according to your testimony now you told not one lie to Colonel Pash, but a whole fabrication and tissue of lies?*

A. *Right.*[84]

This "pure fabrication" and "tissue of lies" was the peg on which the two-person majority of the Board and, subsequently, four of the five AEC commissioners would hang their conviction that Oppenheimer had serious defects of character. At various points on the path to the final AEC decision some would believe that Oppenheimer had, in fact, lied to Pash and others in the 1940s. Others would conclude that he was lying now in 1954 and that the earlier story had been correct. All of these people, regardless of the version of the truth that they accepted, would conclude that Oppenheimer's character was, in some sense, defective. For those people, the evidence supported a conviction on the basis of two violations of security clearance criteria, the problem of character and the problem of past and present associations. These were to be the final basis for the AEC's decision to revoke Oppenheimer's clearance.

Problems of character and association, not loyalty, did in Oppenheimer. Only one AEC commissioner, Thomas E. Murray, would eventually conclude that Oppenheimer was, in fact, disloyal. To come to this conclusion Murray had to construct a heady philosophical argument about the concept of loyalty, grounded in the peculiar political climate of 1954 (which hinged, for him, on "the fact of the Communist conspiracy"), that created, in Murray's words, "a stern test of loyalty." Murray concluded, "Dr. Oppenheimer failed the test."

There was, however, little direct testimony to indicate that Oppenheimer had ever been disloyal within the accepted definitions of loyalty. Even his detractors said so. Edward Teller, for example, in response to the direct question, "Is it your intention in anything that you are about to testify to, to suggest that Dr. Oppenheimer is disloyal to the United States?," said,

> I do not want to suggest anything of the kind. I know Oppenheimer as an intellectually most alert and a very complicated person, and I think it would be presumptuous and wrong on my part if I would try in any way to analyze his motives. But I have always assumed, and I now assume that he is loyal to the United States. I believe this, and I shall believe it until I see very conclusive proof to the opposite.[85]

The AEC Commissioners did not object to the Board's claim that they had before them "much responsible and positive evidence of the loyalty and love of country of the individual concerned."[86]

While Murray may have been alone in his conclusion that Oppenheimer was disloyal, one of his premises—the premise that the system must take precedence over the individual—was accepted by many involved in the decision. Murray wrote, "The requirement that a man in [Oppenheimer's] position should relinquish the right to the complete freedom of association that would be his in other circumstances is altogether a reasonable and necessary requirement. The exact observance of this requirement is in all cases essential to the integrity of the security system."[87] The belief that the integrity of the system comes first, the notion that one who serves the system must submit to it in the name of national security, was unchallenged throughout the proceedings. The Board wrote in their summary, "Whether the incidents referred to clearly indicate a susceptibility to influence or coercion . . . or whether they simply reflect very bad judgment, they clearly raise the question of Dr. Oppenheimer's understanding, acceptance, and enthusiastic support of the security system."[88]

For Oppenheimer the statement that he did not accept and support the security system must have been loaded with irony, since he had played a major role in developing the system. In fact, on the second day of his hearings he had noted that one function of the General Advisory Committee under his chairmanship had been to advise the AEC on matters of security.

> *The Commission reviewed with us [the GAC] its security procedures,* the procedures, *I think,* under which we are now sitting. *I believe their interest in doing that was to find out whether these would seem fair and reasonable to scientists. I don't believe we responded in writing to that, but we probably said that this looked to us like a fair set up.*[89]

The Oppenheimer hearing was a pedagogical event whose point was that even the most presumably responsible of people had to be responsible to the system, not responsible for it. "There remains . . . an aspect of the security system which perhaps has had insufficient public attention," the Hearing Board wrote. "*This is the protection and support of the entire system itself.* . . . It must involve a subordination of personal judgment. . . . It must entail wholehearted commitment to the preservation of the security system and the avoidance of conduct tending to confuse or obstruct."[90]

Oppenheimer was charged and convicted essentially with exceeding the bounds that the system established for him to live within. He was tried for trying to be responsible. In the Chevalier incident, Oppenheimer had exercised an "arrogance of his own judgment with respect to the loyalty and reliability of other citizens." On the matter of advice that Oppenheimer gave, the Board decided either that Oppenheimer had exceeded his range of competence or that the Government had been irresponsible in listening to "the advice of [scientific] specialists relating to moral, military and political issues, under circumstances which lend such advice an undue and in some cases decisive weight."[91] The individual who dared to act individually would pay. The error Oppenheimer made, if we may speak like this, was to assume the responsibility traditionally borne by a responsible person. In fact, the Board cited in a damaging way Oppenheimer's own testimony that, "I felt perhaps quite wrongly that having played an active part in promoting a revolution in warfare I needed to be as responsible as I could with what came of this revolution."[92]

The Oppenheimer case illustrates forcefully the paradoxical position of the individual/expert in complex systems that operate, as Jacques Ellul puts it, "on the basis of purely technical considerations." Ellul's *Technological Society* was published in 1954, the same year as Oppenheimer's trial, so he was on record earlier than most as noting that the rise in technique, progress conditioned only by "its own calculus of efficiency," does not eliminate the individual or devalue individuality. Ellul wrote,

> *On the contrary, progress is made only after innumerable individual experiments. But the individual participates only to the degree that he is subordinate to the search for efficiency, to the degree that he resists all the currents today considered secondary, such as aesthetics, ethics, fantasy. Insofar as the individual represents this abstract tendency, he is permitted to participate in technical creation, which is increasingly independent of him and increasingly linked to its own mathematical law.*[93]

As much as the atomic system enabled the bomb to become what it had been only in potential, so did it enable J. Robert Oppenheimer to become what he had been only in potential before the Manhattan Engineering District was formed. Again Ellul: "when men found themselves going counter to the human factor, they reintroduced— and in an absurd way—all manner of moral theories related to the rights of man, the League of Nations, liberty, justice." We might add to that list the accompanying notions of individual responsibility, moral obligation, and civic duty. But "none of that has any more importance than the ruffled sunshade of McCormick's first reaper. When these moral flourishes overly encumber technical progress, they are discarded—more or less speedily, with more or less ceremony, but with determination nonetheless."[94] For just as the atomic system was free to dispose of its weapons according to its own rules, it was free to dispose of Oppenheimer according to the same set of rules.

And dispose of Oppenheimer is just what the system did.

Some have found it odd that the AEC did not allow, simply, Oppenheimer's contract as a consultant to lapse as it was due to do on June 30, 1954. In fact, the AEC's final decision on Oppenheimer's security clearance had to be rushed into print and was publicly released even before Oppenheimer had seen it so that the decision could be out on June 29, the day before Oppenheimer's contract expired. Oppenheimer himself found it a little strange that the AEC should undertake such an extensive proceeding because as he said in effect, if the Government did not care to have his advice, the Government could simply not ask for it. Some of the Commissioners considered the possibility of just moving on without a decision on the matter of Oppenheimer's security clearance. Commissioner Eugene M. Zuckert wrote that he had "given the most serious consideration to this possibility and concluded that it [was] not practical." Oppenheimer had, in Zuckert's view, built for himself "a unique place . . . in the scientific world and as a top Government advisor." That fact required "that there be a clear determination,"[95] with echoes to Ellul, concerning his status. The system acts with determination and tenacity when an individual becomes too individuated.

A system that creates one's individuality cannot dispose of a person simply by ignoring the person, as in the military practice of "shunning," or by branding, as the good people did with Mistress Pryne. It must dispose by making an extraordinary effort to account for a person's life, including especially those events that are erroneous and that will form the basis for exclusion from the circle of the real and true. There is in the Oppenheimer case an instructive contrast between the way Oppenheimer himself experienced the hearing and the implicit demand of the hearing that Oppenheimer account for himself, that he become accountable.

Recall that in response to Robb's hammering about his role in the Chevalier incident, Oppenheimer said that he had invented the story about Chevalier "because I was an idiot." He called the story itself "a piece of idiocy." Oppenheimer probably was not thinking about the derivation of "idiot" when he uttered this damning term, but the classical meaning of "idiot" as one who is peculiar or alone summarized Oppenheimer's experience of himself and the hearings. He later told *Life* magazine that he had responded to the hearings "the way a soldier does in combat, I suppose. So much is happening or may be about to happen that there is no time to be aware of anything except the next move." Roger Robb, the prosecutor, went home from that fateful second day of the hearing and told his wife, "I've just seen a man destroy himself."[96] Oppenheimer had destroyed himself by effectively showing himself to be alone outside the realm of common discourse and understanding. He admitted to having lived his life, to too great a degree, by himself.

In direct contrast, the hearing wanted a coherent accounting in common, understandable terms. Edward Teller's testimony is regarded by most to have been the most damaging of the trial. Oppenheimer and Teller had started out as good friends and intimate intellectual colleagues. They respected one another. Their relationship had been irreparably strained during the years at Los Alamos as Teller found his Super program supported less than he would have liked and later as he watched the General Advisory Committee, chaired by Oppenheimer, recommend against the "crash" program for the development of "his" bomb. It was against this background that Teller followed his assertion that he had no reason to doubt Oppenheimer's loyalty with the crucial,

> In a great number of cases I have seen Dr. Oppenheimer act—I understood that Dr. Oppenheimer acted—in a way which for me was exceedingly hard to understand. I thoroughly disagreed with him in numerous issues and his actions appeared to be confused and complicated. To this extent I feel that I would like to see the vital interests of this country in hands which I understand better, and therefore trust more. In this very limited sense I would like to express a feeling that I would feel personally more secure if public matters would rest in other hands.[97]

The question for Teller and the Hearing Board generally was whether Oppenheimer was understandable, whether there was a way to make sense of the man and his actions, whether the whole life of the man— the general structure of argument on which Oppenheimer had based his defense and therefore helped to justify—had a narrative structure or a theoretical consistency that would make "confused and complicated" actions, decisions, and behaviors comprehensible.

The Hearing Board had this pivotal concern in mind as they questioned several witnesses about the possibility of "rehabilitation" for those who, in their earlier years, had done things that, were they done in the present, would be clear violations of security regulations. Gordon Gray, the chairman, pushed George Kennan to engage in an exposition of the consideration of a person's "life course" in matters of clearance for security. Kennan tried to impress upon Gray the importance of using "individual judgment" about unusually gifted or bright people by saying, "the really gifted and able people in Government are perhaps less apt than others to have had a fully conventional life and a fully conventional entry . . . into governmental responsibilities." Gray's closing question to Kennan got to the point: "You feel . . . that the unusual person or gifted person who has traveled perhaps a different road than most other people can at one point reach a stability on the basis of which there can be absolute predictability as to no further excursions?" Kennan replied, "Let me say at a point where there can be sufficient predictability to warrant being accepted by the Government for public service."[98] The Board concluded that there was the possibility of rehabilitation for errant individuals by saying, "The necessary but harsh requirements of security should not deny a man the right to have made a mistake, if the recurrence is so remote a possibility as to permit a comfortable prediction as to the sanity and correctness of future conduct."

But the stochastic terms in which all of these arguments about rehabilitation were phrased is the most telling feature of the hearing. The acceptability of a life to the system is never a black-and-white, binary question. As Foucault has noted, the notion of criminality, based on the transgression of a boundary-like law, disappeared in the modern era and was replaced by the notion of delinquency, criminality *omnia in potentia*. In fact, one of the Board members, Ward Evans, tried to argue in his dissenting opinion to the Board that acceptability should be a binary choice, yes or no. He was unsuccessful. Evans noted that Oppenheimer's file had been reviewed several times and that his security clearance had already been granted by the AEC in 1947. The Gray Board was out of line in conducting its review, Evans argued. A person is either qualified or not, Evans seemed to say. Evans wanted to eliminate Primo Levi's "grey zone" so that judgments—human judgments—of a fundamental if inherently flawed sort could still be made. But the Gray Board would not allow that. Evans's view was voted down. And that vote left all lives at all points in their courses open to a negative assessment. As the AEC decision put it, "One inherent difficulty is that *every human being is to some degree a security risk*. So long as there are normal human feelings like pain or emotions like love of family, everyone is . . . a potential risk in some degree to our security."[99] Anyone subject to "the human factor," as Graham Greene used that term, is always a potential outlaw. The best that one could hope for in this new age is to place a life as lived at some point on a probabilistic scale of risk.

In this kind of situation, the person who is at risk can only wait. He waits for the context to change or for a new interpretation of old facts to push him up the scale of probabilities to a point where the risk is, for the system at this time, too great. For Oppenheimer there was never any uncertainty about the outcome of his hearing. He had waited and he knew that his time had come. He understood the risk of being a security risk and said of the hearing, "It was like Pearl Harbor—on a small scale. . . . One knew that something like this was possible and even probable; but still it was a shock when it came." And once the story of his life was started, it had to grind to a conclusive ending. Oppenheimer said that he had "no real hope other than the actual outcome: once a thing like this has been started they couldn't not go through with it to the end; and they couldn't let me win."[100]

Oppenheimer did not go down in a blaze of condemnation or out with the certain nobility of the exiled. He disappeared the way Harry Tuttle disappeared in *Brazil*. All of the paper that constituted the life was assembled, correlated, and hung in its place on the body of the person whose truth the papers contained. After the papers were sorted the man was not there anymore. "Robert Oppenheimer disappeared from the public view and seemed almost to have disappeared from the life of his friends."[101]

If it is true that "a person is named and recognized by another

[and] thereby acquires an individuality which only exists insofar as it is enmeshed with that of others,"[102] it is going only a little too far to say that the Board and the AEC took away the individuality and personhood they had been so influential in creating for Oppenheimer. It is not that they "killed" him. After all, he continued as Director of the Institute for Advanced Study at Princeton and as a productive, roving intellectual. The AEC decision was simply one no longer to foster the life they had allowed Oppenheimer to live.

I. I. Rabi admitted at Oppenheimer's hearing that they were all living in a new age. He added with a measure of melancholy, "You have to become accustomed to life in this kind of life."[103] Oppenheimer had become accustomed to it. He just would not be allowed to continue it.

CHAPTER FOUR:

Narrativity and (Deathly) Silence

In fact, man is a comical creature; there seems to be a kind of jest in it all.

DOSTOEVSKY
Notes from Underground

Edward Teller did not question Robert Oppenheimer's ability, his loyalty, or his effectiveness. He simply could not *understand* Oppenheimer. Un-understandability was Oppenheimer's fatal flaw with respect to the atomic system.

Edward Teller, first among many others, could not accept that Oppenheimer was an idiot, a loner, a person not to be explained. To be understandable, Oppenheimer had to be captured in a narrative structure. In a 1982 foreword to Groves's reissued *Now It Can Be Told*, Teller wrote, "Oppenheimer was so extraordinarily complicated and clever that he could mask those qualities with an appearance of simplicity."[1] Teller's job, as he saw it, was to make Oppenheimer's simple silence speak a true message about its subject. There is a violence in this insistence on understandable talk. Teller made Oppenheimer complex, I suggest, so that he might be simplified by placing him in a narrative structure. Simplification was, as we saw, Teller's wish. It is, I think, our culture's final wish.

Twenty-eight years after his appearance at Oppenheimer's security clearance hearing and fifteen years after Oppenheimer's death, Edward Teller was still trying to make Oppenheimer understandable, to find a message in the man that would make sense. By seeing complexity behind a facade of simplicity Teller made it possible to develop a narrative that would account for Oppenheimer and his actions. Teller's characterization of Oppenheimer as "extraordinarily complicated" is the stuff good stories are made of, for the good story teller is one who will, we can rest assured, break through the surface, find the complexity that must lie below and begin to unravel it, tracing the connections and revealing them to show, in, finally, a simple way, how everything came together to create that which is.

"Narrativity is exciting," says Leo Bersani.[2] The construction of stories that go below the surface is exciting. Narratives apprehend. They put all the little pieces in their places along intersecting and knotted lines in a way that permits us to grasp and hold even that which appears ineffable. Had Teller left his description of Oppenheimer at "simple" or had he and others been satisfied even with "enigmatic" or had they attended to Oppenheimer's description of some of his actions as "piece(s) of idiocy," there would have been little left to say or do except go on. There would have been no excitement, no way to construct a narrative, for there would have been no reason to do so. Teller, and others, would have had to say of Oppenheimer only something like, "Stupid simpleton!" leave the hearing room in 1954, and would have been unable to return there as Teller has apparently kept doing. They would have had no stories to tell, nothing with which to tilt for the rest of their lives.

In point of fact, the security hearing had disposed of Oppenheimer. His story had been told and his life assembled and sorted, if not to Teller's satisfaction and if not to the satisfaction of the troop of biographers that continue to hound the man in death, then at least to the satisfaction of the atomic system. There was, however, a much bigger problem for the impulse to narrativize than Oppenheimer. There remained the problem of the bomb itself. Those first bombs were disruptive, violent events. Those events had to be narrativized, understood, explained.

Bersani and others help us understand that the impulse to place the bomb in some history or other involves an invitation to violence of a second order, violence that is equivalent to the violence done to Oppenheimer by getting his life in order so to judge it. The difference is that the scale is larger and the cultural delirium that such an undertaking effects is more broadly shared.

We must return to our prototypic analyst and our anti-typical systems thinker to begin to appreciate the place, function, and effects of narrativity in understanding. Holmes knew that the story of a crime could always be written. The most complicated of circumstances would, eventually, be understood and could be made understandable to and by a Watson. Every story that ended in a crime had a beginning and a middle. The task of the investigating detective was (is) to separate the story line from the rest of history, expertly to place boundaries dividing the relevant from the irrelevant and the misleading, and to reconstruct a plot as it builds to its climax at the scene of the crime. Holmes used his general knowledge to unravel the specific threads of a particular, usually complex crime. He thereby created tests of his knowledge, reformulated his store of knowledge, and moved on to the next crime with ever more refined tools of apprehension, understanding, and perhaps even control.

Some say the Holmes stories, and all detective fiction, are too neat. Holmes solved the mysteries because Conan Doyle wrote the stories so that Holmes could and would solve them. But to belittle Holmes shifts the attention away from our relationship to such stories. Narratives are exciting to us, the readers, because they let us identify with the process of mastering the melange of reality. Narratives serve a pedagogical function. They reassure us that even the most threatening events in our world, like crime, dastardly crime, can be apprehended by grasping the narrative threads that come together to constitute the textured fabric of experience. The Holmes stories are ultimately comforting because they reassure us that there is an understandable order beneath chaos-threatening crime. We sleep better if we can believe that there are responsible Holmes-like experts in all fields deciphering problems and seeking harmony in a world that is threatening.

Freud is, at first glance, a story teller of the first order. His case studies make marvelous reading and there is a connection between Freud and Holmes that some, including Freud himself, have exploited to explain psychoanalytic "method."[3] But the elaboration that a Freudian story offers gets nowhere except right back to the "I am" with which analysis begins. There is no redemption and certainly no promise that order will overcome chaos. Freudian stories go nowhere and are literally open-ended. As Aaron Green, Janet Malcolm's subject-analyst, says of the stories that patients tell, "their stories are full of . . . arrestingly rich detail, as if a gifted writer had composed them."

Green was attracted to the seeming orderliness that his youthful understanding of psychoanalytic theory provided him as he was confronted with the chaos of the lives his patients reported to him. He
tells us that as he came to understand the "theory" better, the theory
lost its theoretical attractiveness and the patients' stories themselves
became a source of motivation. He became willing to set aside an
interest in orderliness and listen to chaotic individual stories simply
because they moved him.

Patients' stories, which are opposed to Freudian theory, gain one
nothing. They hold no promise. They contain no direction. "Analysis
says nothing about what one ultimately does. Analysis provides one
with the greatest possible freedom regarding what one does," Green
says, but "greatest possible" is often equivalent to "not very much,"
because "we live our lives according to the repetition compulsion and
analysis can only go so far in freeing us from it."[4] One does not arrive,
through analysis, at directive, useful knowledge that might be "helpful" in similar circumstances in the future. Should one live one's life
according to the requirements of culture or according to the dictates
of instinct? Freud's students answered that question in different ways
from the different camps they constructed, but Freud—and orthodox
analysis—is remorselessly silent on the issue.[5]

Stories of lives, which are opposed to theoretical, narrativized
accounts of life, contain no message or moral. They provide "merely
provisional closure," not "definitive" closure.[6] There is no murder
toward which they lead and with which they will definitely conclude.
Instead of building interest in their subject matter as classical stories
must, they may dissipate interest. (Freud said that he found himself,
the subject of the first analytic stories, less interesting as he grew
older and could not understand why anyone would wish to write his
biography.) Such accounts contain no "successes" signalled by one
gaining "control" or developing "authority" or finding a "voice." Indeed, Bersani has written that the "psychoanalytic authenticity of
Freud's work *depends on* a process of theoretical collapse" and he says
his job as a commentator is to "celebrate a certain type of failure in
Freud's thought."[7] The simplicity that results from complexity, the "I
am" of all psychoanalytic stories, is that which subverts a theoretical,
simplifying, analytical, narrative reconstruction of its truth. Freud,
then, could never have been a good detective in the mold of Holmes,
for he has no achievements deriving from his work, nothing useful

that accumulated. He may help one to get the threads of experience in one's hands momentarily, but the analyst knows that experience will always yank most of them back again and unwind any beautiful fabric that one might be tempted to make of them.

Narratives are comforting because they provide continuity through disruptive events. Through their simplifications, they link events to their pasts and provide entrees to the future. They incorporate events into history and into lives so that there may be a sense of coherence. The more disruptive an event, the less understandable an event (or a person, or a life), the more a narrative account is required, at least in our culture. As Bersani notes, narratives provide a perspective and thereby place some things before an event, others behind it.[8] Establishing a theoretical perspective that permits one to find a thing's true place in an order reflects, Bersani is reminding us, a hubris organized around the notion that things that have a place can be placed or replaced. Our passion for narrative coherence betrays an arrogance and serves a function; it serves the process of placement. Crimes must have their place; Oppenheimer got accorded his place; the bomb will get a place. Narrative makes everything find its place.

Bersani is one of only a few writers who have recognized the relationship between the process of narrative placement of people and events, on the one hand, and violence, on the other. His project, as described in his book on Assyrian sculpture, argues that, "the anti-violent tradition of Western humanism has defined violence in ways which may actually have promoted an unintended fascination with violence." He wishes to put in relief "a complicity between narrativity and violence" through the negative tactic of seeing the Assyrian palace reliefs as aesthetic gestures that subvert a possible identification with violence. The reliefs fail to develop a narrative, he points out. They have no beginning and no end. They just present violence, not "violence after violence" or "violence upon violence" as if there were any hope of perceiving an order. They defy attempts to narrativize and, thereby, make sense of them.

In contrast to the Assyrian palace reliefs, a narrative structure, through which we begin to make sense of experience, locates violence in a chain of understanding and thereby stabilizes the world. "We usually think of violence in terms of historically locatable events," writes Bersani,

> *that is, as a certain type of eruption against a background of generally nonviolent human experience. In this view, violence can be made intelligible through historical accounts of the circumstances in which it occurs. . . . [Through narrative,] violence is . . . reduced to the level of a plot; it can be isolated, understood, perhaps mastered and eliminated.*[9]

Narrative re-stabilizes a world that violence threatens (at least) to destabilize. Instead of seeing this outcome as an unalloyed good, it is stability achieved through narrativity, Bersani argues, that "produces the ideal conditions for a mimetic relation to violence."[10] Narratives implicate, either positively or negatively, the tellers and the hearer of the tales. Narratives that involve us in tales of violence invite us to consider seriously our own self's relationship to violence. We cannot be casual anymore and see "the jest in it all"; we must take our selves seriously: For or against. Victim or executioner. Part of the problem or part of the solution. A choice must be made.

But Bersani reminds us that the choices between "for" and "against," between "victim" and "executioner," are not choices. They are equivalents with respect to the narrative structures. "Our choice is not between violence and non-violence, but it is rather between the psychic dislocations of mobile desire and a destructive fixation on anecdotal violence." But in our culture, we tend to take seriously the "choices" offered, assume our roles, and like characters in a Genet brothel, continue to act our parts as the world rages about us. We continue and sustain our own participation in "a certain modernity—a modernity which has defined itself less by protests against the real violence of recent history than by what might be called a taste for noncatastrophic violence."[11] Neither New Mexico nor the oceans were set on fire by Trinity, so let us try to make sense of what we have done, is the invitation to narrativity issued by the rationality of this "certain modernity" in which we live. Let us not eat Oppenheimer, but do let us discover his truth, even if that search may involve a little discomfort (the discomfort of Oppenheimer's personal Pearl Harbor, as he put it) to the man. That is the attitude we are asked to assume today.

Bersani's argument about the relationship between violence and narrativity is mounted negatively. He uses the Assyrian reliefs as an example of how identification with violence is subverted by not narrativizing and by not permitting a narrative to be developed. A positive case for the relationship is found in the work of J. M. Coetzee.

His recent novels, *The Life and Times of Michael K* and *Foe*, both illustrate the seductions to violence involved in the process of constructing narratives to make "silence speak."

Michael K, whose "life and times" Coetzee recounts, is a stupidly simple person. He is born with a hare lip so just speaking is difficult for him. During a civil war he hides out on a farm. For food, he plants pumpkin seeds across the fields in an almost random pattern so that no one will suspect there is an intention or design behind the plantings. He tends his pumpkins by night so that he will not be discovered. Eventually he is captured and associated in the suspicious minds of the soldiers with a band of insurgents that had been seen in the area earlier. Michael is taken to a racetrack whose grandstand has been converted into a prison. There his keepers try all the usual strategies for extracting from him his true story.

"I am not in the war," Michael tells his interrogators after a long series of pleadings that "Michaels," as he is known to the jailers, speak his truth. Michael's assertion of neutrality is unacceptable to the jailers whose notions of life and history—whose *normal* notions of life and history—are dependent on the existence of sides, camps, and prisons: "Of course you are in the war, man, whether you like it or not." "Michaels" must fit into their narrative structures by which their world becomes understandable to them. After being frustrated by Michael's silence, his principal interrogator finally tells a colleague,

> *Don't try twisting a story out of him, because truly there is no story to be had. In the profoundest sense he does not know what he is doing.* Make something up for the report. . . . There is nothing there, *I'm telling you, and if you hand him over to the police they would come to the same conclusion: there is nothing there, no story of the slightest interest to rational people. I have watched him, I know! He is not of our world.*[12]

There is in this renunciation of the impulse to narrativize a hint of respect for Michael K.

But this glimmer of respect dims quickly as this same person invents his own story to account for "Michaels's" "free-spiritedness." He even writes "Michaels" a letter that reads in part,

> *You are precious, Michaels, in your own way. . . . We have all tumbled over the lip into the cauldron of history; only you, following your idiot*

> *light, biding you time in an orphanage (who would have thought of*
> *that as a hiding place?) evading the peace and the war, skulking in the*
> *open where no one dreamed of looking . . . no more trying to change*
> *history than a grain of sand does.*

But this "friend," as he signs the letter, wants to use "Michaels's" story—the story of a hero outside of the war-making machine, outside even of time as he constructs it—to change history. He wants to employ a narrative theory of Michael as a redemption. He wants to put Michael's clothes and his package of pumpkin seeds in a museum. All "Michaels" has to do for this friend to ensure that his story is saved is, as the "friend" puts it at the close of his letter, "yield!"[13]

The construction of a redemptive narrative is necessary to permit the players to persist in their parts. Any narrative will permit the violence that enables everyone to remain in his or her proper place to continue.* The alternative to this kind of violence is the renunciation of all narrative, all categories, all language for the simplicity of idiocy. While there are camps for every category of person, Michael thinks, "Perhaps the truth is that it is enough to be out of the camps, out of all the camps at the same time. Perhaps that is enough of an achievement, for the time being." And he reasons that once he is out of the camps there is one remaining grasp to elude, the grasp of those, like his "friend," who want to know his story so they can be helpfully concerned about him: "I have escaped the camps; perhaps, if I lie low, I will escape the charity too." He concludes, "I was mute and

---

*Some argue that the construction of redemptive narratives is the *duty* of intellectuals. Thus, Zygmunt Bauman writes,

> *The urgency of discursive redemption, if anything, adds to the importance of the*
> *role intellectuals are called to play. Discursive redemption is unmistakably their*
> *duty. The project of modernity had been deposited and still resides in the cultural*
> *tradition the intellectuals perpetuate and develop. As before, the intellectuals must*
> *initiate and guide a process of enlightenment, through supplying an adequate theory*
> *(of history, of social system, or communicative action) which reveals the possibility*
> *of redemption contained in the form of modern society has currently assumed, and*
> *points out realistic strategies of redemptive practice. . . .*[14]

This appeal to the past may be anachronistic. With Drucker, I believe arguments like this come only from books that make a romantic appeal to a territory we have left. To say a polite "no, thank you" to all-too-rational invitations like Bauman's is difficult. My respect for Foucault is based in part on his having done so.

stupid at the beginning, I will be mute and stupid at the end. There is nothing to be ashamed of in being simple."[15]

Coetzee has written elsewhere about the paradoxical position of an author—a narrativizer by trade—in the modern state exemplified, for him, by his own country, South Africa. He asks, "Why are writers *in South Africa* drawn to the torture room?" the rooms within the prisons—those unphotographable buildings that do not appear on any maps—from which "true accounts" have such difficulty emerging. He answers, echoing Bersani, "The dark, forbidden chamber is the origin of novelistic fantasy *per se;* in creating an obscenity, in enveloping it in mystery, the state creates the preconditions for the novel to set about its work of representation." Coetzee is critical, however, of those who would attempt simply re-creations of the violence because their work has an erotic aspect that involves the reader in the spectacle of violence that can never been viewed in fact. "There is something tawdry about *following* the state in this way, making its vile mysteries the occasion for fantasy." The writer faces the problem Michael K faced, the problem of how to remain outside all the camps at once, the problem of

> not *allow[ing]* himself to be impaled on the dilemma proposed by the state, namely, either to ignore its obscenities or else to produce representations of them. The true challenge is how not to play the game by the rules of the state, how to establish one's own authority, how to imagine torture and death on one's own terms.[16]

How can one even write, which is a rule-bound activity, and renounce all rules that necessarily bind?

Coetzee turns to allegory. For example, in *Foe*, Coetzee tells the story of a woman abandoned on an island with Robinson Crusoe and Friday. They are rescued and on the return voyage to England Friday dies. The woman goes in search of an author to write their (her) story. She had to have an author, in particular, because she had to understand a specific historical event, an act of violence, the cutting out of Friday's tongue, something that had happened before the woman arrived on the island. She had to place that event in a narrative structure, since it had no place in her memory and remained only a disruptive "event" in her experience. "On the island I accepted that I should never learn how Friday lost his tongue. . . . Yet the only tongue that can tell Friday's secret is the tongue he has lost," the tongue of her now dead, erstwhile companion. In our time, a seemingly natural substitute for the tongue that tells its own tales is an authoritative teller.

The woman finds her author, of course, in Daniel Defoe. She says to "Foe," as she calls him, "It is for us to open Friday's mouth and hear what it holds." Defoe replies, "That too. . . . I intend something else; but that too. We must make Friday's silence speak, as well as the silence surrounding Friday."[17] Coetzee's fiction alerts us—for it can do little more—to the way narrativity doubles violence and in that doubling mutes it, mutes it by making sense of it, by making it if not acceptable then at least rational by accounting for it.

The doubtful critic may ask now, but how else might we pursue our love for the truth? How else, other than through the construction of asymptotically truthful narrative accounts, might we begin to apprehend what is, in fact, true? There is no reply to this most reasonable question for it shifts the register in which I wish to work. It is one thing to ask whether an account is true or not, or to ask whether the conditions for truth-telling have been met in a particular case, or to try to articulate the conditions that must be met for an account to be judged true. It is another to enquire into the functions of truth and the effects of truth-producing mechanisms.

Michel Foucault has urged us by his several examples always to understand truth, along with truth-producing and truth-verifying mechanisms, as inseparably intertwined with structures of power that operate according to their own rules. "There is a battle 'for truth,' or at least 'around truth,'" Foucault once said. This implies that there is not an "'ensemble of truths which are to be discovered and accepted,' but rather '[an] ensemble of rules according to which the true and the false are separated and specific effects of power attached to the true.'" It also implies that "it's not a matter of a battle 'on behalf' of the truth, but a battle about the status of truth and the economic and political roles it plays."[18] Foucault's anecdotal accounts of the play of power, like that of "Alexina," *aka* Herculine Barbin the "hermaphrodite," illuminate the specific violences exacted not just in the name of truth but by the operation of truth itself.[19] The impulse to narrativize is an impulse to violence, in Foucault's thinking.

We need not involve ourselves in Foucault's philosophical gymnastics to grasp the point when a popular novel will serve. As the library burns at the end of Umberto Eco's *The Name of the Rose*, William of Baskerville recounts for Adso the chain of violences that brother Jorge brought upon his monastery through his battles "on behalf" of the truth, a battle he waged in devout opposition to another truth that was contained in the copy of Aristotle's volume on comedy that the monastery owned. William says, "The Antichrist can be born from piety itself, from excessive love of God or of the truth. . . . Jorge did a diabolical thing because he loved his truth so lewdly that he dared anything in order to destroy falsehood."

The reader is tempted, as Adso was tempted, to think William a hypocrite, since he has just solved the mystery of the monastery in a manner linked explicitly to Holmes's analytical approach. William is, after all, a classical detective in a seemingly classical detective story. Adso tries to console William by telling him, "you have defeated Jorge because you exposed the plot." That is, he narrativized everything and laid out the chain of events in their true order so that they might be understandable. But William has a different view of his "success": "There was no plot . . . and I discovered it by accident." The point is not quite a variant of the apothegm "the truth will out." The point is more like, "to the victor goes the rights to truth." William admits that he had tried all along to construct a narrative that would account for all the crimes that had occurred, a narrative in which there was a responsible person, the criminal, and a design of criminal intention. But this pursuit was futile and a result more of the stubbornness of rationality than of wisdom or intelligence. "I arrived at Jorge pursuing the plan of a perverse and rational mind," William says, "and there was no plan, or, rather, Jorge himself was overcome by his own initial design and there began a sequence of causes, and concauses, and of causes contradicting one another, which proceeded on their own, creating relations that did not stem from any plan."[20]

William concludes that truth itself, when held lewdly, may be a serious problem if it is not seen as only a temporary solution to local, particular problems: "The order that our mind imagines is like a net, or like a ladder, built to attain something. But afterward you must throw the ladder away, because you discover that, even if it was useful, it was meaningless. . . . The only truths that are useful are instruments to be thrown away."[21] Holding onto a truth—"lewdly" as William characterizes Jorge's seizure of his truth—and nailing it down through coherent, rational narratives is violence itself, not, as we tend to think, one answer to violence.

This kind of reasoning gives little indication of what one ought to do besides be cautious in one's attachment to true facts and true accounts. Foucault, of course, has been of little help (and it is in his failure to be helpful that *I* find his work so helpful). In an early essay he seemed to be directive when he aligned himself with a "philosophy of non-positive affirmation." His 1963 "Preface to Transgression" was one of his first attempts to articulate what it means to engage in a continuous critique. He cites Bataille's wish "to implicate (and to question) everything without possible respite" and without finding anything positive—not even the act of negation—in this strategy. He wrote,

> *Transgression is neither violence in a divided world (in an ethical world) nor a victory over limits (in a dialectical or revolutionary world). . . . Transgression contains nothing negative, but affirms limited being. . . . But correspondingly, this affirmation contains nothing positive: no context can bind it, since, by definition, no limit can possibly restrict it.*[22]

If one tries to render this into a directive one is left only with enigmatic notions like "transgress in the name of nothing" or "use the positive voice to say 'no.'" Foucault's later work is equally (un)helpful. What can it mean to take as a "rallying point" against the operations of sex and sexuality, operations that seek to penetrate the last refuges of individuality and subjectivity, a "different economy of bodies and pleasures"?[23] There is little coherent truth here to grasp, lewdly or otherwise. But that is, for me, the essence of a permanent critique that begins and ends in laughter, in the renunciation of an impulse to construct true narratives. Perhaps that is why some find Foucault's "call for 'permanent critique' either too subversive or too empty"[24] with little ground between the extremes. It leaves little room for action. But we can outline the almost orgiastic search for truth that occurs in specific instances and, perhaps, suggest some of the effects of that passion. After the violence of the first bombs there was a violence of a second order, the violence of trying to make sense out of the first violence by giving it a narrative place in history in order to stabilize the world.

Bomb Stories:
Making "Deathly Silence" Speak

Richard Rhodes recounts D. R. Inglis's memory of the Trinity test. He recalled the flash, the hemispherical fireball "like a half-risen sun," the column of smoke and debris that rose quickly, and at twenty miles from Ground Zero, he thought, "The feeling of the remoteness of this thing which had seemed so near was emphasized *by the long silence* while we watched the grey smoke grow into a taller and taller twisting column."[25] Oppenheimer recalled that after the blastwave had passed everyone walked outside "and then it was extremely solemn. . . . A few people laughed, a few people cried. Most people were silent."[26] "Not until [the car loads of scientists] reached the guarded gates of Los Alamos did the flood of talk burst loose."[27]

The "flood of talk" was slower to come after the detonation of the second atomic bomb. In Hiroshima,

> those who were able walked silently toward the suburbs in the distant hills, their spirits broken, their initiative gone. . . . They were so broken and confused that they moved and behaved like automatons. Their reactions had astonished outsiders who reported with amazement the spectacle of long files of people holding steadily to a narrow rough path. . . . The outsiders could not grasp the fact that they were witnessing the exodus of a people who walked in the realm of dreams.

Robert Jay Lifton says that "rather than wild panic" the seemingly dead but real survivors of Hiroshima reported only a "deathly silence" following the blast.[28]

Since Trinity, since Hiroshima, we have been hard at work filling the silences that the bombs left as their legacy. We have tried to make that "deathly silence" speak using various narrative apparatuses. We have invented bomb stories to try to contain and localize the bomb. We have been so persistent in this effort that the flood of talk among the scientists as they returned from the Trinity test became for one cultural historian, Paul Boyer, a "Niagara of evidence." Boyer, in his effort to "recover [a] lost segment of our cultural history" by reporting on the earliest American responses to the bomb, found that all the stories we currently tell about nuclear weapons—"the visions of atomic devastation, the earnest efforts to rouse people to resist such a fate, the voices seeking to soothe or deflect those fears, the insistence that security lay in greater technical expertise and in more and bigger weaponry"—were all present in the earliest days of our new age. Along with the explosions of the bombs came an "explosion in men's minds" that attempted to locate this new device on the cultural landscape.[29] Multiple narratives tried to stabilize this most destabilizing instrument.

The bomb was destabilizing because it marked a radical discontinuity in experience. "We knew the world would not be the same."[30] This is how Oppenheimer recalled the rupture that the bomb caused for him and others. Trinity was a point of discontinuity for those who saw it and Hiroshima marked the appearance of "an unsettling new cultural factor," a factor that "transformed . . . the fundamental ground of culture and consciousness."[31] The stories that emerged tried to fit this fundamental discontinuity into the stable, narrative continuity of history. For some the bomb became a beginning, the beginning of a new age in which people must willfully and purposefully reformulate their relationships to technology, to one another, to their deaths, and so on. For others, the bomb was an ending, the terminus of three hundred years of physics as Hans Bethe once put it to Oppenheimer, or the end of a progressive era of reason and sanity. For others it was a logical development in the business of war, one more incremental step up the ladder of destructive capability. For virtually everyone, it was something that had to be placed somewhere in some narrative structure.

The bomb is a device that sets everything in motion. It homogenizes. It is the ultimate boundary-breaching device, a keen reflection of the new logic to which the bomb is tied. It would be easy to say our stories become our defense against this new device. It is more accurate to say that our stories give definition to that which threatens to obliterate all definition. The challenge is to understand where these stories leave their tellers.

FINDING CONTINUITIES

There are many kinds of stories about the bomb. They all serve to provide some continuity through the historical discontinuity that the bomb was.

The previous chapter discussed the difficulty of attributing responsibility when systems make people their agents. But a narrative that names the people deemed responsible for violence is one way to provide continuity through the disruptions of the violence. The bomb may have marked a discontinuity, but, this narrative form would go, people had made the bomb, and so, the bomb can be accounted for by the history of people's thoughts, their cleverness, their decisions and their actions.

Perhaps the most radical statement of this view came from the French writer Andre Malraux during a dinner conversation with Haakon Chevalier in September 1954, following Oppenheimer's security hearing. Malraux had met Oppenheimer during his and Kitty Oppenheimer's visit with Chevalier the previous December. Malraux had been as impressed by Oppenheimer as most people were. At this dinner Chevalier told Malraux of what he called Oppenheimer's "impotence" at his hearing. Malraux was intrigued. He said, "The trouble was, he accepted his accusers' terms from the beginning. He should not have allowed them to shift the battle to their ground, where they were sure to destroy him. . . . He should have just told them at the very outset, *'Je suis la bombe atomique!'* "[32]

Malraux's *post hoc* counsel assumes that authority rests with the person and retains the relative continuity that the person enjoys. It assumes that the life of the expert has a continuity and integrity even if the history that unfolds around that life does not. Oppenheimer was for Malraux, and many others, an overwhelming figure. Many people wanted Oppenheimer to assert his responsibility in a place where he had, in fact, none. For Chevalier Oppenheimer was "a towering intellectual giant, . . . a model of moral rectitude." He knew Oppenheimer to be

> a sage who, by the vastness of his culture, by his profound humanism, by his love of humanity, by the power of his personality and his gift of persuasion could, and very possibly would, on the occasion of some future international crisis involving the fate of mankind, tip the scales in favor of life rather than of death.[33]

The great man, who was the atomic bomb, remained great if he would have but asserted his greatness, according to this narrative account that people constructed on Oppenheimer's behalf. The greatness that led him to make the bomb could be relied upon to unmake, in good Newtonian fashion, its effects. Chevalier's is not the portrait of an "idiot," a man alone without the connections in civic associations he would need to be able to continue in his greatness. Robb's extraction of Oppenheimer's admission of his idiocy was devastating to those who wanted Oppenheimer, the man they had invented for themselves, to remain himself, comparable in stature to the device he had "fathered." *"Je suis la bombe atomique!"* would have preserved the old order. It would have assured everyone that responsible people might continue to be responsible. It would have sustained a fantasy that is valuable in our new age.

The impulse to narrativize often aims at different levels of analysis than the personal, but the same function—the function of providing continuity through a disruption—is served. If the man whose extraordinariness in the moral realm accounted for the discontinuity was, perhaps, driven to acknowledge acts that were "out of character" with that extraordinariness, something else must be operating to effect such an act and to extract such an admission. Some narrative forms focus attention on factors that cause men of extraordinary character to act, for the moment, out of character. Philip Stern, for example, takes his cue for the construction of an account from a comment by the Gray Board's chairman. Gray said in his summation that even though Oppenheimer was the object of their investigation it was the security system of the United States that was on trial in 1954. Stern makes a case that the security system was the factor that led to Oppenheimer's out-of-character acts that led to the bomb. Under a narrative account of this sort, one need not lower one's estimation of the great man from whose abilities the past was fashioned and on whose (continuing) abilities the future might depend. The great man remains great. It is the system that would tarnish his greatness that is corrupt. And that corruption of the system can be located by historian narrativizers like Stern at the end of the causal chains of history that included Senator McCarthy's activities, that included a change in public opinion about those who had built the bomb, that included a change in the status of the scientist in political circles.[34] Stern's story sees the security system as the essential menace that stands in the way of good works by extraordinary men like Oppenheimer. Stern's story accounts, at least in part, for the continuation of evil in the post-bomb world and implies that if the causes of the *aberration* that the security system is were controlled, the progressive sanity of the past enacted through the great people of the past or through their contemporary counterparts might be reinstated. This narrative form, of course, is at odds with the view, probably held by Oppenheimer, that the security system, like the Holocaust, might mark an advance in culture, but the principals' views are sometimes not important to those in need of narrative.

Oppenheimer provided his own form of continuity through the silencing effect of Trinity. Actually, he provided two loosely linked stories that gave the bomb a place in history, one based in Bohr's concerns for openness and one based on a historical notion of the place of the expert in a democratic society. Both emphasized not the greatness or the moral and humane qualities of a man or even several men but relied instead on a faith in the reasonableness of people generally.

"What the expert does for society—and the scientist is a good example—is to increase knowledge—the techniques of knowledge—and the power to control the natural world. . . . It is not his function to make the choice [of how knowledge and technique are to be used], but to define and illuminate it." In a democracy, this story, with its echoes from Szilard through Kemeny's thoughts on the place of experts following Three Mile Island, says the continuing wisdom of the people provides the continuity. Particular men and women, good or evil, great or not, may come and go, but the people, the *demos*, will remain. The choices of a citizenry are historical constants and history is written in terms of those factors that block and those factors that facilitate the democratic exercise of an informed choice. This is a popular narrative form for providing continuity over the long haul of this "certain modernity."

Several of Oppenheimer's speeches in the years immediately following the war express his concern that the secrecy in which the construction of the bomb was conducted not be continued, that people in all nations be given access to the information they needed to understand the extent and the character of "the new powers, the new alternatives, of an advancing mastery of nature"[35] that science had provided. "Change is permanent" was the rhetorical device Oppenheimer used to bridge the past to the post-war present: "When it went off, in the New Mexico dawn, that first atomic bomb, we thought of Alfred Nobel, and his hope, that dynamite would put an end to wars. . . . We knew that it was a new world, but even more we knew that novelty was itself a very old thing in human life, that all our ways are rooted in it." One cannot prevent change, Oppenheimer's narrative ran, but there is a very real threat that the development of an understanding of change by the many would be blocked by the few.

> *We were concerned . . . that these weapons, which would we knew some day be a possibility, should be manifest to all men to see and understand, that they might know what future war would be, that they might bring to bear this knowledge, and the insight that derives from it, in shaping their ways. It would not have been a better world if the unrealized possibility of these terrible weapons had been a secret shadow on our future.*[36]

If government is open with its people and the people are permitted to know the true nature of the weapons the experts could not help but enable to come from their organic necessity, then all will (probably) be well. This historical narrative is written not in terms of impediments to the actions of a few good men but in terms of impediments to general understanding and in terms of the democratic education of the populace.

Oppenheimer's concern for openness came directly from Bohr. Bohr extended his notion of complementarity at the atomic level to an understanding of the atomic bomb itself. The bomb was *both* a peril and a hope as Oppenheimer, playing his Plato to Bohr's Socrates, put it in his Los Alamos speech of November 1945:

> *It is clear to me that wars have changed. . . . I think the advent of the atomic bomb and the facts that will get around that they are not too hard to make, that they will be universal if people wish to make them universal, that they will not constitute a real drain on the economy of any strong nation, and that their power of destruction will grow and is already incomparably greater than that of any other weapon—I think these things create a new situation. . . . The point is that atomic weapons constitute . . . a field, a new field, and a new opportunity for realizing preconditions. I think when people talk of the fact that this is not only a great peril, but a great hope, this is what they should mean. . . . [They should mean that] in this field, because it is a threat, because it is a peril, and because it has certain characteristics, . . . there exists a possibility of realizing, of beginning to realize, those changes which are needed if there is to be any peace.*[37]

In Bohr's view, the bomb's power would either become the great equalizer *qua* leveler by destroying everyone, everything, every nation with absolute equality, or the bomb's light would illuminate existing inequalities, it would open the secrets of the international order to the view of all, and would thereby set the stage for the improvement of humanity. The novelty of the situation created by the bomb could, in Bohr's words to President Roosevelt, "offer a unique opportunity of appealing to an unprejudiced attitude, and it would appear that an understanding about this vital matter might contribute most favorably towards the settlement of other problems where history and traditions have fostered divergent viewpoints." Bohr insisted that only "the free access to information" could set the stage for the solution of the many problems the post-war world faced. His memo to Roosevelt concluded,

> it need hardly be stressed how fortunate in every respect it would be if, at the same time as the world will know of the formidable destructive power which has come into human hands, it would be told that the great scientific and technical advance has been helpful in creating a solid foundation for a future peaceful cooperation among nations.[38]

Bohr was not given to a strict Cartesianism nor was he one to shy away from paradox. That the bomb could be the solution to the problem it is was not an unacceptable conclusion to the man who declared the laws of classical physics inoperable at the atomic level.

In Bohr's scheme the bomb became a beginning to a new narrative. His dialectical story placed the bomb at the start of a new history. People around Bohr were swept up by this view and their accounts of their reactions to the bomb reflect Bohr's sensibilities, sensibilities that admitted seeming confusions or contradictions. Robert Wilson, for example, recalls his two "almost simultaneous" reactions to the Trinity explosion. His first was one of relief that the job of the scientists was now complete. The second "was one of horror at what we had done and at what such a bomb could do." These reactions, he says, made him appreciate completely "the kind of responsibility that Bohr had so perceptively been preaching about." The lives of some of the scientists "changed gears almost immediately" as they began the mobilization they hoped would lead to an international control of atomic weapons.[39] If history had started anew, people's actions had to conform to the new narrative. People will have to "change gears" and begin life anew, with a new *aufklärung*.

From its starting point at Trinity, this narrative of the emergence of an embryonic morality and of a sense of responsibility is constructed in terms of clouded consciousnesses—Oppenheimer's "selling out" to the side of power against the urgings of his scientific colleagues, for example—and in terms of missed opportunities like that of the U.N. conference. In an interview Oppenheimer suggested that the postwar era was the result of one major missed opportunity, the failure to choose the narrative plot that led to peace at the precise moment that the story opened. The interviewer asked Oppenheimer, "[Can you tell us] what your thoughts are about the proposal of Senator Robert Kennedy that President Johnson initiate talks with the view to halt the spread of nuclear weapons?" He responded, "It's twenty years too late. It should have been done the day after Trinity."[40] The story is also written in terms of diplomats and statesmen misreading Bohr's message as a call for an all-or-nothing solution to the problem of atomic weapons and refusing to adopt a strategy of incrementalism that would build trust in a world that Bohr realized would probably remain less than totally open. Even Richard Rhodes was captivated by Bohr's view and concludes his fine history of these events with an appeal that we should all rediscover the virtues of Bohr's open world.

Oppenheimer is reported to have tried to mount one other narrative and to involve President Truman in it. This story, if true, would be a sophomoric twist on the "great man" narratives. It is reported that Dean Acheson took Oppenheimer to see Truman so that the President might persuade Oppenheimer to help Bernard Baruch plan for the United States' participation in the United Nations Atomic Energy Commission. Oppenheimer, recall, was bothered by Baruch's appointment. He expressed his disappointment to the President and "suddenly he blurted out, 'Mr. President, I have blood on my hands.'" Some people say Truman offered Oppenheimer a handkerchief so that he might wipe them. Peter Goodchild says only that the President later told Acheson never to bring Oppenheimer to the White House again. "After all, all he did was make the bomb. I'm the guy who fired it off,"[41] Truman is reported to have said. Oppenheimer was trying to involve Truman in a story of "evil in our time." The efforts of great men lead to evil if those efforts are not implemented with wisdom, this story usually goes. Oppenheimer was opening the way for the President to engage in acts of ablution, but Truman did not rise to the bait. His history was written more in terms of Oppenheimer's own experts-in-society story but with an emphasis on the independence of elected representatives from the entreaties of the experts.

Oppenheimer's view that experts ought to remain independent of political considerations has retained its currency. Some scientists have accepted it as a narrative that enables them to continue work in the weapons field. Robin Crews, a sociologist, interviewed seventy-three physicists who received the Ph.D. in physics in 1983. He divided his sample into fifty-three "weapons scientists," people who either worked in defense related jobs or in weapons research or would do so in the future, and twenty "non-weapons scientists." Crews concludes, "there is a positive correlation between belief in the values of the traditional image of science [as objective, value neutral, non-social] and participation in weapons or defense related research." For Crews the traditional image of science is "a metaphor that has become confused with reality." Those who embrace it are delusional,[42] still of clouded consciousness. But they are in good historical company. If this is a metaphor, then it is a sustaining metaphor, and while it may be helpful to point out the "error" in which these young scientists persist, I think it is more helpful to recognize the service done by these narrative structures, both for those who invoke them and for the rest of us who hear them.

All of these narrative forms serve the same double function. At once they provide a bridge across an event that people experienced as fundamentally disruptive and discontinuous and they close off the event from the lives it threatens by locating it at a precise, unchanging point in some history or other. Narratives complicate in order to explain. They tie together human talents, wills, and desires with moral notions of individual responsibility, duty, and the overarching categories of good and evil into structures that highlight certain lines of reason, reasonableness, and truth in order to account for the simple fact that Oppenheimer stated so simply: "we have made a thing, a most terrible weapon."[43]

Through their explanations, these narrative structures develop a "redemptive discourse," as Bauman calls it (see the footnote on page 183). They seek to apprehend those forces—human forces and structural forces—that helped create the "thing" and they outline the dynamic operations of these forces. They serve up the fantastic image that, in a Newtonian way, those forces, once harnessed, could be used to reverse the processes that led to the creation of the thing, or at least they hold out the promise that these forces might be directed to attenuate the thing's effects. If the bomb is a product of human prowess, then human prowess can be marshalled against the bomb. Alternatively, these narratives locate redemption in the logical structure of the narrative itself. The bomb will either obliterate us all or it will save us from itself. Regardless of its form, a narrative focuses our attention on certain factors and forces and encourages us not to look elsewhere and everywhere for the presence of a device that is so pervasive as to be considered, without being hyperbolic, the grounding of any characterization of our time.

By focusing our attention on those forces and factors that promise a measure of control and mastery, our fascination with the bomb itself is necessarily invigorated. The scientists grasped the nature of nature and created the bomb which, when set off, is uncontrollable, and that sparks no small measure of fascination. As Freeman Dyson put it,

> *I have felt it myself. The glitter of nuclear weapons. . . . To perform these miracles—to lift a million tons of rock into the sky. It is something that gives people an illusion of illimitable power and it is . . . this, what you might call technical arrogance that overcomes people when they see what they can do with their minds.*[44]

The power of the promise that you can master the very power of nature is compelling. That promise, though, is empty now for we are in the realm of management, not mastery.

Perhaps we can forgive the arrogance of those who developed the thing itself, but those of us who come after the bomb's originators and who tell our bomb stories are more arrogant still. We—both those who construct their narratives in the name of advocacy and those who use them for critique—are, in effect, imagining controlling the uncontrollable, limiting the illimitable, and we double the technical arrogance experienced by the scientists. In the construction of narrative accounts one experiences the glitter of a power more powerful than these devices of the greatest power. The promise of redemption that is embedded in the narratives that account for the bomb seduce one into the very logic of the bomb itself. As Coetzee might put it, there is something tawdry in following the logic this way.

MORALITIES AND THE CRITICS

To be able to construct an interesting narrative there must be some dark and unknown space which only the story will, eventually and in its own good time, illuminate. A narrative must have an ending that gives meaning to all the strange circumstances that come before. Conversely, all the little events of a narrative must point unerringly toward the end. Apocalyptic ends make for good moralities. If a narrative convinces us that our actions are aimed toward a particularly unacceptable end, then that narrative might persuade us to rethink the strange circumstances we are living day to day and redirect our actions toward some other end. Some narratives beget moralities and their accompanying moralists. Novelist Tim O'Brien has terrorist Sarah confront William Cowling, anti-hero of The Nuclear Age, with: "Nixon was sweet. Oppenheimer was sweeter. Einstein—sweetest old geezer who ever lived." Cowling replies, "Yes, but Einstein warned us," to which Sarah snaps, "That's how sweet he was! Invents the end of the world, then sounds the alarm," as she drifts into a reverie.[45] The sweet old guys who invented the end of the world made it possible for their stories to have a moral. They were laying the ground for the development of moralities from which we might all learn how to live our lives. Instead of a narrative that holds out the promise of mastery and redemption, theirs are stories full of moral imperatives that tell one how to structure one's life and imagination in this new age.

It is not surprising that physicians would mount the first major collective effort, following the atomic scientists, against the bomb. Physicians are our premier narrativizers, who encourage us to understand a life in terms of "life course trajectories" and a death as "the final stage of growth," and who hold out the promise of a "good death" if we live according to the narrative plots for a good life that medical science maps.[46] Physicians for Social Responsibility (PSR) began in Boston in 1961. That small group of medical doctors was concerned primarily with the effects of atmospheric tests of nuclear weapons. Their initial efforts involved the publication of two essays, one on the likely effects, human and ecological, of a nuclear attack on the United States and the other on "The Physician's Role in the Post-Attack Period."[47]

The tactics of writings such as those produced by Physicians for Social Responsibility are familiar by now. These experts will out-expert other experts in the hopes of turning members of the educated public into experts themselves. There are always the famous contour charts showing levels of devastation at various distances from a hypothetical nuclear blast. There are the elongated contours showing radiation dosages from the blast and from drifting fallout coupled with the graphs, to which Slotin's personalized "experiment" contributed much, showing the relationship between radiation dose and the probability of dying from that dose.

After the reinvigoration of Physicians for Social Responsibility in 1979, their writings followed the path that medical logic had cleared. Medical textbooks and practices expanded the medical domain from the strictly physiological to the social and psychological dimensions of disease (and thence into "wellness").[48] In their turn, PSR began to sponsor papers on the "psycho-social trauma" of living with nuclear weapons in our collective cultural background as well as on the physical and environmental effects of nuclear explosions. Following the logic of systems theory, which had become the basis for medical work after mid-century, these experts even started exploring the rather distant and multiply mediated relations between spending on defense and the money that might otherwise be available for spending on health care and disease prevention. They were becoming, as they had to become under the regime of systems, specialists in the general.

All of this group's work is organized in the idiom of medical expertise even though their work branches across traditional academic disciplines. One collection of papers, for example, is structured like a report on a clinical encounter. There are the "symptoms"—a review of the muted anxiety and the rush to spend ever more on defense, the "causes"—an assessment of the "strategic capabilities" of world powers, and of the "pathogenesis" of imaginable explosions, the "prognosis"—the effects on individuals and essays on the encompassing vision of a nuclear winter, and the "treatment." "The baton in the relay race against a nuclear Armageddon is being passed from physicist to physician," writes Bernard Lown. Why? Because

> the physicians' analysis is precise, clinical and exorcises the mystifying verbiage, Manichean oversimplifications and sanitized statistics of the strategic experts. The physicians' movement is compelled by a growing conviction that nuclear war is the number one health threat and perhaps constitutes the final epidemic for which the only remedy is prevention.

And physicians are schooled in the constructions of complex narrative accounts of all facts as they are known.

The modern would-be critic of nuclear armament tries both to be precise and clinical and also to put a human face on the potential destructiveness of the weapons. "Many people recognize in some way and at some level that the continuation of the nuclear arms race is a threat to the survival of civilization, nothing less—maybe even . . . to the survival of the human species," says Lester Grinspoon. He continues that while "it is easy to repeat such words. . . , the difficult thing is to make ourselves feel what we know and determine our actions by it." Knowledge of the effects of nuclear weapons, effectively assimilated, "demands that we redirect our lives in small and large ways."[50] In contrast to Gertrude Stein, who said she "had not been able to take any interest in the bomb. Surely it will kill a lot, but it's the living that are interesting, not the way of killing them,"[51] Physicians for Social Responsibility and others who have followed their efforts are trying, we might say, to make the bomb interesting, to get us all interested, and move us to do the right thing.

It would be a little foolish to argue that doing the right thing is wrong, but we may examine the effects of so many people agreeing that now is the time to do the right thing and doing it. The physicians' morality is a powerful organizer. In this case, it has organized the opposition well. We can say without irony that the opposition to nuclear build-up is a classical democratic movement (so long as we do not confuse "classical" with "ideal"). As William Connolly puts it in *Politics and Ambiguity*, "Democracy makes the state accountable to the people; . . . it encourages a healthy skepticism toward rules, authority, laws, experts, and regulations; it enables skeptical citizens to curtail governmental officials bent upon a destructive course." But along with this critical aspect comes an incorporative thrust. Every contemporary theory of democratic practice has in common with every other theory, Connolly says, an "ontology of concord." "Each [theory] assumes that when properly constituted and situated the individual or collective subject achieves harmony with itself and with the other elements of social life." There is no room for ambiguity. Even criticism—perhaps especially criticism—must be mounted in terms of dominant, endorsed, recognized discourses so that the legitimacy of an argument or an opposing position might be fairly judged. "The humanist critics of repressive politics and the overt agents of coercive control are . . . Siamese twins. . . . These twin strategies function together (behind the backs of intellectuals who constitute them as oppositional) to extend the tentacles of order more deeply into the self."[52]

Confrontations of the state with its radical opponents are rarer now that confrontation has shown itself to be a blunt instrument. Police now arrive at demonstrations critical of the state not in riot gear with clubs swinging; they arrive causally dressed and with video cameras. How nice, we can hear them saying, that the opposition has become so loyal that it too organizes photo opportunities. And, in their turn, critics always film everyone with a camera in case some of them turn out to be from the police. There is a certain equivalence effected in all this.

Both the expert nuclear warriors and expert critics of nuclear war serve the same pedagogical purpose. The elaborators of nuclear winter and other end- or near-end-of-the-world scenarios give the anxiety felt by so many moderns an object, a focus. We are assured by the good doctors of both types on both sides that our anxiety is justified. Look at tables and graphs and grasp the meaning, the human meaning, of your concern! Then you will be able to understand the ambiguous feelings of unease that pervade life. And if you are moved to speak against anxiety, here are the terms in which to cast that speech. Use your imaginations, but imagine *this*. Such are the instructions we regularly receive from our expert instructors who fancy themselves critics. One may join the opposition but like all loyal oppositions this one requires the payment of dues and the carrying of cards. Helen Caldicott and Carl Sagan are only part of a long line of intellectuals who serve as our modern "therapeutic authorities" who "first translate our dreams, wishes, and anxieties into clinical vocabularies [the vocabularies of elongated contour charts and dose-fatality curves] and then hand them back to us as officially prescribed avenues to freedom."[53] They will take our fears, make them rational, and then permit us all to become part of *their* body count at the massings of the opposition in appropriately monumental cities.

But what is the nature of this opposition? The language of the opposition is not fundamentally different from the language of the strategic experts themselves. It is little wonder that Physicians for Social Responsibility receives "hundreds" of requests for reprints from the Department of Defense, as they tell us they do. In addition to organizing the opposition, firming the terms of the debate, and bring-ing all the critics out into the light of a brilliant New York day for an orderly march and moving speeches, they are providing data and analyses useful to the Department, essential data in the calculus of strategy and warfare. Critic and expert meld together, and, just as Siamese twins threaten the common-sense notion of "individuality," the meeting of minds that has occurred on the terms of debate and the rules of relevance threatens the very notions of "criticism" and "opposition."

The equivalence of expert critic and expert advocate makes soci-ological arguments about the authority of experts, or about the re-lationship between expertise and influence, or other normative arguments about the proper and "necessary" relationship between expertise and the political arena, seem a little meretricious and su-perficial. At least these arguments are premature. Ought one to be a more or less willing servant of the state or should one's expertise manifest itself in thoughtful criticism? This is the choice that socio-logical experts tell us that experts face. But these are one in the same question. They are simply two sides of the one question, to what should one be loyal and how should that loyalty be expressed? In all the moralizing about the bomb, in Oppenheimer's efforts to achieve rational, international control over atomic energy, in the guilt-ridden hand wringing over Hiroshima, in the PSR material on how to talk properly to critique well, we can hear only varied efforts to find the proper means by which to express one's loyalty. All these rhetorical efforts are attempts to help one find one's place in systems that make experts their agents and in which all ultimately serve those systems and the structures of power they deploy. In a world where proper talk is structured by systems of expertise or by *their subsystem* of criticism, where the choice is between being an expert expert or an expert critic, I am inclined to share that "deeply lodged suspicion of the times . . . that events and individuals are unreal, and that the power to alter the course of the age, of my life and your life, is actually vested nowhere."[54] I am inclined to take the advice of Javitt, "this man who never existed," one of whose aphorisms was, "Be disloyal. It's your duty to the human race. The human race needs survival and it's the loyal man who dies first from anxiety or a bullet or overwork. If you have to earn a living, boy, and the price they make you pay is loyalty, be a double agent—and never let either of the two sides know your real name."[55]

Twenty years after the Trinity test, Oppenheimer wrote an article for the *Washington Post* called "Alpha or Omega was 20 Years Ago." Next to the text was a picture of the mushroom-shaped cloud over which was imposed remarks from two observers. The first was by William Laurence, the press representative at the test who wrote, "One felt as though one were present at the moment of creation when God said: 'Let there be light.'" The other was from George Kistia-kowsky: "I am sure that at the end of the world—in the last milli-seconds of the earth's existence—the last man will see what we have just seen." Oppenheimer's article was a rehearsal of his peril-and-a-hope idea. He wrote of the scientists' increased attention, as the war wound down, to "the peril and the hope that our work would bring to human history: the peril of these weapons and their almost in-evitable vast increase; and the hope of limiting and avoiding war, and of new patterns and institutions of international cooperation, insight and understanding." His assessment after twenty years was that little had changed since he had first offered this characterization of the new situation: "The last two decades have been shadowed by danger, ever changing, never really receding. Looking to the future, I see again no ground for confidence; but I do see hope." Then, in conclu-sion, he wrote, "it is not the mood of hope, but hope itself, that is part of our life, and thus part of our duty. We are . . . testing whether men can both preserve and enlarge life without war as the great arbiter of history. This we knew early in the morning of July 16, 20 years ago."[56]

Oppenheimer was, like most commentators since 1945, trying to locate the bomb in some narrative structure. He was making it either a beginning or an ending in order to accord Trinity its place. There is something forced about this strategy, however, and throughout Oppenheimer's writing and speeches, we can sense the tension as he struggles to be as good a maker of meaning as he was a maker of bombs. The struggle is especially clear in 1962 as he tried to recall for General Groves how he came to the name "Trinity" for the test. He remembers two John Donne poems that may have been on his mind, but beyond that, he says, he does not have a clue about the origin of the name. But the name is apt and metaphorically forceful. The test was neither a beginning nor an end, not an alpha *or* an omega, as the *Post* would have it. Trinity was and is both at once, beginning and end. It is that which defies narrative, that about which many stories are told but none can capture. To know how to live, to develop a morality for our time, we probably have to construct narratives that give the bomb a place in our history and our lives and develop a little loyalty to whatever they require. But maybe Oppenheimer knew more than he knew as he gave the first bomb the name of an enigma, veiled, tempting, ultimately impenetrable.

FAILED NARRATIVES

We act as if we must come to grips with the bomb. We must formulate an understanding. At least intellectuals must, for it is their duty. But in the era of complex systems, where the critic is indistinguishable from the able advocate, where responsibility and power are vested nowhere, where moralities serve their systems, I want, somewhat in line with Bersani, to celebrate certain failures. It is the failure to grasp, the failure to appreciate, the failure to construct a narrative account of the bomb, the failure to engage our interests that interests me. In response to the deathly silence of the bomb, we have a history of labored silences that merits attention without turning that attention into an attempt to fill those silences with various narrative truths.

Narratives that put the bomb in its place, from the dialectics of Bohr and Oppenheimer to the charts and graphs of Physicians for Social Responsibility, have an institutional locus. Even if some of them are intended to help us put a human face on the phenomenon of our time, they are not narratives that occur on a human scale or have a human appeal. The failure of these stories to find a human locus is reflected, first, in the appeal to myths that many of the scientists made to express something of their personal situation.

Oppenheimer, for example, invoked the myth of Prometheus to describe his feelings and the feelings of some of his colleagues at Trinity: "We thought of the legend of Prometheus, of that deep sense of guilt in man's new powers, that reflects his recognition of evil, and his long knowledge of it."[57] Or he interpreted the actions of the scientists through the ancient language of sinfulness, a language that proffers an understanding of human essence, not a social-psychological or pseudo-physical explanation of human behavior. He had said during an address at MIT that the physicists had "known sin" and this was a knowledge difficult to lose. When asked to explain this comment he said, "We were all aware of the fact that we in one way or another were intervening explicitly and heavy-handedly in the course of human history; that is not for a physicist a natural professional activity. . . . That's the sin of pride."[58]

Freeman Dyson relied on the legend of Faust:

> *The Faustian bargain is when you sell your soul to the devil in exchange for knowledge and power. That, of course, in a way is what Oppenheimer did. There's no doubt. He made this alliance with the United States Army, in the person of General Groves, who gave him undreamed-of resources—huge armies of people and as much money as he could possibly spend—in order to do physics on the grand scale, in order to create this marvelous weapon. And it was a Faustian bargain if ever there was one. And of course we are still living with it. Once you sell your soul to the devil, there's no going back on it.*[59]

Others, including Oppenheimer's brother Frank Oppenheimer, conjured the image of a Frankenstein monster that held its maker in its grasp:

> *Amazing how the technology tools trap one. They're so powerful. . . . I was impressed because most of the sort of fervor for developing the bomb came as a kind of anti-fascist fervor against Germany. But when V-E day came along, nobody slowed up. . . . We all kept working. And it wasn't because we understood the significance against Japan. It was because the machinery had caught us in its trap and we were anxious to get this thing to go.*[60]

All the popular myths of our time have been mustered in vain attempts to give human meaning to this event that occurred on a scale unimaginable to human beings.

Some argue that myths are explanations of last resort in the modern era, metaphorical reconstructions of situations that cannot be described in the language of linear causality on which our culture chiefly relies.[61] But this reasoning is reductive. It forces myth to fit the needs of a people dependent on explanations that apprehend cause-and-effect relations that imaginably might be used to redeem us. Myths are not conventional narratives. They are stories without context and without closure. They describe a situation but they open up the future. They are without redeeming effect even though a particular myth may hold out the promise of redemption. The myths the scientists used to describe their situation do not point backward and highlight certain lines of causality that brought them to the place they find themselves. The myths do not locate the scientists and their works at a particular place in the technological and socio-political landscape of the mid-twentieth century. The scientists' myths described with elegance the inherent simplicity of the situation in which these men found themselves and from which they were bound by their existence to move on unencumbered. The record shows that part of their "moving on" involved encumbering themselves with narrative explanations of their accomplishments, their feelings, their guilt, and so on. But narrative activity is different from a description that gains one nothing in the way of prescriptive knowledge.

The nature of the difference between a narrative constructed to explain and to begin to master a phenomenon like the bomb, on the one hand, and a mythic response, on the other, is illustrated by the general artistic response to the bomb. Narratives are neat. They tidy up an event. They let one know what is important and worthy of one's attention. They also provide a measure of closure by sealing an event in its history and by suggesting how the event is to be dealt with. The general artistic response to the bomb has not been so neat. There has been no closure as even some artists have hoped for. Artists have not been able to capture the bomb and pin it to a place and time, often to their own dismay. Their subject has remained pervasive and evasive. The bomb keeps opening up those artistic spaces that narrative renderings would close off.

Robert Lifton has described in considerable detail the difficulty some Japanese artists have had in using the bomb as a subject for their art. Lifton himself even has some difficulty finding ways to write about the difficulties of the artists. One of the most awkward sections in his unusually well-written *Death in Life* comes as he tries to suggest that the artistic "failures" of the Japanese are, in fact, "successful" and in some sense "useful" artistic efforts. He tries to link the artistic response to "an overwhelming historical experience" and to "the question of mastery." "In Hiroshima," Lifton writes,

> the relationship between the quality or popularity of artistic works and the degree of collective mastery is imprecise and difficult to evaluate. But an important relationship does exist. For these works are special

distillations of group psychic response, and in the accomplishments and
failures can both reflect that response and profoundly influence it.[62]

Lifton is fighting to find success in failure. He is fighting the battle
of the narrative accountant who must, for whatever reason, bring the
bomb to account.

In fact, Lifton finds himself writing mostly of artistic "failures."
One of his informants told him that the bomb was "an alien object
removed from human beings," an object that seemed to have no
"special significance" in the ordinary world of ordinary men and women.
The scale of destructiveness led one person to recall, "One was not
allowed to have his own way of dying but was simply annihilated
with everyone else." "What [this writer] could not emotionally absorb
or creatively transform," Lifton comments, "was the massive anonymity and the *irrelevance* of A-bomb deaths. Unable to relate these
deaths to any cosmology or vision of human continuity, he (and A-
bomb writers in general) could not render them either dramatic or
tragic."[63]

There was considerable debate in Japan about how the bomb should
be represented and about whether it should be represented at all.
Lifton recalls that a Hiroshima newspaper article in 1953 called on
writers not to single out the bomb for special literary attention: "Now
that seven years have passed, isn't it about time to stop writing in
this fashion and instead to deal with the more essential things of life?"
Lifton notes that the author of this plea was very close to one of
Coetzee's "options," the option that comes "close to advocating that
Hiroshima's unique history be totally ignored," of ignoring the horrors of the state. In the debate that followed the publication of this
article, however, "just about everything that could be said about A-
bomb literature was said . . . but this did not necessarily produce any
A-bomb literature." The debate went through all the options—making
the bomb stand for evil, finding the responsible people and making
them be responsible, looking at the effects of the bomb from the
victims' points of view, looking at the bomb from a political point of
view. But in the end, the "A-bomb literature was meaningless."[64]

Essential meaninglessness did not stifle the meaning-making apparatus, though. But the stunning feature in the instant case is the
failure of that usually successful mechanism. People in Japanese culture continued their attempts to construct narratives for precisely the

same reason the scientists and others here did. They wanted to penetrate to the meaning of the event, place the bomb in history, and provide continuity through an irrevocable rupture. One writer, reflecting on the situation of the artists generally, began, "None of my work goes deep enough," as if the effects of the bomb had an interior that could be apprehended by narrative.

> At the beginning I tried to give an objective presentation of misery.
> Then I realized that I couldn't just dwell on the past, but had to connect
> the past with the future. Then, as a means of dealing with the future, I
> became interested in communism. . . . And then I realized that social
> institutions were not everything and that we must consider what goes
> on in individual human lives.

And yet, after running the course from the misery of the past to a redemptive, humane vision of the future, this writer, Kokubo by name, remained trapped in the dilemma experienced by artists who rely on the bomb for their material. As put by Lifton, he heard "voices which sometimes insist that he must create from the atomic bomb and sometimes that he has no right to do so; which sometimes suggest that the death-saturated Hiroshima environment confers special powers upon him and sometimes that it inflicts him with a debilitating curse."[65] The creative response, in its efforts to give human meaning to the bomb, was suspended between these poles.

Paul Boyer documents a similar creative response to the bomb on this side of the Pacific. "Apart from a few isolated voices," he says, "the initial literary response to the atomic bomb was, to say the least, muted." There were, of course, calls to artistic action and a few tentative attempts to capture the meaning of this new event by polishing up old works so that they showed a gleam of prophecy or by trying to focus on some human aspect of this event, an event that impressed people from those in the Enola Gay through the present day as fundamentally impersonal and lacking of human content. Boyer summarizes the American reaction to the bomb by noting that American artists faced the same question the Japanese struggled with:

> What was the appropriate aesthetic for the bomb? If an air raid on a
> small Spanish town could inspire one of Picasso's greatest canvases, or
> the individual brutalities of Napoleon's invasion of Spain Goya's most
> powerful work, how was one to respond imaginatively to Hiroshima and

Nagasaki and, still more, to the prospect of world holocaust? The question haunted writers in 1945, and it would continue to do so. As one linguistic specialist asked in 1965: "Is it possible that in spite of our vast and ever-growing vocabulary we have finally created an object that transcends all possible description?"[66]

Boyer titles his survey of the literary response to the bomb, "Words Fail."

Boyer is quite taken with a work by James Agee called "Dedication Day." This "rough sketch for a moving picture" depicts the dedication of a new monument in Washington, D.C., in the spring of 1946. To be dedicated is the Arch, a Frank Lloyd Wright work made of "fused uranium." The dignitaries assemble, the bands play, the speeches are spoken, and this dedication becomes a little more earnest than most because "it was not clear either to the speakers or the listeners precisely why or to what purpose or idea the Arch had been raised and was to be dedicated." Nothing is clarified as Dedication Day climaxes with the unveiling of the inscription on the Arch. With much pomp, the curtain drops to reveal the appropriately indefinite words "THIS IS IT." There is no human meaning that anyone can attach to this new creation.

Below ground, under the Arch, a complementary drama plays out in Agee's effort to put human beings into this story. There American disabled soldiers, all winners of military decorations, labor on one twelve-hour shift while "depreciated but surviving [Japanese] collaborators in the experiments at Hiroshima and Nagasaki" work the other shift manufacturing the Eternal Fuse which rises through the middle of the Arch. These Keepers of the Flame, as the laborers are called, are joined by "one of the more elderly of those scientists who contributed their genius towards the perfecting of the bomb," one who had gone "a little queer in the head." As he works with the war heroes and the Japanese survivors his derangement increases so much that he is eventually told that "his services . . . would no longer be required, and that he had his choice of lifelong residence and treatment, gratis, in whatever sanitarium in the nation he might prefer." This announcement brings him, apparently, to his senses, and he asks that he be allowed on Dedication Day to throw the switch that would set the Eternal Fuse rolling and hissing. We are told that neither Einstein nor Lise Meitner were available for this job so the honor had finally been offered to Leslie Groves. Groves withdraws in favor of the scientist who elects to remain underground during the ceremonies. Shortly after the festivities the old scientist is found dead by his own hand next to the Fuse's spool. He has a note pinned to his jacket saying that his death was obligatory and was meant to endow the monument with "special significance," the human significance, perhaps, that the monument to "THIS IS IT" did not have—indeed, could not have— previously. After much hand-wringing and lesson-learning from this "pathetic incident," the scientist is buried at Ground Zero in New Mexico, where "this gifted scientist, and his colleagues, first saw the light of the New Age." Agee concludes,

> *For misguided and altogether regrettable though his last days were—a sad warning indeed to those who turn away from the dictates of reason, and accept human progress reluctantly—he was nevertheless, perhaps, our last link with a not-too-distant past in which such conceptions as those of "atonement," and "guilt," and "individual responsibility," still had significance.*[67]

Boyer calls Agee's story "tantalizingly incomplete." Indeed, at an institutional level, at the level of providing a narrative understanding, there is no terminus to the piece. Agee himself told a friend that this "rough sketch" was to be a "book about the atomic bomb—so far as an amateur could see the consequences," so perhaps this is in fact an unfinished story for a book or a movie never made.[68] But perhaps the incompletion of this story is the point to which we ought to attend; perhaps its incompletion is all that a narrative using the bomb as its point of departure could ever achieve.

Certainly, the sense one gets from Lifton's assessment of the current situation—a situation in which "our legacy of holocausts and dislocations have left us confused about limits, no longer certain where anything begins or ends"—is that our efforts to give shape, meaning and definition to events in our time are bound to fail. The age is, for Lifton, characterized by a "series of breakdowns and blurrings of boundaries"—boundaries between life and death, boundaries around the extent of possible violence, boundaries of the self, the boundaries, in short, that give definition to living.[69]

The new age is a time when only Lifton's "Protean Man" is comfortable. "Protean Man" is modeled after Proteus, the god who could change his shape to fit the circumstance. Proteus's one aversion was to assuming a single shape and fulfilling his function of prophecy. Lifton sees Proteus as the model for modern people living without boundaries and who act, as one of Lifton's patients did, with "polymorphous versatility" as the circumstances warrant.[70] In the months following the announcement of the bomb, Agee experienced himself to be a "Protean Man": "I ought to go crazy but probably won't. It seems possible to 'adjust' to anything short of atomic liquefaction, and I'll probably keep right on adjusting." Adjusting, not completing. His new world was one without end. There was left to people only two forms of boundary breaching totalization: "At the end of the next war we either survive or don't survive total annihilation (i.e., of everyone, everywhere) or: we survive either as 'victors' or vanquished under a world tyranny."[71] To individual people conducting their affairs on a human scale, this "choice" remains, following Stein, uninteresting.

Narrative structures that provide a sense of continuity through disruptions in history are as easy to construct. They stabilize the world and give us a sense of vitality and, often, a little redemptive knowledge. The only continuity that can be perceived in mythic descriptions or in the general artistic response to the bomb is the banal continuity of continued existence. "We either survive or don't survive" is an opening onto the future that carries the small and humorous consolation that at least we may have more time to invent more narratives to get us over. Living in the midst of constant human inventiveness, when that inventiveness is bound to failure and need not be taken too seriously, is not a wholly bad way to live.

Inconclusion

Some years after the war, Niels Bohr was invited to give a lecture at Harvard. Robert Wilson, then a young associate professor of physics at Harvard, wondered whether Bohr would remember him from their few days together at Los Alamos. Wilson knew it would be coup of significant proportions in academic circles if the great man even raised an eyebrow of recognition in his direction. Bohr not only recognized Wilson but insisted on a private conference with him. Once behind closed doors, no doubt with the senior faculty agog outside, Wilson listened as Bohr told him he wanted to talk about the work of the Federation of Atomic Scientists, chaired by Wilson, on international control of nuclear arms. Bohr said he thought the Federation could help achieve peace in their time. Wilson recalls,

> I replied that we in the FAS had only been doing what he had inspired us to do back at Los Alamos. Then he dropped his voice a few decibels and said that he wanted me to carry out a mission for him, so important (his voice falling a few more decibels) that peace in the world depended on it.
>
> I assured him that I was eager to carry out the mission, but would he please speak a little louder so that I could clearly understand what I was to do. Bohr lowered his voice even more. I hitched my chair closer now because I knew that this was genuinely crucial, since it was Bohr's style to give emphasis by lowering his voice—and I could barely hear him at that point. He began to discuss his talks with Churchill and Roosevelt, and went on to further, more fruitful developments. I turned one ear toward him, the better to hear. He started to instruct me on what to do, just as someone knocked at the door and announced that his lecture was to begin. Bohr lowered his voice and continued his instructions—inaudibly.
>
> In desperation, I pressed my ear actually into contact with his lips. Knock, knock, knock. "The lecture, Dr. Bohr! The lecture! It's past time." Tears streaming down my face, I pleaded, "For God's sake, man, speak up!" Alas, the instructions had been delivered. Bohr got up and gave himself over to the importunate professor who should have introduced him 15 minutes earlier.[72]

It is against such intrusions of the human, the "all too human" as we say, in the affairs of rationality that sociologists like Arthur Stinchcombe have tried to warn us.

> Social structures that make information available to decision makers and protect the quality of information reaching those decision makers are essential to the operation of reason as a social institution. . . . The achievement of civilization could be formulated as the successful detachment of the faculties that make people rational from the limiting context of personal goals [or, we might add, from the limiting context of personal quirks such as lowering one's voice for emphasis], so that they can be applied to the improvement of social life.[73]

The problem with Wilson's encounter with Bohr was that it was personal. It was motivated by Bohr's genuine but unfortunately, we might say, personal concern for peace, and it was sustained by Wilson's pride in his personal recognition by Bohr. It was as if Wilson had learned nothing by being part of the machine at Los Alamos or by being part of the complementary machine of criticism being formulated by the disaffected scientists. It was as if both parties believed that people still mattered. We who have had the benefit of expert sociological instruction should know better.

In the age of systems, the problems of being a person and of acting as if people mattered may be moot. Benjamin DeMott, the essayist who suggests that "power . . . is actually vested nowhere," captures the problem of developing an identity by the people who "command" our war-making machine, men who are "unlikely to show images or attitudes of war, only sites and cycles, partial glimpses of The Ultimate Plant." Over the hum of The Plant, the lieutenant general asks, "Who am I?," and is answered,

> *I am not a maker of events but a remover of obstructions. For progress's sake, and in acknowledgment of the insuperable uncontrollability of "forces," I march with affairs—and am in truth hardly a man of war at all. Patron of industry? supporter of research? Even these titles imply an improper separation from the huge machine that encompasses all. I am simply "of the community," and in the service of things as they are.*

A systems person has no place except as an enabler of the potential resident in the system itself. He or she can achieve a sense of "ritual participation" in making things happen by identifying with others who appear to have control over minor aspects of the system[74] or by otherwise narrativizing one's circumstances to try to give them human meaning. This is the place of the expert person and it is, by now, familiar.

In our efforts to participate in the affairs of our time, there seem to be two choices before us. These choices are offered both to expert persons and those of us who struggle to be just persons in this life. These "choices" might be called the madness of rationality, on the one hand, and the rationality of madness, on the other. The choice is not an inviting one to people, but it must be examined.

Just months after the end of the war Lewis Mumford weighed in with a *Saturday Review* article called, "Gentlemen: You Are Mad!" The way of the new reason is madness, he said.

> *We in America are living among madmen. Madmen govern our affairs*

> in the name of order and security. The chief madmen claim the titles of
> general, admiral, senator, scientist, administrator, Secretary of State,
> even President. And the fatal symptom of their madness is this: they
> have been carrying through a series of acts which will lead eventually to
> the destruction of mankind, under the solemn conviction that they are
> normal responsible people, leading sane lives, and working for
> reasonable ends.

Our leaders, Mumford wrote, do nothing exceptional to merit the designation "mad." They carry on in the most rational of ways. Their actions "seem the normal motions of normal men, not the compulsions of people bent on total death." Instead of Feynman's Dragon or Frisch's elephant, our leaders, Mumford said, had a "comet by the tail" which their rationality mandated that they treat as a "child's skyrocket."

According to Mumford, no willful act of identification with this mad reason or with its embodiment in rational actors is necessary. Indeed, it is the inaction of the populace that proves our own mass madness. "Why do we keep our glassy calm in the face of this danger? There is a reason: We are madmen, too. We view the madness of our leaders as if it expressed a traditional wisdom and a common sense."

Mumford's call from inaction is based on his belief that the path of this reason leads necessarily to total destruction.

> Even now, in the middle of the Pacific Ocean, they plan a further
> madness, with a monkey-like curiosity to discover a new secret that is
> no secret. One mad act has led to a second, the second to a third: and
> the end will be a morbid compulsion to achieve the last irretrievable act
> of world madness—in the interests of security, peace, and truth.[75]

Once you become rational you seemingly have no choice but to be rational and to follow your rationality where it leads, even unto madness.

The madness of which Mumford wrote is the madness Yossarian sees everywhere around him in *Catch-22*. Yossarian's leaders and his colleagues are people who are all "identified by their totally mechanical attitude toward human life," as one critic put it.[76] The only thing available for anyone to do in the face of such rationality is, short of Agee's "atomic liquefaction," adjust. As DeMott has it, it is only a matter of cultivating a little "maturity," a little "disinterestedness," or a little "sophistication" so that we might continue to "half-live."[77]

The other option is no longer to live, or settle for "half-living," in the madness of rationality but to surrender to the madness that seems the only rational thing to embrace.

James Agee gives way to a cliche to close his "Dedication Day." The great mad scientist is said to have given a gift "greater, perhaps, than that of his more stable colleagues. For, though 'sacrifice' is a word to be used only with apologies, it would be hard to define what, if anything, they 'sacrificed' in the giving; but he gave up his sanity."[78] William Cowling of O'Brien's *Nuclear Age* has a backyard that talks to him. He listens to his backyard as it commands him to come outside and dig a deep hole. And keep digging, the hole tells him, because that is the only rational thing to do in these times. Eventually, Cowling puts his wife and daughter into the hole, wires it with explosives, and sits with his fingers playing over the detonator as he listens to the hole tell him, *"Push the fucking button!"* He doesn't. He comes to his senses, we might say, long enough to console himself with the thought that at the last moment, "when Kansas burns, when what is done is undone, when fail-safe fails, when deterrence no longer deters, when the jig is at last up . . . *E* will somehow not quite equal mc^2, . . . that the terminal equation will somehow not quite balance,"[79] which, of course, is madness of a higher order than listening to the commands of holes in your yard, as sane physicists would probably quickly assure us. There is the problem of "how to live *in* this world," Philip Roth wrote, and not even our most creative people have an answer to that problem, unless, he says, "the answer is that we cannot." The heroes of modern fiction proffer only the advice that we should all "be charming on the way to the loony bin."[80]

Some have found some direction from the refusals of fictional characters, like Yossarian, to participate in systems. "Yossarian's obsessive concern for survival makes him not only *not* morally dead, but one of the most morally vibrant figures in recent literature—and a giant of the will beside those weary, wise and wistful prodigals in contemporary novels who always accommodate to American life." Yossarian chose, we are told, "a new morality based on an old ideal, the morality of refusal."[81] Yossarian is the modern-day Bartleby, Melville's scrivener who, with his simple "I would prefer not to," repulsed his employer's every effort, humane and otherwise, to move him from his chosen routine, through which he had lived a life, into the systems that could sustain and support him.

Refusal might be a very old ideal, but it may not translate well into the age of systems. Norbert Wiener tried the tactic of refusal in 1947 when he acted against the custom of his profession and turned down a request from a person in the Department of Defense for a reprint of a paper he had written during the war. Recognizing that his work would undoubtedly be used in furtherance of Department of Defense programs, he wrote in an open letter, "The interchange of ideas which is one of the great traditions in science must of course receive certain limitations when the scientist becomes an arbiter of life and death." Noble, but Wiener was the first to understand that his refusal was also a little silly. The scientist who prompted Wiener's letter was connected with the defense establishment and, Wiener noted, "Since it is obvious that with sufficient effort you can obtain my material, even though it is out of print, I can only protest pro forma in refusing to give you any information concerning my past work."[82] Expertise is fluid and systems managers are able to remove the obstructions, make knowledge available, and make the necessary connections. Moral indignation and refusal are hardly blocks before well-functioning systems. That is why the Pentagon's chief of Strategic Defense Initiative contracts could respond confidently, when asked why he gave contracts to scientists morally opposed to SDI, that he was interested in a scientist's knowledge, not his morals.

Indeed, there is something a little silly even about the notion that there are two choices, the madness of rationality or the rationality of madness, before us. These "options" are, in fact, more like Connolly's Siamese twins of humanist criticism and coercive control than they are like opposed ways of acting. Over a century ago, Dostoevsky's *Notes from Underground* suggested that one of these "choices" is inevitably tied to the other. Indeed, one begets the other. Madness is not just a reasonable response to rationality, it is *the* response. The "positiveness" of "twice two makes four," says the nameless narrator, "is not life, gentlemen, but is the beginning of death." And in response to such positiveness that turns people into piano keys or organ stops, the nineteenth century analogues of our agents of complex systems, human beings will assert their humanness through madness, if that is what it takes. A person

> *would desire the most fatal rubbish, the most uneconomical absurdity,*
> *simply to introduce into all this positive good sense his fatal fantastic*
> *element. It is just his fantastic dreams, his vulgar folly, that he will*
> *desire to retain, simply in order to prove himself—as though that were*
> *necessary—that men are still men and not the keys of a piano.*

Following this line, it becomes impossible to tell whether the "mad-men" against whom Mumford rails are acting out of a concern for rationality or out of the perversity that marks them as human, for Dostoevsky says,

> *if he does not find the means [to prove himself not the key of a piano] he*
> *will contrive destruction and chaos: He will launch a curse upon the*
> *world, and as only man can curse (it is his privilege, the primary*
> *distinction between him and other animals) it may be by his curse alone*
> *that he will attain his object—that is, to convince himself that he is a*
> *man and not a piano key!*[83]

These choices that are not choices and this rationality that is mad-ness have been explored by others,[84] and it is not necessary to rehearse their ideas and arguments here. It is sufficient to understand our situation a little better. We can predict what will likely happen as we move on. The experts and their opposite numbers, the expert critics, will continue to stake out the sides that we might take. We will continue to follow Dostoevsky's sick, spiteful man and invent adventures for ourselves and make up our lives "so as at least to live in some way."[85] We will continue to make the "deathly silence" of the bomb speak and we will continue to make Bohr's "silence" speak on the matter of world peace as we re-invent imaginative paths from our troubled situation to something better. Some will stand by, remain "of the community," and serve "things as they are." Others, like Op-penheimer, will try to apply their critical powers, which events have proven effective once in modifying history, to the improvement of our collective lot. Others will refuse to serve and stand naked to receive their medals (or the bullets before the open pit, whichever the stochastic elements of the systems that support us happen to serve up). Others will listen to the holes in their lives commanding them to dig deeper. In one way or another, we will all probably continue to look to the experts of both sorts and, with Robert Wilson, cry and scream, "For God's sake, man, speak up!" We will, like Eco's mysterious author/conveyor of the Adso of Melk manuscript, search the shelves of burned-out libraries and assemble their *disecta membra* in search of a message that is true.

The risk is that we will conclude, with Eco's author, that finally there is no message, that the assemblage of symbols to which we have looked hopefully for truth "is the result of chance." And we will be, with Bohr, silent, and unable to tell whether our silence is the result of will, reason, or circumstance. But then, with our search for truth suspended, we may have the chance to find one another.

When asked on "Meet the Press" if it was true there was no defense against atomic weapons, Robert Oppenheimer responded without hesitation, "Peace."[86] He did not elaborate, narrativize or play out the plot. There was nothing more to say. Perhaps it is time to entertain the possibility that all of our truth-telling talk and all of our rational efforts to apprehend reality—our efforts to shine a bright light into every crevasse of nature to make her yield a message that is true— is the foundation of our current, violence-prone situation. If so, that would be a joke of a very high order. A lot may depend on whether we get the joke and learn to laugh.

Notes

Opening

1. Arney, William Ray, *Power and the Profession of Obstetrics*, Chicago, Ill.: University of Chicago Press, 1982; Arney, William Ray, and Bernard J. Bergen, *Medicine and the Management of Living: Taming the Last Great Beast*, Chicago, Ill.: University of Chicago Press, 1984.

2. Bloom, Allan, *The Closing of the American Mind*, New York, N.Y.: Simon and Schuster, 1987, p. 297.

3. Levi, Primo, *The Drowned and the Saved*, New York, N.Y.: Summit Books, 1988.

4. Cohen, John, ed., *The Essential Lenny Bruce*, New York, N.Y.: Random House, 1967, p. 112.

5. Lang, Candace, *Irony/Humor: Critical Paradigms*, Baltimore, Md.: Johns Hopkins University Press, 1988.

6. Ibid., p. 2.

7. Ibid., p. 195.

8. Greene, Maxine, *The Dialectic of Freedom*, New York, N.Y.: Teachers College Press, 1988, p. 115.

9. Foucault, Michel, *The Archeology of Knowledge*, New York, N.Y.: Harper Colophon, 1972, p. 17.

10. Including Barbara Duden, Wolfgang Sachs, Jean Robert, and a host of others I met at Foster Avenue.

11. A biologist with whom I taught responded to a student's question about the meaning of "life" on the second day of class with, "For a biologist, 'life' is not a very useful term."

12. Illich, Ivan, "The institutional construction of a new fetish: Human life," talk given at a "planning event" of the Evangelical Lutheran Church in America on March 29, 1989, Chicago.

13. Cf. Arney and Bergen, op. cit.

14. This with thanks to Jutta Mason.

CHAPTER ONE : *Introduction to Extremity*

1. Freidson, Eliot, "Are professions necessary?," pp. 3–27 in Thomas L. Haskell, ed., *The Authority of Experts: Studies in History and Theory,* Bloomington, Ind.: University of Indiana Press, 1985, p. 15.

2. Ibid., p. 25.

3. Illich, Ivan, *Medical Nemesis: The Expropriation of Health,* New York: Pantheon, 1976; Illich, Ivan, *Toward a History of Needs,* New York: Bantam New Age Books, 1980; Illich, Ivan, *Gender,* New York: Pantheon, 1985. The latter is his strongest statement yet about the damage done by moving away from a subsistence-oriented economy.

4. Stinchcombe, Arthur L., "Reason and rationality," *Sociological Theory* 4 (Fall 1986): 151–66, pp. 161–62.

5. Ibid., p. 163.

6. Haskell, Thomas L., "Introduction," pp. ix–xxxix in Haskell, op. cit., pp. xxxvi–xxxvii.

7. See, for example, Levy, Bernard-Henri, *Barbarism with a Human Face,* New York, N.Y.: Harper and Row, 1977.

8. Megill, Allan, *Prophets of Extremity: Nietzsche, Heidegger, Foucault, Derrida,* Berkeley, Calif.: University of California Press, 1985, p. 183.

9. Foucault, Michel, "Confessions of the flesh," in Colin Gordon, ed., *Power/Knowledge: Selected Interviews and Other Writings [of Michel Foucault],* New York: Pantheon, 1980, p. 198.

10. "Revolutionary action: 'Until now'—A discussion with Michel Foucault, under the auspices of Auriel," pp. 218–33 in Donald F. Bouchard, ed., *Language, Counter-Memory, Practice: Selected Interview and Essays by Michel Foucault,* Ithaca, N.Y.: Cornell University Press, 1977, p. 220.

11. Blanchot, Maurice, "Michel Foucault as I imagine him," pp. 61–109 in *Foucault/Blanchot,* New York, N.Y.: Zone Books, 1987, pp. 90–91.

12. Ibid., pp. 73, 76.

13. Blanchot, op. cit., p. 80.

14. "Intellectuals and power: A conversation between Michel Foucault and Gilles Deleuze," pp. 205–217 in Bouchard, op. cit., p. 208.

15. Megill, op. cit., p. 184.

16. Walzer, Michael, "The politics of Michel Foucault," *Dissent* 30 (Fall 1983): 481–90, p. 482.

17. Roth, Philip, "Writing American fiction," *Commentary* 31 (March 1961): 223–33, pp. 227, 224.

18. Blanchot, op. cit., p. 93.

19. Poirier, Richard, *The Renewal of Literature: Emersonian Reflections,* New York, N.Y.: Random House, 1987, p. 72, emphasis added.

20. Foucault, Michel, *Discipline and Punish: The Birth of the Prison,* London: Allen Lane, 1977.

21. Foucault, Michel, "The political function of the intellectual," *Radical Philosophy* 17 (1976): 12–14, p. 13.

22. Hoy, David Couzens, "Introduction," pp. 1–25 in David Couzens Hoy, ed., *Foucault: A Critical Reader*, New York, N.Y.: Basil Blackwell, 1986, p. 13.

23. Blanchot, op. cit., p. 69.

24. Foucault, "The political function of the intellectual," op. cit., p. 12.

25. Jacoby, Russell, *The Last Intellectuals: American Culture in the Age of Academe*, New York, N.Y.: Basic Books, 1987.

26. Foucault, "The political function of the intellectual," op. cit., p. 12.

27. Oppenheimer, J. Robert, "The atomic age," *New York Philharmonic Symphony Radio Program*, December 23, 1945.

28. Cousins, Norman, "Modern man is obsolete," *The Saturday Review of Literature* 28 (August 18, 1945): 5–9, p. 5.

29. Lifton, Robert Jay, *Boundaries: Psychological Man in Revolution*, New York, N.Y.: Random House, 1970, p. 96.

30. Larson, Magali Sarfatti, "The production of expertise and the constitution of expert power," pp. 28–79 in Haskell, op. cit., p. 56.

31. Drucker, Peter F., *The New Realities: In Government and Politics/In Economics and Business/In Society and World View*, New York, N.Y.: Harper and Row, 1989, p. ix.

32. Barber, Benjamin, "Turning off the Enlightenment," *New York Times Book Review*, September 10, 1989.

33. Wiener, Norbert, *Cybernetics: Or Control and Communication in the Animal and the Machine*, 2nd ed., Cambridge, Mass.: MIT Press, 1961, p. 39.

34. Walzer, op. cit., p. 481.

35. Davis, Nuel Pharr, *Lawrence and Oppenheimer*, New York, N.Y.: Simon and Schuster, 1968, p. 190.

36. Foucault, *Discipline and Punish*, p. 304.

37. Rieff, Philip, *Fellow Teachers*, New York, N.Y.: Dell, 1972 p. 6.

38. From the Latin *perspicere*, to see through, *perspicx*, clear-sighted.

39. Rousseau, Jean-Jacques, *Emile, or On Education*, translated by Allan Bloom, New York, N.Y.: Basic Books, 1979, p. 342.

CHAPTER TWO : *The Complex and the Simple*

1. Drucker, Peter, *The New Realities: In Government and Politics/In Economics and Business/In Society and World View*, New York, N.Y.: Harper and Row, 1989, p. 3.

2. Ibid., p. 13.

3. Davis, Philip J., and Reuben Hersh, *Descartes' Dream: The World According to Mathematics*, San Diego, Calif.: Harcourt, Brace, Jovanovich, 1986.

4. Descartes, Rene, *Discourse on Method and Meditations*, Indianapolis, Ind.: Bobbs-Merrill, 1960, p. 31.

5. Ibid., p. 15.

6. Prigogene, Ilya, *Order Out of Chaos: Man's New Dialogue with Nature*, New York, N.Y.: Bantam Books, 1984, pp. 7, 11, emphasis in the original.

7. Arendt, Hannah, *The Human Condition*, Chicago, Ill.: University of Chicago Press, 1958, p. 263.

8. Holmes, Sherlock, "The Book of Life," quoted in John H. Watson, *A Study in Scarlet: Being a Reprint from the Reminiscences of . . .* , in Sir Arthur Conan Doyle, *The Complete Sherlock Holmes*, Volume 1, Garden City, N.J.: Doubleday, 1930, p. 23.

9. Ibid.

10. Blois, Marsden S., "Conceptual issues in computer-aided diagnosis and the hierarchical nature of medical knowledge," *Journal of Medicine and Philosophy* 8 (1983): 29–50, p. 34.

11. Foucault, Michel, *Discipline and Punish: The Birth of the Prison*, London: Allen Lane, 1977, p. 223.

12. There are many new references on this subject. See, e.g., Patricia Cline Cohen, *A Calculating People: The Spread of Numeracy in Early America*, Chicago, Ill.: University of Chicago Press; Theodore M. Porter, *The Rise of Statistical Thinking, 1820–1900*, Princeton, N.J.: Princeton University Press, 1983; and Stephen M. Stigler, *The History of Statistics: The Measurement of Uncertainty Before 1900*, Cambridge, Mass.: Harvard University Press, 1986.

13. Watson, op. cit., p. 21.

14. It will be recalled that Watson's introduction to Holmes involved a report of how Holmes was beating corpses to determine the extent of bruising that might be induced after death.

15. Bordo, Susan, "The cultural overseer and the tragic hero: Comedic and feminist perspectives on the hubris of philosophy," *Soundings* 2 (1982): 181–205, p. 183. The Rorty quote, in Bordo, is from Rorty, Richard, *Philosophy and the Mirror of Nature*, Princeton: Princeton University Press, 1979, pp. 317–18.

16. Frank H. Hankins, *Adolphe Quetelet as Statistician*, New York, N.Y.: AMS Press, 1968, originally presented as a thesis at Columbia University, 1908.

17. Arendt, op. cit., pp. 305–6.

18. Ibid., p. 304.

19. Hunt, Robert, "The science of the exhibition," in *The Crystal Palace Exhibition, The Art Journal Illustrated Catalogue*, London, 1851, p. v.

20. Jungnickel, Christa, and Russell McCormmach, *The Intellectual Mastery of Nature: Theoretical Physics from Ohm to Einstein*, Volume 2, Chicago, Ill.: University of Chicago Press, 1986, p. 347.

21. Arendt, op. cit., p. 321.

22. Rinearson, Peter, "The quest for simplicity," *Seattle Times/Seattle Post-Intelligencer*, June 19, 1983, D4–5, p. D4.

23. Ibid.

24. Prigogene, op. cit., p. 2; Alvin Toffler, "Foreword: Science and change," ibid., pp. xi–xxvi, p. xiii.

25. Forrester, Jay W., *Urban Dynamics*, Cambridge, Mass.: MIT Press, 1969, p. 10.

26. Ibid., pp. 9.

27. Sachs, Wolfgang, "On the Archeology of the Development Idea: Six Essays," STS Program, Penn State University, November 1989. Published in German in *epd-Entwicklungspolitick* [Frankfurt], June–September 1989, and in Italian in *Il Manifesto* [Rome], 22 August–12 September 1989.

28. Petersen, Aage, "The philosophy of Niels Bohr," *Bulletin of the Atomic Scientists* 19 (September 1963): 8–14.

29. Rhodes, Richard, op. cit., p. 56.

30. Laslo, Ervin, *The Systems View of the World: The Natural Philosophy of the New Developments in the Sciences*, New York, N.Y.: George Braziller, 1972, pp. 27–75.

31. Churchman, C. West, *The Systems Approach and Its Enemies*, New York, N.Y.: Basic Books, 1979, p. 8.

32. Arendt, op. cit., pp. 248, 259, 250.

33. Laslo, op. cit.

34. Forrester, op. cit., p. 108.

35. Ibid., pp. 9–10.

36. Perrow, Charles, *Normal Accidents: Living with High-Risk Technologies*, New York, N.Y.: Basic Books, 1984, pp. 27–29.

37. Prigogene, op. cit., p. 9.

38. Ophuls, William, *Ecology and the Politics of Scarcity: Prologue to a Political Theory of the Steady State*, San Francisco, Calif.: W. H. Freeman, 1977, pp. 6, 231.

39. Post, H. R., "Against Ideologies," inaugural lecture, London, Chelsea College, 1974, p. 9.

40. Wallace, Walter L., *The Logic of Science in Sociology*, Chicago, Ill.: Aldine, 1971.

41. Truesdell, C., "The computer: Ruin of science and threat to mankind," pp. 594–631 in C. Truesdell, *An Idiot's Fugitive Essays on Science: Methods, Criticism, Training, Circumstances*, New York, N.Y.: Springer-Verlag, 1984, pp. 622–23.

42. Post, op. cit., p. 12.

43. Forrester, op. cit., pp. 113–114.

44. Ophuls, op. cit., p. 6, emphasis added.

45. Freud, Sigmund, "Analysis Terminable and Interminable," *The Standard Edition of the Psychological Works of Sigmund Freud*, London: Hogarth Press, 1968, vol. 23: 209–253.

46. The words are from Forrester, op. cit., p. 113.

47. Ophuls, op. cit., pp. 244, 228.

48. Dirac, Paul A. M., "The relation between mathematics and physics," *Proceedings of the Royal Society of Edinburgh* 59 (1938/1939): 122–29.

49. Teller, Edward, *The Pursuit of Simplicity*, Malibu, Calif.: Pepperdine University Press, 1980, p. 13.

50. Laslo, op. cit., pp. 74–75.

51. Ophuls, op. cit., interleaf between pages 244 and 245.

52. Forrester, op. cit., p. 129.

53. Prisig, Robert M., *Zen and the Art of Motorcycle Maintenance*, New York, N.Y.: Bantam Books, 1974, p. 340.

54. Teller, op. cit., pp. 13–14.

55. Ibid., p. 152.

56. Szasz, Ferenc Morton, *The Day the Sun Rose Twice: The Story of the Trinity Site Nuclear Explosion, July 16, 1945*, Albuquerque, N.M.: University of New Mexico Press, 1984, p. 90, emphasis added.

57. Quoted in Marx, Joseph L., *Seven Hours to Zero*, New York, N.Y.: G. P. Putnam's Sons, 1967, p. 157.

58. Tibbets, Paul W., "Training the 509th for Hiroshima," *Air Force Magazine*, August 1973, p. 55, quoted in Rhodes, Richard, *The Making of the Atomic Bomb*, New York, N.Y.: Simon and Schuster, 1986, p. 708.

59. Gullemin, Victor, *The Story of Quantum Mechanics*, New York, N.Y.: Charles Scribner's Sons, 1968, p. 15.

60. Rhodes, op. cit., p. 70.

61. Snow, C. P., *The Physicists*, Boston, Mass.: Little, Brown and Company, 1981, p. 58.

62. Ibid., p. 67.

63. Ibid., p. 70.

64. Oppenheimer, J. Robert, *Science and the Common Understanding*, New York: Simon and Schuster, 1953, p. 44.

65. MacKinnon, Edward M., *Scientific Explanation and Atomic Physics*, Chicago: University of Chicago Press, 1982.

66. Oppenheimer, op. cit., pp. 46–47.

67. Rhodes, op. cit., pp. 263–264.

68. Rutherford, Ernest, and Frederick Soddy, in Rutherford, *Collected Papers* I, London: Allen and Unwin, 1962, quoted in Rhodes, op. cit. p. 43.

69. Aston, Francis, "Forty years of atomic theory," pp. 101–126 in Joseph Needham and Walter Pagel, eds., *Background to Modern Science*, New York, N.Y.: Macmillan, 1938, p. 114.

70. Joliot, Frederic, "Chemical evidence of the transmutation of the elements," Nobel lecture, 1935.

71. Snow, op. cit., p. 100.

72. Davis, Nuel Pharr, *Lawrence and Oppenheimer*, New York, N.Y.: Simon and Schuster, 1968, p. 11.

73. Blumberg, Stanley A., and Gwinn Owens, *Energy and Conflict*, New York, N.Y.: G. P. Putnam's Sons, 1976, p. 89.

74. Groves, Leslie R., *Now It Can Be Told: The Story of the Manhattan Project*, New York, N.Y.: DaCapra Press, 1962, pp. xiii, xiv.

75. Quoted in Goodchild, Peter, *J. Robert Oppenheimer: 'Shatterer of Worlds,'* London: British Broadcasting Corporation, 1980, p. 48.

76. Quoted in Goodchild, op. cit., p. 54.

77. Groves, op. cit., pp. 54–55.

78. Ibid., pp. 62–63.

79. United States Atomic Energy Commission, *In the Matter of J. Robert Oppenheimer: Transcript of the Hearing before Personnel Security Board and Texts of Principal Documents and Letters, Washington, D.C., April 12, 1954, through May 6, 1954*, Government Printing Office, reprinted by Cambridge, Mass.: MIT Press, 1970, p. 712.

80. Ibid, pp. 770–805, passim.

81. Hawkins, David, *Project Y: The Los Alamos Story, Part I: Toward Trinity*, Los Angeles, Calif.: Tomash Publishers, 1983, p. 5.

82. Atomic Energy Commission, op. cit., p. 28.

83. Groves, op. cit., p. 167.

84. Atomic Energy Commission, op. cit., p. 12.

85. Hawkins, op. cit., p. 40.

86. Public Broadcasting Service, "The Day After Trinity: J. Robert Oppenheimer and the Atomic Bomb," transcript of the broadcast, April 29, 1981, p. 10.

87. Hawkins, op. cit., p. 34.

88. Filipkowski, Paul, "Postal censorship at Los Alamos, 1943–1945," *The American Philatelist* (April 1987): 345–50.

89. Rhodes, op. cit., p. 460.

90. Atomic Energy Commission, op. cit., p. 14.

91. Public Broadcasting Service, op. cit., p. 6.

92. Alsop, Stewart, and Ralph E. Lapp, "The strange death of Louis Slotin," pp. 8–18 in Charles Neider, ed., *Man Against Nature: Tales of Adventure and Exploration*, New York, N.Y.: Harper and Row, 1954, p. 11.

93. Hawkins, op. cit., p. 164.

94. Davis, op. cit., p. 225.

95. Ibid, p. 226.

96. Alsop and Lapp, op. cit., pp. 10–11.

97. Davis, op. cit.

98. Alsop and Lapp, op. cit., p. 12.

99. Froman, Darol, "Preliminary report on the accident in Parajito laboratory, Los Alamos, on 21 May, 1946," memo to Norris E. Bradbury, edited, declassified report from Los Alamos Laboratory, October 16, 1986, pp. 2–4.

100. Ibid., p. 5.

101. Davis, op. cit., pp 234–235.

102. Groves, op. cit., pp. 296–297.

103. Quoted in Groves, General Leslie, "Memorandum for the Secretary

of War," July 18, 1945, pp. 47–55 in Williams, Robert C., and Philip Cantelon, eds., *The American Atom: A Documentary History of Nuclear Policies from the Discovery of Fission to the Present, 1939–1984*, Philadelphia, Pa.: University of Pennsylvania Press, 1984, p. 52.

104. Goodchild, op. cit., p. 162.

105. Ticknor, George, untitled poem, copyright 1955 by Trustees of Dartmouth College, Hanover, N.H.

106. Rabi, I. I., *Science: The Center of Culture*, New York, N.Y.: The World Publishing Company, 1970, p. 138.

107. Groves, "Memorandum . . . ," op. cit., p. 48.

108. Davis, op. cit., p. 240.

109. Laurence, William T., Boxed material in an article "Atomic power: A bitter and growing controversy," *New York Times*, July 16, 1970, p. 20.

110. Quoted in Groves, op. cit., p. 52.

111. Los Alamos Scientific Laboratory, *Los Alamos: Beginning of an Era, 1943–1945*, Los Alamos National Laboratory, n.d., p. 53.

112. Quoted in Groves, op. cit., pp. 52–53.

113. Public Broadcasting Service, "Confessions of a Weaponeer," transcript of the broadcast, March 3, 1987, p. 8.

114. Public Broadcasting System, "The Day after Trinity," op. cit., p. 19.

115. Oppenheimer, J. Robert, "The atom bomb and college education," *The General Magazine and Historical Chronicle*, General Alumni Society, University of Pennsylvania (Summer 1946): 9.

116. McPhee, John, *The Curve of Binding Energy*, New York, N.Y.: Farrar, Straus, and Giroux, 1973, pp. 146–48.

117. Pringle, Peter, and William Arkin, *SIOP: The Secret U.S. Plan for Nuclear War*, New York, N.Y.: W. W. Norton, 1983, p. 45.

118. Draper, Theodore, "American Hubris: From Truman to the Persian gulf," *New York Review of Books* 34 (July 16, 1987): 40–48, pp. 42–43.

119. Pringle and Arkin, op. cit., p. 91, emphasis added.

120. Ibid., p. 104.

121. Ibid., pp. 21–22.

122. Ibid., pp. 241–52.

123. Bracken, Paul, *The Command and Control of Nuclear Forces*, New Haven, Conn.: Yale University Press, 1983, p. 31.

124. Ibid., p. 33.

125. Ibid., p. 55.

126. Ibid.

127. Ibid., p. 64.

128. Heims, Steve J., *John von Neumann and Norbert Wiener: From Mathematics to the Technologies of Life and Death*, Cambridge, Mass.: MIT Press, 1980, p. 287.

129. Powers, Thomas, "How nuclear war could start," *New York Review of Books* 31 (June 17, 1985): 33–36, p. 33.

130. Oppenheimer, 1946, p. 9.

131. Ibid.

132. Oppenheimer, 1946, pp. 262–66.

133. Meadows, Donnella H., and others, *The Limits to Growth: A Report for the Club of Rome's Project on the Predicament of Mankind*, New York, N.Y.: Universe Books, 1972.

134. Sharp, Marilyn, *Masterstroke*, New York, N.Y.: R. Marek, 1981.

135. Borgmann, Albert, *Technology and the Character of Contemporary Life: A Philosophical Inquiry*, Chicago, Ill.: University of Chicago Press, 1984, p. 15.

136. Ibid., p. 246.

137. Oppenheimer, J. Robert, "A speech given by J. R. Oppenheimer at a meeting of the Association of Los Alamos Scientists," Los Alamos, N.M., November 2, 1945, J. Robert Oppenheimer Papers, Library of Congress, Box 266, p. 2, emphasis added.

138. Marrus, Michael, "The impossible and unspeakable: Review of Yitzhak Arad, Belzec, Sorbibor, Treblinka: The Operation Reinhard Death Camps," *New York Times Book Review*, June 28, 1987, p. 14, emphasis added.

139. "Interview with Dr. Oppenheimer for 'The Building of the Bomb,'" British Broadcasting Corporation transcript, n.d., J. Robert Oppenheimer Papers, Library of Congress, Box 246, p. 2.

140. Lifton, Robert Jay, *Death in Life: Survivors of Hiroshima*, New York, N.Y.: Basic Books, 1967, pp. 74–75.

141. Heisenberg, Werner, "Research in Germany on the technical application of atomic energy," *Nature* 160 (August 16, 1947): 211–15.

142. Alvarez, Luis W., *Alvarez: Adventures of a Physicist*, New York, N.Y.: Basic Books, 1987, p. 75.

143. Paraphrased from Public Broadcasting Service, "A is for Atom, B is for Bomb," broadcast transcript, WGBH Educational Foundation, 1980, p. 17.

144. Kemeny, John G., "Saving American democracy: The lessons of Three Mile Island," The Compton Lecture, Massachusetts Institute of Technology, April 1980.

145. Oppenheimer, "A speech given by . . . ," op. cit., p. 2; "Atomic weapons," op. cit., pp. 7–8.

146. Oppenheimer, "A speech given by . . . ," op. cit., p. 1.

147. Marrus, op. cit, emphasis added.

148. Freud, Sigmund, *Civilization and Its Discontents*, New York, N.Y.: W. W. Norton, 1961, p. 37.

149. Deighton, Len, *London Match*, New York, N.Y.: Knopf, 1985, p. 259.

150. Sartre, Jean-Paul, *Iron in the Soul*, New York, N.Y.: Bantam Books, 1963, pp. 217–25.

151. Weart, Spencer R., "The heyday of myth and cliche," pp. 81–90 in Len Acklund and Steven McGuire, *Assessing the Nuclear Age*, Chicago, Ill.: Educational Foundation for Nulcear Science, 1986, p. 82.

152. "Let sleeping plants lie," *Time*, January 19, 1987, p. 53.

153. Gapay, Les, "Preserved trees look alive, thanks to Weyerhaeuser," *Seattle Post-Intelligencer*, January 7, 1987, pp. B6, A1.

154. McPhee, op. cit., p. 107.

155. Quoted in "The Day after Trinity," PBS, op. cit., pp. 13–14.

156. Teller, op. cit., pp. 18–19, 152.

157. Public Broadcasting System, "A is for Atom, B is for Bomb," op. cit., p. 17.

158. Dr. Tom Grissom, Olympia, Washington.

159. Glover, Jonathan, "Am I my brain?," *New York Review of Books*, April 9, 1987, pp. 31–34, p. 34.

160. Heims, op. cit., p. 197

CHAPTER THREE : *Responsibility and "Life in This Kind of Life"*

1. Rubenstein, Richard L., *The Cunning of History: The Holocaust and the American Future*, New York, N.Y.: Harper and Row, 1975, p. 95.

2. Ibid., p. 6.

3. Ibid., pp. 2, 91, emphasis in the original.

4. Ibid., p. 87.

5. Ibid., p. 88.

6. Ibid.

7. Ibid., pp. 94–95.

8. Dorfman, Ariel, "Adios, General: Saying Good-Bye to Pinochet," *Harper's Magazine* 279 (December 1989): 72–76, p. 73.

9. Wolfe, Tom, *The Right Stuff*, New York, N.Y.: Farrar, Strauss, Giroux, 1979, p. 180.

10. Perrow, Charles, *Normal Accidents: Living with High-Risk Technologies*, New York, N.Y.: Basic Books, 1984, pp. 271–281.

11. Monkman, Carol Smith, "The super plane no man can fly: Strain KO's pilots: Projected jet can tolerate strong G force," *Seattle Post-Intelligencer*, July 24, 1986, pp. A1, A12, emphasis added.

12. Skinner, B. F., *Walden Two*, New York, N.Y.: The Macmillan Company, 1948, p. 320.

13. Ibid., pp. 7–9.

14. Ibid., pp. 29–31, 97.

15. Ibid., pp. 78, 29.

16. Ibid., pp. 296–299.

17. Ibid., pp. 54–55, 263.

18. Ibid., pp. 104–105.

19. Malcolm, Janet, *Psychoanalysis: The Impossible Profession*, New York, N.Y.: Alfred A. Knopf, 1981, p. 6.

20. Freud, Sigmund, "Observations on transference-love: Further recommendations on the technique of psycho-analysis III," *The Standard Edition*

of the Psychological Works of Sigmund Freud, London: Hogarth Press, 1958, vol. 12: 159–171, p. 162.

21. Ibid., p. 163.

22. Lacan, Jacques, *The Four Fundamental Concepts of Psycho-Analysis*, New York, N.Y.: W. W. Norton, 1981, pp. 230–243.

23. Schneiderman, Stuart, ed., *Returning to Freud: Clinical Psychoanalysis in the School of Lacan*, New Haven, Conn.: Yale University Press, 1980, p. vii.

24. Freud, "Observations on transference-love," op. cit., p. 170.

25. Malcolm, op. cit., p. 108.

26. Malcolm, Janet, *In the Freud Archives*, New York, N.Y.: Alfred A. Knopf, 1984, p. 25.

27. Rogers, Carl R., *Client-Centered Therapy: Its Current Practice, Implications, and Theory*, Boston, Mass.: Houghton Mifflin, 1951, pp. 53–54.

28. Ibid., p. 29.

29. Ibid., p. 38.

30. Ibid., p. 221.

31. Ibid., p. 513.

32. Ibid., p. 19.

33. Ibid., p. 12.

34. Jacoby, Russell, *The Repression of Psychoanalysis: Otto Fenichel and the Political Freudians*, New York, N.Y.: Basic Books, 1983, p. 46.

35. Simon, Herbert A., *The New Science of Management Decision*, revised edition, Englewood Cliffs, N.J.: Prentice-Hall, 1977, p. 106.

36. Wiener, Norbert, *The Human Use of Human Beings: Cybernetics and Society*, New York, N.Y.: Avon Books, 1954, p. 216.

37. Kemeny, John G., "Man viewed as a machine," *Scientific American* 192 (April 1955): 58–67, p. 67.

38. Simon, op. cit., p. 68.

39. Ibid., p. 107.

40. Ibid., pp. 132–33.

41. Ibid., p. 133.

42. Kanter, Rosabeth Moss, *The Change Masters: Innovation for Productivity in the American Corporation*, New York, N.Y.: Simon and Schuster, 1983, pp. 202–203.

43. Ibid., p. 56, emphasis added.

44. Ibid., p. 204.

45. Ibid., pp. 142, 61.

46. Ibid., pp. 366–67.

47. Ferguson, Kathy E., *The Feminist Case Against Bureaucracy*, Philadelphia, Pa.: Temple University Press, 1984, p. 56.

48. Ibid., p. 206.

49. Foucault, Michel, *The History of Sexuality, Volume 1—An Introduction*, New York, N.Y.: Pantheon, 1978, p. 138 ff.

50. Ferguson, op. cit., p. 25.

51. Wiener, op. cit., pp. 56–58.

52. This with thanks to David Abrahms.

53. Smith, Alice Kimball, and Charles Weiner, eds., *Robert Oppenheimer: Letters and Recollections*, Cambridge, Mass.: Harvard University Press, 1980, pp. 241–42.

54. Smith and Wiener, op. cit., pp. 243–46.

55. Goodchild, Peter, *J. Robert Oppenheimer: 'Shatterer of Worlds,'* London: British Broadcasting System, 1980, p. 73.

56. Smith and Wiener, op. cit., p. 249.

57. Ibid., p. 262.

58. Ibid., pp. 257–59.

59. Ibid., p. 242.

60. Ibid., p. 221.

61. Ibid., p. 264.

62. United States Atomic Energy Commission, *In the Matter of 'J. Robert Oppenheimer: Transcript of Hearing before Personnel Security Board and Texts of Principal Documents and Letters*, Cambridge, Mass.: The MIT Press, 1971, p. 28.

63. United States AEC, op. cit., pp. 14, 70.

64. Smith and Wiener, op. cit., p. 275.

65. Ibid., p. 289.

66. Goodchild, op. cit., p. 179.

67. Smith, Alice Kimball, *A Peril and a Hope: The Scientists' Movement in America: 1945–47*, Cambridge, Mass.: The MIT Press, 1970, pp. 373–74.

68. Ibid., p. 338.

69. Williams, Robert C., and Philip L. Cantelon, *The American Atom: A Documentary History of Nuclear Policies from the Discovery of Fission to the Present, 1939–1984*, Philadelphia, Pa.: University of Pennsylvania Press, 1984, p. 94.

70. Goodchild, op. cit., p. 182.

71. Ibid., p. 185.

72. Groves, Leslie R., *Now It Can Be Told: The Story of the Manhattan Project*, New York, N.Y.: Da Capo Press, 1962, p. 63.

73. Goodchild, op. cit., pp. 95–96.

74. United States AEC, op. cit., p. 470.

75. "The GAC Report of October 30, 1949," printed as an appendix at pp. 150–59, York, Herbert, *The Advisors: Oppenheimer, Teller, and the Superbomb*, San Francisco, Calif.: W. H. Freeman and Company, 1976.

76. Oppenheimer, J. Robert, "Atomic weapons and American policy," *Foreign Affairs* 31 (July 1953): 525–35, p. 529.

77. Oppenheimer, J. Robert, *Science and the Common Understanding*, New York, N.Y.: Simon and Schuster, 1953.

78. Chevalier, Haakon, *Oppenheimer: The Story of a Friendship*, New York, N.Y.: George Braziller, 1965.

79. United States AEC, op. cit., p. 3.

80. Ibid., pp. 4–5.

81. Ibid., p. 7, emphasis added.

82. Ibid., p. 137, emphasis added.

83. Ibid., p. 146.

84. Ibid., p. 149, emphasis added.

85. Ibid., p. 710.

86. Ibid., p. 1011.

87. Ibid., p. 1061.

88. Ibid., p. 1018.

89. Ibid., p. 67, emphasis added.

90. Ibid., p. 1013, emphasis added.

91. Ibid., p. 1018.

92. Ibid., pp. 1016.

93. Ellul, Jacques, *The Technological Society*, New York, N.Y.: Random House, p. 74.

94. Ibid.

95. United States AEC, op. cit., p. 1054.

96. Coughlan, Robert, "The tangled drama and private hells of two famous scientists," *Life*, December 13, 1963, p. 102.

97. United States AEC, op. cit., p. 710, emphasis added.

98. Ibid., pp. 365, 377.

99. Ibid., pp. 1012, 1054, emphasis added.

100. Coughlan, op. cit., pp. 88, 98.

101. Ibid., p. 103.

102. Kovel, Joel, "Things and words: Metapsychology and the historical point of view," *Psychoanalysis and Contemporary Thought* 1 (1978): 21–88.

103. United States AEC, op. cit., p. 466.

CHAPTER FOUR : *Narrativity and (Deathly) Silence*

1. Teller, Edward, "Introduction," pp. iii–ix in Leslie Groves, *Now It Can Be Told: The Story of the Manhattan Project*, New York, N.Y.: Da Capo Press, 1962, 1983, p. ix.

2. Bersani, Leo, and Ulysse Dutoit, *The Forms of Violence: Narrative in Assyrian Art and Modern Culture*, New York, N.Y.: Schocken Books, 1985, p. 40.

3. Letter from Sigmund Freud to C. G. Jung, June 18, 1909, pp. 234–35 in William McGuire, ed., *The Freud/Jung Letters*, Princeton, N.J.: Princeton University Press, 1974.

4. Malcolm, Janet, *Psychoanalysis: The Impossible Profession*, New York, N.Y.: Knopf, 1981, pp. 48, 102, 108.

5. Rieff, Philip, *The Triumph of the Therapeutic: Uses of Faith after Freud*, Chicago: University of Chicago Press, 1987; Berger, Louis, *Freud's Unfinished Journey: Conventional and Critical Perspectives in Psychoanalytic Theory*, London:

Routledge & Kegan Paul, 1981; see especially Bergen, Bernard J., *Illumination by Darkness: Freud and the Work of Consciousness*, forthcoming.

6. Bersani and Dutoit, op. cit., p. 41.

7. Bersani, Leo, *The Freudian Body: Psychoanalysis and Art*, New York, N.Y.: Columbia University Press, 1986, pp. 3–6.

8. Ibid., p. 43.

9. Bersani and Dutoit, op. cit., pp. v, 51.

10. Ibid., p. 52.

11. Bersani, op. cit., p. 70.

12. Coetzee, J. M., *Life & Times of Michael K*, New York, N.Y.: Viking, 1983, pp. 138.

13. Ibid., 151–52.

14. Bauman, Zygmunt, *Legislators and Interpretors: On Modernity, Post-Modernity and Intellectuals*, Ithaca, N.Y.: Cornell University Press, 1987, p. 191.

15. Ibid., p. 182.

16. Coetzee, J. M., "Into the dark chamber: The novelist and South Africa," *New York Times Book Review*, January 12, 1986, pp. 12, 35.

17. Coetzee, J. M., *Foe*, New York, N.Y.: Viking, 1986, p. 67, 142.

18. Foucault, Michel, "Truth and Power," pp. 109–133 in Colin Gordon, ed., *Power/Knowledge: Selected Interviews and Other Writings [of Michel Foucault]*, New York, N.Y.: Pantheon, 1980, p. 132.

19. Foucault, Michel, *Herculine Barbin: Being the Recently Discovered Memoirs of a Nineteenth-Century French Hermaphrodite*, New York, N.Y.: Pantheon, 1980.

20. Eco, Umberto, *The Name of the Rose*, San Diego: Harcourt Brace Jovanovich, 1983, pp. 491–92.

21. Ibid., p. 492.

22. Foucault, Michel, "A preface to transgression," pp. 29–52 in Donald F. Bouchard, ed., *Language, Counter-Memory, Practice: Selected Essays and Interviews*, Ithaca, N.Y.: Cornell University Press, 1977, pp. 35–36.

23. Foucault, Michel, *The History of Sexuality, Volume 1—An Introduction*, New York, N.Y.: Pantheon, 1978, pp. 157–59.

24. Hoy, David Couzens, "Introduction," pp. 1–25 in David Couzens Hoy, ed., *Foucault: A Critical Reader*, New York, N.Y.: Basil Blackwell, 1986, p. 23.

25. Rhodes, Richard, *The Making of the Atomic Bomb*, New York, N.Y.: Simon and Schuster, 1986, pp. 673–74, emphasis added.

26. Giovannitti, Len, and Fred Freed, *The Decision to Drop the Bomb*, New York, N.Y.: Coward-McCann, 1965, p. 197.

27. Hawkins, David, *Project Y: The Los Alamos Story*, Los Angeles, Calif.: Tomash Publishers, 1983, p. 247.

28. Lifton, Robert Jay, *Death in Life: Survivors of Hiroshima*, New York, N.Y.: Basic Books, 1967, p. 25.

29. Boyer, Paul, *By the Bomb's Early Light: American Thought and Culture at the Dawn of the Atomic Age*, New York, N.Y.: Pantheon, 1985, p. xix.

30. Giovannitti and Freed, op. cit.

31. Boyer, op. cit.

32. Chevalier, Haakon, *Oppenheimer: The Story of a Friendship*, New York, N.Y.: George Braziller, 1965, pp. 115, 116.

33. Ibid., p. 113.

34. Stern, Philip M., *The Oppenheimer Case: Security on Trial*, New York, N.Y.: Harper and Row, 1969, p. 495.

35. Oppenheimer, J. Robert, "The atom bomb and college education," *The General Magazine and Historical Chronicle*, University of Pennsylvania, General Alumni Society, 1946, p. 263.

36. Ibid., pp. 265, 264.

37. Oppenheimer, J. Robert, "A speech given by J. R. Oppenheimer at a meeting of the Association of Los Alamos Scientists," Los Alamos, N.M., November 2, 1945, pp. 3–4.

38. In Oppenheimer, J. Robert, "Niels Bohr and atomic weapons," transcript of a talk given at Los Alamos, May 18, 1964, Papers of J. Robert Oppenheimer, Library of Congress.

39. Wilson, Robert R., "Niels Bohr and the young scientists," pp. 35–42 in Len Ackland and Steve McGuire, eds., *Assessing the Nuclear Age*, Chicago, Ill.: Educational Foundation for Nuclear Science, 1986, p. 39.

40. Else, John, producer, "The Day After Trinity: J. Robert Oppenheimer and the Atomic Bomb," Public Broadcasting Service, April 29, 1981, p. 29.

41. Goodchild, Peter, *J. Robert Oppenheimer: 'Shatterer of Worlds,'* London: British Broadcasting System, 1980, p. 80.

42. Crews, Robin Jeffrey, "Scientific values and physical scientists' participation in weapons research," a paper given at the American Sociological Association meeting, August 1985.

43. Oppenheimer, J. Robert, "Atomic weapons," *Proceedings of the American Philosophical Society* 90 (January 1946): 7–10, p. 7.

44. Else, op. cit., p. 30.

45. O'Brien, Tim, *The Nuclear Age*, New York, N.Y.: Knopf, 1985, pp. 272–73.

46. Arney, William Ray, and Bernard J. Bergen, *Medicine and the Management of Living: Taming the Last Great Beast*, Chicago, Ill.: University of Chicago Press, 1984.

47. See Ervin, Frank R., Jon B. Glazier, et al., "Human and ecological effects in Massachusetts of an assumed thermonuclear attack on the U.S.," pp. 1–20 in Aronow, Saul, Frank R. Ervin, and Victor W. Sidel, eds., *The Fallen Sky: Medical Consequences of Thermonuclear War*, New York, N.Y.: Hill and Wang, 1963, and Sidel, Victor W., H. Jack Geiger, and Bernard Lown, "The physician's role in the post-attack period," pp. 21–41 in the same volume.

48. Arney and Bergen, op. cit.

49. Lown, Bernard, "The physician's commitment," pp. 237–40 in Ruth Adams and Susan Cullen, eds., *The Final Epidemic: Physicians and Scientists on*

Nuclear War, Chicago, Ill.: Educational Foundation for Nuclear Science, 1981, p. 237.

50. Grinspoon, Lester, "Introduction," pp. 1–6 in Lester Grinspoon, ed., *The Long Darkness: Psychological and Moral Perspectives on Nuclear Winter*, New Haven, Conn.: Yale University Press, 1986, p. 3.

51. Boyer, op. cit., p. 38.

52. Connolly, William, *Politics and Ambiguity*, Madison, Wis.: University of Wisconsin Press, 1987, pp. 3, 10, 104.

53. Ibid., p. 108.

54. De Mott, Benjamin, "Looking for intelligence in Washington," *Commentary* 30 (October 1960): 291–300, p. 291.

55. Greene, Graham, "Under the garden," pp. 3–61 in Graham Greene, *A Sense of Reality*, New York, N.Y.: Viking, 1963.

56. Oppenheimer, J. Robert, "Alpha or omega was 20 years ago: Physicist Oppenheimer sees atomic bomb as great test of whether man can live without war," *Washington Post*, July 11, 1965, p. E1.

57. Oppenheimer, "The atomic bomb and college education," 1946, op. cit., p. 265.

58. "Interview with Dr. Oppenheimer for 'The Building of the Bomb,'" transcript of British Broadcasting System interview dated February 24, 1965, Papers of J. Robert Oppenheimer, Library of Congress, Box 246.

59. Else, op. cit., p. 14.

60. Ibid.

61. Kirk, G. S., *Myth: Its Meaning and Function in Ancient and Other Cultures*, Cambridge: Cambridge University Press, 1970.

62. Lifton, op. cit., pp. 397.

63. Ibid., pp. 400, 401.

64. Ibid., p. 414.

65. Ibid., pp. 38–39.

66. Boyer, op. cit., pp. 246, 250.

67. Agee, James, "Dedication day," pp. 103–117 in Fitzgerald, Robert, ed., *The Collected Short Prose of James Agee*, Dunwoody, Georgia: N. S. Berg, 1978.

68. Agee, James, *Letters of James Agee to Father Flye*, New York, N.Y.: George Braziller, 1962, p. 152.

69. Lifton, Robert Jay, *Boundaries: Psychological Man in Revolution*, New York, N.Y.: Random House, 1969, pp. xi, 3, 44, 45.

70. Ibid., pp. 44, 45.

71. Agee, *Letters of James Agee to Father Flye*, op. cit., p. 160.

72. Wilson, op. cit., pp. 40–41.

73. Stinchcombe, Arthur L., "Reason and rationality," *Sociological Theory* 4 (Fall 1986): 151–66, pp. 158, 165.

74. DeMott, op. cit., pp. 292, 294, 296.

75. Mumford, Lewis, "Gentlemen: You Are Mad!," *The Saturday Review of Literature* 29 (March 2, 1946): 5–6, p. 6.

76. Brustein, Robert, "The logic of survival in a lunatic world," *New Republic* 145 (November 11, 1961): 11–13, p. 12.

77. DeMott, op. cit., p. 291.

78. Agee, "Dedication day," op. cit., p. 117.

79. O'Brien, op. cit., pp. 302, 312.

80. Roth, Philip, "Writing American fiction," *Commentary* 31 (March 1961): 223–33, p. 228.

81. Brustein, op. cit., p. 13.

82. Wiener, Norbert, "A scientist rebels," *Atlantic Monthly* 170 (1947): 46, p. 46.

83. Dostoevsky, Fyodor, *Notes from Underground*, New York, N.Y.: Dell Publishing, 1960, pp. 52, 50.

84. Weisskopf, Victor, "A race to death," *New York Times*, May 14, 1978, p. E19; Schelling, Thomas C., *Arms and Influence*, New Haven, Conn.: Yale University Press, 1966.

85. Dostoevsky, op. cit., p. 37.

86. Oppenheimer, J. Robert, "Meet the Press," audio tape of November 26, 1945, broadcast, Library of Congress.

Index

Acheson, Dean, 158, 195
Acheson-Lilienthal Report, 156–57
aesthetics. *See* simplicity
Agee, James, 209–10, 215
Alvarez, Louis, 89, 114–15
ambiguity, 6–13
analysis, 37–44; and the atom, 63–66
Arendt, Hannah, 42–43
art, and bomb. *See* narrative
associations, 137–40, 168
atom, models of, 64–81
atomic bomb, and the structure of thought, 63–74; first test (*see also* Trinity), 27; international control, 157; making, 61–111; simplicity of, 61
authority, 16–17
"average man," 41

Bacher, Rober, 152
Baruch, Bernard, 157
Bauman, Zygmunt, 183, 196
Bersani, Leo, 177, 180–81; and psychoanalytic theory, 179–80; on violence, 180–82
Bethe, Hans, 151, 154
Blanchot, Maurice, 25
Blois, Marsden, 39

Bloom, Allan, 6
Bohr, Niels, 8–9, 49, 52, 73, 80, 110–11, 193–94, 211–13; and atomic physics, 68–70
bomb, artistic response to, 206–11. *See also* atomic bomb
bomb delivery system, 101–11
bomb stories, 188–211
Borden, William Liscum, 162–64
Bordo, Susan, 40
Borgmann, Albert, 112–15
boundaries, 8, 28–29, 103–4; and expertise, 131–38
Boyer, Paul, 188, 208–9
Bracken, Paul, 107–10
Brazil, 34, 174
Bruce, Lenny, 9–11, 23, 124, 161
bureaucracy, 146–49
Byrnes, James, 157

Caldicott, Helen, 201
Catch-22, 214–15
Chadwick, James, 75
character, 137–40, 168
Chevalier, Haakon, 159–63, 190
Chevalier incident, 159–62, 166, 169–70
choice, 181
Churchman, C. West, 49

237